WHEN THE BUBBLE BURSTS
Clinical Perspectives on Midlife Issues

WHEN THE BUBBLE BURSTS
Clinical Perspectives on Midlife Issues

Eda G. Goldstein

THE ANALYTIC PRESS
2005   Hillsdale, NJ   London

Published by
The Analytic Press, Inc., Publishers
    Editorial Offices:
    101 West Street
    Hillsdale, NJ 07642

    www.analyticpress.com

Typeset in Goudy and Zurich by
Christopher Jaworski, Bloomfield, NJ
Photograph "Blue Ridge" © 2004 by
Christopher Jaworski

Index by Leonard S. Rosenbaum, Washington, DC

Library of Congress Cataloging-in-Publication Data

Goldstein, Eda G.
    When the bubble bursts : clinical perspectives on
    midlife issues / Eda G. Goldstein
      p. cm.
    Includes bibliographical references and index.
    ISBN 0-88163-348-8
    1. Middle age—Psychological aspects. 2. Middle-
      aged persons—Mental health. 3. Psychotherapy.
      I. Title.

RC451.4.M54G66 2005
618.97'8914—dc22

                        2005048018

Printed in the United States of America
10 9 8 7 6 5 4 3 2 1

CONTENTS

ACKNOWLEDGMENTS

I am indebted to the many colleagues, students, mentors, and patients who have made contributions to this book. The Dean, faculty, and both Ph.D. and M.S.W. students of the New York University School of Social Work have been an important source of intellectual stimulation and support. I am particularly appreciative of my colleagues, Drs. Jeffrey Seinfeld, Carol Tosone, RoseMarie Perez Foster, Judith Mishne, Theresa Aiello, and Judith Siegel. My past association with Dr. Otto Kernberg at the New York State Psychiatric Institute and New York Hospital–Cornell Medical Center, Westchester Division and the late Dr. Marjorie Taggart White, a passionate, inspiring, and early proponent of self psychology, contributed to a broad and diverse theoretical base that has served me well in trying to understand and treat narcissistic vulnerability. My connection to the Association for Psychoanalytic Self Psychology has played a significant role in keeping me abreast of current psychoanalytic contributions in the study of subjectivity and relational theory.

I would not have been able to sustain the lonely process of writing without the encouragement of my friends, Dr. Lucille Spira, Enid Ain, Hannalyn Wilkins, Phyllis Taormina, Carole Vitale, Jeff Ponnell, Tom Ambrosole, Sinai Waxman, Harvey Nussbaum, Sean Cody, Mario Dilione, Jerry Douglas, and John Stellar. My life partner, Patricia Petrocelli, deserves special thanks for her steadfast support.

I would like to thank John Kerr, formerly of The Analytic Press, who was a staunch supporter of my interest in writing a book about psychotherapy and midlife. Likewise, the staff of The Analytic Press, including Dr. Paul Stepansky, Eleanor Kobrin, and Joan Riegel, have been wonderful in their encouragement of my writing projects and in their efforts to bring this book to fruition.

Finally, my clinical work with midlife patients has taught me a great deal about vulnerability and resilience. It has expanded my own world view, caused me to be more sensitive to others' life experiences, caused me to scrutinize my own values and beliefs about the human condition, and affirmed the positive potential of midlife.

PREFACE

This book describes how midlife events disturb people's equilibrium, thwart their healthy self-needs, and trigger varying degrees of weakness in the self. It identifies and illustrates crucial foci in the treatment process of a range of midlife patients who enter psychotherapy. The treatment approach that is employed is primarily self-psychological. Self psychology is applicable to a range of treatment modalities that can be placed on a continuum between supportive work on one pole and psychoanalysis on the other. There is not always a clear dividing line between these two poles, however, and supportive techniques and other nontraditional uses of the self are found in psychoanalysis and psychoanalytic psychotherapy (Wallerstein, 1986; Fosshage, 1991; Miller, 1991). Readers may differ with respect to where on this continuum they place the numerous treatment examples contained in the book. I have attempted to write in a user-friendly style. The case vignettes are based on my clinical and supervisory experiences. In some instances, I have condensed session material and used composite examples of similar types of patients.

Chapter 1 presents an overview of the nature of midlife and its impact on the self and implications for psychotherapy with people in midlife.

Chapter 2 discusses theoretical perspectives on adult development and midlife.

Chapter 3 illustrates the impact on the self of 10 common midlife events and situations.

Chapter 4 considers the vicissitudes of narcissism and narcissistic vulnerability in midlife.

Chapter 5 describes the nature of assessment with midlife patients.

Chapter 6 explores the process of helping patients to modify the grandiose self, facilitate mourning of various types of losses, and diminish feelings of guilt, badness, and fraudulence.

Chapter 7 examines the process of helping patients to reshape and strengthen their self-concept, improve their self-esteem regulation,

expand their capacity for empathy, and find new selfobjects and outlets for self-expression.

Chapter 8 discusses some countertransference issues that arise
when midlife therapists treat midlife patients. It discusses use of therapist self-disclosure and the rewards of treatment.

This book is intended as an aid to clinicians who are interested in
the psychotherapy of persons in midlife and in the particular problems that they confront. Even though it mainly addresses the treatment of patients who are having significant difficulty dealing with
the issues and events of midlife, it is a hopeful book. It shows how the
psychotherapeutic process can enable midlifers to understand their
own reactions, needs, and difficulties; strengthen their sense of who
they are and what they can be; and overcome obstacles to their moving on in their lives.

1
ISSUES IN MIDLIFE AND THE PSYCHOTHERAPEUTIC PROCESS
An Overview

This book is about contemporary psychodynamic psychotherapy with patients who are experiencing major difficulties in coping with the stresses, challenges, and opportunities of midlife. It stems from the author's interest in the impact of current life on the personality and is based on her clinical experiences. She has been impressed by two distinctive and somewhat contradictory observations of midlife. On one hand, it can be a time of enjoyment and satisfaction and a period that stimulates growth and positive changes. Alternatively, midlife events can cause severe stress and crises and may result in the emergence of mental and physical symptoms and cause some people to become chronically anxious, depressed, angry, or depleted. Research has shown that the presence or absence of meaningful support systems and resources undoubtedly plays a role in these outcomes (Eckenrode and Gore, 1990; Eckenrode, 1991), but it is likely that other internal factors within the personality, as well as external influences within the culture, are significant as well.

Although most, if not all, of us are susceptible to the disappointments, stresses, and blows of midlife, many people come to this period with significant areas of narcissistic vulnerability (Goldstein, 1995b). This term refers to a "particular weakness in an individual, created by past injuries to certain aspects of the self" (Jacobowitz and Newton, 1999, p. 455). Such weakness makes people highly reactive to perceived threats to self-esteem and identity and makes the navigation of midlife difficult. Rather than being able to enjoy the fruits of this era, meeting its challenges, and recovering from its assaults, some people experience acute distress or begin a downward cycle of chronic dysfunction. One only has to look at the incidence of emotional disorder, substance abuse, divorce, marital infidelity, the frantic search for symbols of youth and attractiveness, and the extensive use of psychotropic drugs to recognize that the midlife epoch takes its toll. Olfson and his colleagues (2002) found that the percentage of Americans aged 55 to 64 receiving psychotherapy doubled in the decade between 1987 and 1997. Moreover, almost 50 percent of those who sought mental health treatment during this period were taking antidepressants in 1997, compared with 14 percent in 1987.

A major theme of this book is that, whatever the symptoms or presenting problems of midlife patients, the psychotherapy of those who enter treatment in midlife invariably must address self issues. It is important to consider how current stressors are frustrating healthy self-needs and the degree to which they are triggering narcissistic vulnerability. Treatment can provide an experience in which patients can regain their equilibrium, find new ways of affirming and expressing their sense of self, and rework and strengthen their self-structures.

Defining Midlife

Midlife is not just a point in time nor is it merely a transition or passage from youth to old age. It spans many years, and people differ in their perceptions of its precise boundaries. Lachman and James (1997, p. 2) observe that because it is customary to view midlife as the middle phase of adulthood, its beginning and end depend on how long one expects to live. For example, the authors note that, although many people think of midlife as starting as early as age 35 and extending to age 65, older adults tend to see midlife as ranging from age 40 to the 70s, whereas younger adults place it from ages 30 to 55. Hunter and Sundel (1989) suggest that one reason for the expansion of midlife's boundaries is that people are living longer generally. Because of the wide time span that this epoch encompasses, people who are at the beginning of this period face different challenges than did those who are much older (p. 2). As Helson (1997) commented ironically, "We enter the adult world with abundant energy but little experience; we approach our exit with abundant experience but little energy" (p. 21).

Frequently, people's exact chronological age is less important in ushering in the middle years than is their perception of themselves in relation to time. In the 1970s, it was popular to view midlife as constituting a period of crisis because of the awareness of the passing and limitations of time.

> No gong rings, of course. But twinges begin. Deep down a change begins to register in those gut-level perceptions of safety and danger, time and no time, aliveness and stagnation, self and others. It starts with a vague feeling. . . . I have reached some sort of meridian in my life. I had better take a survey, reexamine where I have been, and reevaluate how I am going to spend my resources from now on. Why am I doing all this? What do I really believe in? . . . I have only so much time before the dark to find my own truth [Sheehy, 1974, p. 242].

In contrast to popular views, however, the awareness of being middle-aged does not appear to prompt a crisis for some men and women, nor does becoming middle-aged always signify loss and decline (Pearlin, 1985; Lachman et al., 1994; Kimmel and Sang, 1995; Kertzner and Sved, 1996; Stewart and Ostrove, 1998; Aldwin and Levenson, 2001; Heckhausen, 2001; Lachman, 2001; Hunter and Sundel, 2002). Moreover, there are numerous paths in midlife and more opportunities for growth and positive changes today than was true in previous periods. Nevertheless, "midlife appears to be a time to look back and a time to look ahead, a time to ask how things are going and what is left to do" (Lachman and James, 1997, p. 3).

The Positive Edge of Midlife

It is not uncommon for those who enter midlife to feel that they are in the prime of their lives and at their peak (Sze and Ivker, 1987; Mitchell and Helson, 1990). Many people have attained long-sought-after goals and satisfying relationships. They feel a sense of emotional and physical well-being and a sense of safety. They enjoy personal and financial security, as well as status and power. They have a renewed or redirected sense of generativity and are optimistic about making changes and finding new possibilities for personal fulfillment and creative expression. Societal changes have resulted in recent generations of men and women being reared with expectations about the aging process and with societal opportunities far different from those of previous generations. In many respects, Baby Boomers are recreating midlife. Perhaps signaling this trend is that "progressive lenses" and "continuous vision" have come into parlance to replace the popularity of the older concept of bifocals.

There are numerous myths about midlife men and women that should be discarded, especially in the wake of the dramatic shifts that have taken place since the mid-1960s and early 1970s regarding women's place in society (Colarusso and Nemiroff, 1981; Hunter and Sundel, 1989). These changes have afforded women new opportunities to actualize themselves and to choose diverse life options. Women can now enter arenas formerly typically occupied only by men, and women now interact with men on different terms. For example, recent studies of college-educated women in their 40s showed them to have a strong sense of personal identity, a broadened vision of the self in the social world, and a capacity to be effective and have an impact (Stewart and Ostrove, 1998, p. 1189). Concurrently, concepts of masculinity have been redefined and men's roles have expanded. Many men view themselves less traditionally. They are more expressive and able to communicate their needs, hold different values about their involvement in family life, and are able to relate in a more egalitarian manner. On the negative side, not all men have welcomed or embraced these developments. Some are confused by and resistant to the changes that have occurred and women's expectations of them. Many midlife women face more complicated choices and stressful demands than previous generations. Now they have to balance multiple roles; they experience new frustrations and disappointments when their expectations clash with the reality around them; and they must negotiate new ways of relating to men without prior role models.

In spite of midlife's positive potential, it raises compelling concerns and contains events that involve significant disappointments and losses and that may challenge or undermine one's values, ideals, self-esteem, and even safety. Yet many people display an astonishing degree of flexibility and confidence in coping with life stressors and taking on new roles and challenges (Heckhausen, 2001). One study revealed that, although most people believed that midlife involved more responsibility and increased stress than did other periods, they also viewed persons in midlife as more competent and as having more social supports to manage stress than they had at other ages (Lachman et al., 1994).

Maintaining Self-Esteem and Identity in Midlife

It has been said that the fundamental developmental task of adult life involves the maintenance of self-esteem and identity in the face of the biological, psychological, and social stresses and losses that occur as we grow older (Lazarus, 1991, p. 35). In putting forth a self-psychological theory of personality development, Heinz Kohut recognized that people exhibit healthy self-needs all through life. He emphasized that maintaining self-esteem and identity always requires the presence of responsive and sustaining others (selfobjects) and does not entail true autonomy from the environment. Kohut (1984) proposed:

Self–selfobject relationships form the essence of psychological
life from birth to death, [and] that a move from dependence
(symbiosis) to independence (autonomy) in the psychological
sphere is no more possible, let alone desirable, than a corresponding move from a life dependent on oxygen to a life independent of it in the biological sphere [p. 47].

Kohut focused on self-development in early life, however, and did
not describe how healthy selfobject needs manifest themselves and
find outlets and responsiveness in older adults. Although he identified the presence of archaic selfobject needs in so-called narcissistic
adults, he did not address how weakness in the self influences the successful negotiation of developmental tasks and stressful events in
mid- and later life (Galatzer-Levy and Cohler, 1990, p. 95).

Threats to self-esteem and periods of disequilibrium may stem
from the impact of internal as well as external sources and from gratifying as well as disturbing life events (Jacobowitz and Newton, 1999,
p. 456). There may be the loss of significant relationships or minimizing of occupational or family roles. Financial, romantic, and career
opportunities may have passed them by. Midlifers may undergo physical changes that lessen feelings of femininity or masculinity, attractiveness, and prowess; sexuality may decline or press for new outlets.
Illness may strike. The limitations of one's life partner, the prospect
of never finding a mate, or the reality of being childless may seem
more acute. The coming of age of their children and their children's
life choices may create major disappointments. The need to be a caretaker of ailing parents and the illness, disability, and death of parents,
siblings, and friends may result in burdensome responsibilities and
necessitate changes in self-concept or a reworking of relationships,
or these events may touch off earlier developmental issues.

Whether one sees the door opening or closing in midlife (Brooks-
Gunn and Kirsh, 1984, p. 11), this period tends to be fraught, even
for those with relatively firm intrapsychic structures. Few people, if
any, are insulated from the stresses of midlife. In this sense, we all are
vulnerable to a degree particularly when the world today confronts us
with unsettling and sometimes frightening conditions and potential
threats in the work, personal, and societal spheres. Those reared earlier than some others and who have a different set of values and

expectations may feel out of step with life; the rules may seem to have changed in the middle of the game.

The prolonged downturn in the economy and corporate corruption that occurred early in this century seriously weakened the financial well-being of many segments of the population. These changes produced a staggering degree of unemployment and underemployment and forced drastic change in people's occupational and personal lives and plans for the future.

The shocking and tragic terrorist attack on the World Trade Center on September 11, 2001 shattered our collective sense of safety. It not only cut short the lives of thousands of people and thrust their families into a state of grief, but it also left millions of people in an ongoing state of worry and fear. Suicide bombings and retaliation in the Middle East, the prelude to and actual war in Iraq and its violent and uncertain aftermath, and the buildup of weapons of mass destruction in other countries disrupted and threatened people's sense of safety and security and ability to plan for the future. The disclosure of the government's policies about and actual treatment of prisoners in the Mideast challenged our moral authority. As a result of all these events, many people from all walks of life are fearful that the world is out of control, a state of affairs that may not cease any time soon.

Narcissistic Vulnerability and Midlife

Midlife events are potentially stressful and disruptive, however, not only because of the realistic challenges that they present but also because of their subjective meaning in causing injuries to the self and their role in triggering underlying personality difficulties. There has been some, but not very much, attention to the fate of weakness in the self in mid- and later life (Cath, 1963; Kernberg, 1977; Colarusso and Nemiroff, 1981; Gottschalk, 1990; Lazarus, 1991; Goldstein, 1992, 1995b; Pearlman, 1993; Ellman, 1996; Ruth and Coleman, 1996; Jacobowitz and Newton, 1999). Although some people develop compensatory mechanisms that enable them to overcome weakness in the self and function reasonably well, others are unable to do so. Instead, their narcissistic vulnerability is part of a more pervasive faulty or deficient structural organization that affects self-esteem regulation, interpersonal relationships, perceptions of reality, and identity (Jacobowitz and Newton, 1999, pp. 455–456).

Even positive achievements may create distress if one feels undeserving or fraudulent or does not seem to receive the anticipated approval, recognition, love, or respect that one has been seeking, consciously or unconsciously, from significant others. Positive changes and new adaptations that challenge core identifications may seem treacherous or unattainable for those who lack parental or other significant role models (Barnett, 1984, pp. 341–357). Major, or even seemingly minor, disappointments may cause some people to experience acute disequilibrium followed by chronic symptoms, prolonged distress, and ongoing difficulties coping. Relationships may cause disappointment or fail to relieve a sense of inner emptiness and loneliness.

Some who have a difficult time in midlife may appear to have functioned well and to have attained major successes. For them, the bubble of perfection, self-sufficiency, and control of others and life may seem to erode or suddenly burst (Modell, 1975, pp. 275–282) as children and partners display unacceptable characteristics or behavior or show disturbing emotional problems: aging parents make new demands or die without expressing love and approval; the need for new and greater achievements brings overwork and exhaustion and does not relieve the feelings of emptiness, depression, and anxiety; increased competition, aging out of certain careers, forced unemployment, early retirement, illness, or disability undermines the mainstays of their self-esteem and identity.

The bubble bursts not only for those who have sought perfection but also for those who have underfunctioned or behaved in a self-destructive manner while maintaining the belief that they will eventually succeed and achieve their dreams and ambitions. Feelings of regret or pressure to make changes may arise as a person becomes acutely aware of the limitations of time, the paths that have not been traveled, and the life that has not been led. It may be necessary for them to shed certain illusions about themselves and their lives that have kept them going. Change seems necessary but is not always possible. A deep sense of regret, envy of those who made different choices and seem to have achieved more success, dread of the future, and a feeling of futility about ever being able to attain one's ambitions may set in.

Theories of Adult Development

Embodying the view that child development almost totally shapes the adult personality, traditional Freudian psychoanalytic theory, early ego psychology, and British and American object relations theories were static in their concept of adulthood. They did not consider adult development in its own right and saw adults as merely replaying past conflicts and living out previously formed personality characteristics, defenses, and internalized relational patterns. Carl Jung (1933), who initially was a member of Freud's inner circle, and Erik Erikson (1950, 1959) were the first psychoanalysts to discuss midlife as a distinctive phase that has its own developmental tasks and themes. Their writings, however, tended to be philosophical and focused narrowly on a few key ideas. Subsequently, others have studied the adult life cycle more systematically (Neugarten and Associates, 1964; Gould, 1978; Levinson et al., 1978; Lifton, 1979; Pollock, 1987). Others have described the evolution of identity, defenses, and character traits over time and in response to role transitions (Benedek, 1970; Vaillant, 1977; Elson, 1984). The coping demands of stressful and traumatic life events have been identified (Coehlo, Hamburg, and Adams, 1974; Parad and Parad, 1990), and new psychoanalytically based formulations about adult development have been offered (Colarusso and Nemiroff, 1981).

Despite these contributions, several writers have noted that, prior to the last 20 years, much of the major work on adult development ignored the life course of women, viewed women in only traditional ways, or described women of earlier generations (Williams, 1977; Rossi, 1980; Brooks-Gunn and Kirsh, 1984). Since then, a significant body of theory and research about the unique life course issues that women face and their coping and adaptation has accumulated (Baruch and Brooks-Gunn, 1984; Brooks-Gunn and Kirsh, 1984; Hunter and Sundel, 1989, 2002; Wainrib, 1992; Lachman and James, 1997; Stewart and Ostrove, 1998; Lachman, 2001). Likewise, more is known about midlife gays and lesbians, although knowledge about the life course of people of color and other ethnic minorities is still at an early point (Spurlock, 1984; Gibson, 1989; Sang, 1993; Kimmel and Sang, 1995; Kertzner and Sved, 1996).

Nevertheless, theories about normal adult development and of healthy and pathological narcissism, as well as other types of adult psychopathology, have not been well integrated. Having originated largely out of distinctive interests and concerns, those two bodies of knowledge often appear to constitute different realms of discourse.

Psychotherapy in Midlife

It is noteworthy that the emergence of theories about and burgeoning research into midlife have not led to significant changes in clinical work or to a clear conceptualization of the therapeutic task with midlife patients (Ellman, 1996, p. 353). In this regard, it bears mentioning that, within the psychoanalytic community, a long-standing prejudice existed against treating people of a certain age with intensive psychotherapy or psychoanalysis. Ellman notes that Freud's famous cases involved younger patients and that he held a negative view of the ability of mid- and later life persons to engage in psychoanalysis. "The age of patients has this importance in determining their fitness for psychoanalytic treatment . . . near or above the fifties the elasticity of the mental processes, on which the treatment depends, is as a rule lacking—old people are no longer educable" (Freud, 1905, p. 264). Nevertheless, it is common today for middle-aged patients to enter both psychotherapy and psychoanalysis, where they likely are treated by middle-aged therapists. Although most analysts today probably no longer hold the more extreme views of earlier generations about midlife persons' inability to change, many may still hold other stereotypical views of midlifers. These therapists may consequently be limiting their understanding of their midlife patients, with the result that they impose their own expectations about and experiences with the aging process on their patients (McQuaide, 1998a, b).

When people come for treatment in midlife, they usually are seeking relief from anxiety, depression, burnout, confusion and uncertainty, feelings of loss, physical symptoms, loneliness, or a general of malaise and angst. They may feel overwhelmed in trying to deal with the stresses in their lives. Some may wish to make positive changes in their lives but either are unable to do so or develop disabling symptoms in the process of trying to achieve their goals. Others feel trapped and cannot free themselves from painful relationships or life situations. What are the goals, focus, and nature of psychotherapy of midlife patients? Moreover, because so many therapists are midlifers who also may be encountering the stresses, disruptions, and concerns of this period, it is important to consider the transference–countertransference issues that arise when therapists and patients alike are dealing with similar midlife concerns and events. Therapists' personal struggles around self-esteem and identity cannot help but influence their therapeutic stance and countertransference reactions.

From a broader perspective, as the health care system is overburdened and there are serious threats to clinical work in both agency and private practice, the task of being available to patients is ever-more difficult. Just as it is difficult for a parent to establish a good enough holding environment for a child when the child is surrounded by a nonnurturing and stressful environment, it may be difficult for therapists to be emotionally present and to show empathy for patients when they feel under siege in their professional lives. A parallel process may take place in which therapists may pass along to their patients what they experience from their surrounding environment.

2
THEORIES OF MIDLIFE

Although the classical psychoanalytic method aimed at bringing about changes in so-called neurotic adults by making their unconscious childhood conflicts conscious and working through their effects on patients' current functioning, as noted in chapter 1, Freud and his followers neglected adulthood as a developmental phase in which growth and change occur. The writings of the early ego psychologists and British and American object relations theorists reflect a similar thrust. Although Jung (1933) and Erikson (1950) introduced fresh perspectives on midlife into psychoanalytic theory, the more systematic study of adulthood is a relatively recent occurrence. This chapter reviews selected contributions to adult developmental theory and research on midlife.

Early Psychoanalytic Theorists

As part of his general theorizing, Jung (1933) put forth a distinctive view of personality development. He considered midlife as constituting

13

a developmental phase that ushered in a crisis. Jung believed that about age 35 or 40 saw a turning point that offered opportunities for growth and change but that could instead lead to derailments as a result of poor preparation (Colarusso and Nemiroff, 1981, p. 23). He wrote that midlife required a shift in goals and values because "we cannot live the afternoon of life according to the program of life's morning; for what was great in the morning will be little at evening, and what in the morning was true will at evening have become a lie" (Jung, 1971, p. 17).

Jung (1933) believed in the possibility for greater individuation and transcendence in midlife (see also Lachman and James, 1997, pp. 5–7; Staudinger and Bluck, 2001, pp. 11–12). By individuation he meant that a person could realize, express, integrate, and balance parts of himself or herself that were dormant or neglected previously and thus make the emergence of a unique self possible. For example, a man who had developed his masculinity could bring out the more feminine aspects of his personality, or an extrovert could develop the more introverted parts of himself or herself. By transcendence Jung meant that midlife adults must overcome their preoccupation with the physical strength, attractiveness, sexuality, and other concerns of youth. They must learn to live in harmony with themselves and come to value humanity and the laws of nature. Despite his belief in the positive potential of midlife, Jung saw people as erecting blocks to the full expression of their personalities and as often hampered in meeting the demands of this phase.

Although Erikson identified himself as a psychoanalyst within the Freudian and ego-psychological tradition, he achieved prominence through his extensive theorizing about the epigenesis of the ego during the entire life cycle. Unlike Freud, however, he conceived of development as continuing throughout adulthood, which he saw as a dynamic rather than a static time. Some theorists outside of psychoanalysis put forth similar ideas (Havighurst, 1968; Riegel, 1975), but Erikson's views had considerable appeal because of their innovative, philosophical, and psychological thrust. Unfortunately, like that of other adult developmentalists of the time, Erikson's thinking reflected a traditional view of sex role behavior and a male bias.

Erikson (1950, 1959) described personality development as psychosocial in nature, as involving progressive mastery of developmental tasks in each of eight successive stages of the human life cycle. He described the beginning of each stage as constituting a normal, or healthy, crisis, in the sense that it caused a temporary state of disequilibrium resulting from the insufficiency of usual coping skills and the need to acquire new ones. He saw each stage as encompassing not only the mastery of specific developmental tasks but also the resolution of a core developmental crisis, which centers on a basic change in one's attitude or perspective toward oneself, others, and the world. Erikson argued that resolution of each crisis leads to a progressive consolidation of a sense of ego identity, or sense of self. Although he believed that success in each stage depends greatly on one's degree of accomplishment in earlier ones, he nevertheless thought that one could repair earlier developmental difficulties by mastering later stages (Goldstein, 1995a, pp. 88–95).

Erikson described three adulthood stages. He and some other authors viewed midlife as bringing about a generativity versus stagnation crisis (Colarusso and Nemiroff, 1981, p. 32; Lachman and James, 1997, pp. 6–7; Staudinger and Bluck, 2001, pp. 14–16). As midlife proceeds, it can be argued that this period also contains elements of both earlier and later adulthood stages that involve a crisis centering on the attainment of intimacy versus self-absorption and ego integrity versus despair, respectively.

Erikson (1959) wrote that the main task of the middle years had to do with parenthood and the attainment of generativity, by which he meant

> the interest in establishing and guiding the next generation, although there are people who, from misfortune or because of special and genuine gifts in other directions, do not apply this drive to offspring but to other forms of altruistic concern and creativity, which may absorb their kind of parental responsibility [p. 97].

He went on to say, however, that merely wanting or having children does not guarantee generativity and that the "majority of young parents seen in child guidance work suffer, it seems, from the retardation of or inability to develop this stage" (p. 97).

For Erikson, ego integrity, which he saw as belonging to the final stage of adulthood, accrued from success with all earlier stages:

It is the acceptance of one's own and only life cycle and of the people who have become significant to it as something that had to be and that, by necessity, permitted of no substitution. It thus means a new different love of one's parents, free of the wish that they should have been different, and an acceptance of the fact that one's life is one's own responsibility. It is a sense of comradeship with men and women of distant times and of different pursuits, who have created orders and objects and sayings conveying human dignity and love [p. 98].

Adult Developmental Theories

Since Jung and Erikson, others have developed theories of and studied adult life more systematically. They have expanded our understanding of the stages of the life cycle and shed light on the nature of personality change in adulthood. They have described the ways in which adults cope with stressful and traumatic life events. Moreover, they have put forth new perspectives on the nature of women's development and their life course and offered fresh views of the lives of members of culturally diverse populations.

Research on the Adult Life Cycle

Daniel Levinson and his colleagues (1978) made a major contribution by delineating the "seasons of a man's life." Like Erikson, Levinson and his colleagues used a psychosocial perspective and viewed the transitions to different life stages as constituting a developmental crisis. They based their thinking on studies of the life course of 40 men and accounts of men's lives as portrayed in literature.

The four major eras that Levinson et al. described include preadulthood (ages 0–20), early adulthood (ages 20–45), middle adulthood (ages 45–65), and later adulthood (ages 65+). Each era can be further subdivided and poses its own developmental tasks, the overriding one of which is the need to evolve a life structure that integrates one's external situation (roles, interests, goals, and lifestyle) with one's internal state (personal meaning of these external factors, identity, values, psychodynamics, and capacities). Levinson et al. wrote about a second era, early adulthood, which is marked by a transitional crisis at around age 30, at which time men feel the impetus to make changes in their lives and to build a more stable and complete life structure. It is only then that they settle down in a committed love relationship, move into a more satisfying job situation, and start a family. Transitional periods usually come about when tension develops between the external situation and internal needs, causing the person to alter his life structure to achieve a better fit (Colarusso and Nemiroff, 1981, pp. 36–42; Goldstein, 1995a, pp. 105–106).

When men approach the third era of middle adulthood, which begins around age 40, their earlier success, which often was accompanied by increasing pressures and responsibilities, may cause them to question where they have been, what they want, and where they are going. This self-questioning ushers in a midlife transition. Individuation in this period involves confronting and integrating four pairs of polarities: youth versus age, destructiveness versus creativity, masculinity versus femininity, and attachment versus separateness (Colarusso and Nemiroff, 1981, p. 41). In the sample that was studied, the men's reordering of priorities in midlife often led them to emphasize relationships more than career, which was their main focus in earlier periods (Staudinger and Bluck, 2001, p. 12).

Dynamic processes in adult life that are unrelated to life transitions per se also can generate personality change. Robert White (1966), a nonpsychoanalytic ego psychologist who wrote extensively about the concepts of competence and mastery, described five growth trends in adult life: (1) the stabilizing of ego identity in which one's sense of identity becomes richer on the basis of accumulated experiences involving a sense of competence and self-esteem; (2) the freeing of personal relationships in which the capacity to perceive, accept, and value people in their own right increases, permitting more gratifying and intimate relationships; (3) the deepening of interests, whereby one acquire greater skills, knowledge, and competence; (4) affirmation of and commitment to a value system that involves social purposes; and (5) the expansion of caring, in which egocentrism is transcended and the welfare of others becomes important (Goldstein, 1995a, pp. 102–104).

Interested in the evolution of ego defenses and their role in adaptation, George Vaillant (1977) based his views on the study of 95 men in addition to accounts of men's lives in the literature. His findings lent support to the idea that defenses mature as adults grow older and that adults with more mature, in contrast to more primitive, defenses show more success in adapting to the developmental tasks of Erikson's (1959) life cycle stages.

In a different set of studies of a large sample of psychiatric outpatients and normal subjects, psychiatrist Roger Gould (1978) focused on the steps by which individuals overcame the childhood assumptions or consciousness that could potentially interfere with their developmental progression and acquire an adult consciousness instead. Although this process contributed to self-definition, Gould believed it was terrifying because it threatened illusions about absolute safety and security. He wrote that prior to the midlife period (ages 28–34), the main false assumption that the adult must relinquish is the idea that life is simple and controllable, whereas in the midlife decade (ages 35–45) the adult must let go of the belief that evil does not exist in the world. The latter false assumption has numerous components: the illusion that safety can last forever; the belief that death cannot happen to one or one's loved ones; the idea that it is impossible to live without a protector; the view that there is no life beyond one's family; and the conviction that one is an innocent (Colarusso and Nemiroff, 1981, pp. 47–49).

On the basis of his cross-cultural studies of men and women, Guttman (1975) made some interesting, albeit controversial, observations about the differences between young and older men and between men and women in midlife. He identified the tendency of older men, in contrast to younger men, to be more concerned with love than with conquest or power. The younger men were more interested in taking pleasure from food, pleasant sights, sounds, and human associations rather than being narrowly focused on sexual pleasures and instrumental goals (pp. 44–45). Guttman also described women's aging process as taking them in an opposite direction from men psychologically. Across cultures, women become more aggressive in later life, less sentimental, more managerial, less interested in communion, and more turned toward agency (p. 45). He offered an interpretation of marital disharmony, male marital infidelity, and divorce based on what he believed to be the lack of fit between men and women in later life.

Another significant contribution to adult developmental theory can be found in the work of Bernice Neugarten (1968; Neugarten et al., 1964). On the basis of her studies of relatively successful normal men and women (ages 45–55), Neugarten identified seven salient issues as typical of middle adulthood: (1) middle-aged adults look to themselves rather than to others as the instrument for achieving their goals; (2) they monitor and devise strategies for maintaining their bodies because of their increased sense of physical vulnerability; (3) they view their lives in terms of how much time they have left; (4) they see death as personal and as happening to themselves and their loved ones; (5) they increase their self-understanding and understanding of earlier and later generations because of their position of being in the middle; (6) they view ongoing and future accomplishments as possible because of their accumulated expertise; and (7) they increase their self-reflection, introspection, and restructuring of their lives, processes that culminate in a life review that can result in personality changes in later life (Butler, 1963). Neugarten (1968) also highlighted the "central importance of the executive processes of personality in middle age: self-awareness, selectivity, manipulation, control of the environment, mastery, competence, and a wide array of cognitive strategies" (p. 98).

Sharing Neugarten's view that awareness of death is a significant feature of midlife, psychiatrist and psychohistorian Robert Lifton (1979) wrote extensively about the need for persons in midlife to grow from their awareness of death, which he believed to be more acute in contemporary society, without becoming incapacitated by their anxiety about its inevitability or becoming numbed and stagnated. He believes that integrating death awareness in a healthy manner can result in midlife adults' becoming more loving and caring and more able to parent and mentor the next generation. They are more productive and creative in their work and professional pursuits, and show more humor and appreciation of the absurd. For many people, the process of coming to terms with the passage of time and the inevitability of death may engender mourning, which goes beyond grief for the loss of meaningful relationships. Mourning can encompass grieving for lost opportunities, for experiences, and for the future. Nonetheless, although painful, mourning can be liberating and growth-enhancing (Pollock, 1987).

The Impact of Role Transitions

In a related vein, some theorists have addressed the influence of role transitions, such as becoming a spouse or life partner, parent, supervisor, or caretaker of one's parents, on the adult personality. This impact may stem from the social pressure that one may experience from family, peers, and society about the need to take on certain roles, having to meet the actual requirements of a particular role, and the change in self-concept involved in taking on a major new role.

For example, in her early work, Neugarten (1968) drew attention to the expectations that adults of different social classes and ethnic groups share about the age at which significant events in life should occur that involve taking on new roles. There is a social clock that exerts pressure on people to make certain types of changes. Sometimes roles that are thrust on individuals at times that are not in keeping with their own or others' expectations create both disequilibrium and opportunity for growth.

Neugarten also viewed the changes in self-concept and identity as constituting a critical issue in adult life. She described how taking on a new role requires not only special coping skills but also the expansion or changes in one's self-concept. For example, it is not unusual for new parents to begin to see themselves as more adult and act in more adult ways. Or getting a promotion or position that puts one in a more senior rather than junior role in relationship to others may call forth a new way of viewing the self.

Interested in the effect of the parenting process on the adult personality, Therese Benedek (1970) described its positive and negative potential. She noted that different phases of parenting may evoke different parental conflicts that stem from the parents' own childhood. She believed not only that parents relive and become possibly stymied by their own earlier difficulties during child rearing but that they also rework and resolve those difficulties, thus reaching a new level of maturation themselves. In this connection, Miriam Elson (1984), drawing on self-psychological concepts, wrote about the transformation of parental narcissism that optimally occurs during the parenting process.

Although Benedek (1970) focused on the effect of the parenting role, her ideas provided a framework for understanding the growth potential inherent in taking on other roles that reiterate earlier conflicts throughout life. For example, becoming an adult caretaker of an aging parent may stir up unresolved conflicts and long-standing resentments but also may provide opportunities for repairing, coming to terms with, or transcending them. Rapoport (1963), even earlier than Benedek and Elson, described the transition points in the family life cycle that could be both disorienting and growth-producing.

Reconceptualizing Adult Development and Its Vicissitudes

Synthesizing the general thrust of the major adult developmental theorists just discussed, Colarusso and Nemiroff (1981) offered seven hypotheses about the psychodynamic theory of adulthood: (1) the developmental process is basically the same in the adult as in the child; (2) development in adulthood is an ongoing, dynamic process; (3) adult development is concerned with the continued evolution of existing structures and their use rather than on the formation of psychic structures, as is characteristic of childhood; (4) the fundamental developmental issues of childhood continue as central aspects of adult life but in altered form; (5) adult development is influenced by both the adult and the childhood past; (6) development in adulthood is greatly influenced by the body and physical change; and (7) a major developmental crisis and phase-specific theme of adult development is the recognition and acceptance of time and inevitability of personal death (Goldstein, 1995a, pp. 102–103).

In one of the uncommon instances in which a clinician applied adult developmental theory to the treatment situation, Ellman (1992) developed a hospital midlife crisis treatment unit for a subgroup in the middle-aged population for whom the universal phase-specific tasks of midlife were experienced as pathogenic trauma (p. 564). The most common midlife issues seen in the patients on this unit concerned

reappraisals in many areas of life. These areas had to with relationships, work identity, and self-concept, particularly related to physical
changes. As might be expected, these patients gave much thought to
the passage of time and the meaning of life and of one's past and the
need to come to terms with it (p. 564).

Effect of Life Events and Crises

The literature on adulthood discussed so far emphasized the normal
and expected developmental and role-transition crises of adult life
that cause disequilibrium and contain the potential for growth.
Stressful and traumatic events in midlife that shake a person to the
core may also result in positive changes despite their potential for
stimulating a spiraling downward course. This effect became the focus of crisis theory, which originated, in part, from the study and
treatment of soldiers who had developed so-called war neuroses and
combat fatigue during World War II and of those veterans and their
families who needed to readjust to civilian life after the completion
of military service (Grinker and Spiegel, 1945). Additionally, some
investigators became interested in the reactions of individuals to disasters and stressful life events (Selye, 1956; Hill, 1958; Janis, 1958;
Tyhurst, 1958; Parad and Caplan, 1960; Kaplan, 1962; Caplan,
1964; Strickler, 1965; Lazarus, 1966; Langsley and Kaplan, 1968).
    Lindemann's (1944) classic paper, "Symptomatology and Man-
agement of Acute Grief," delineated identifiable stages of the grief
process of the survivors of the tragic Coconut Grove nightclub fire in
Boston, in which hundreds of persons lost their lives or were injured.
According to Lindemann, an important component of grief resolution is the survivor's ability to master various affective, cognitive,
and behavioral tasks. He observed that people could resume and
even improve their precrisis level of functioning after a crisis, or they
could deteriorate. Lindemann believed that those who showed mal-
adaptive solutions to their grief could be helped through intervention to cope more effectively with their mourning.
    Crisis theory is based on the assumption that a person strives to
maintain equilibrium through an ongoing series of adaptive measures and problem-solving techniques. A crisis represents an upset of

that equilibrium in which the person's customary coping strategies are inadequate to deal with the task at hand. A belief underlying crisis work is that people are capable of making positive changes even when they have endured catastrophic situations. Although some crisis theorists have suggested that all people who experience a similar event will respond in a like manner, others have focused on the unique meaning that a person attaches to a particular situation. For example, Jacobson, Strickler, and Morley (1968) differentiated between generic and individual intervention, the former focusing on the common reactions of all the people who experience the same event and the latter emphasizing the unique reactions of each person.

There is a vast literature on the impact of such traumatic events as natural or manmade disasters; marital separation and divorce; illness, disability, and death; sexual and physical violence; war and captivity; emigration; and even terrorism (Parad, 1965; Coehlo et al., 1974; Parad and Parad, 1990). Most of this literature, however, looks at the usual recovery process and at the significance of social supports in fostering coping and adaptation. It tends to minimize the impact of personality characteristics and dynamics on the recovery process and does not address the reasons for the inability to regain one's equilibrium and move forward.

Gender, Generation, and Diversity

Most, but by no means all, seminal writing on adult development has been based on studies of men and either ignored the life course of women or described them according to their marital and maternal roles, loss of attractiveness, experience of menopause, and empty-nest syndrome (Bart, 1971; Adelmann et al., 1989; Dan and Berhard, 1989; Greer, 1992; McQuaide, 1998a, b). For example, almost 20 years elapsed from the writing of his book on men's life cycle before Levinson (1996) turned his attention to adult women. It should be noted, however, that the lack of differentiation between male and female development was characteristic of most psychodynamic theories generally. Moreover, much of the theorizing about women that did exist derived from observations of those who were reared at a

particular historical time and who may have been different from
those born later (Williams, 1977; Rossi, 1980; Brooks-Gunn and
Kirsh, 1984).

It is beyond the scope of this chapter to review the entire body of
work about women's development generally and their adult life
course specifically (see, e.g., Barnett, 1984; Baruch and Brooks-
Gunn, 1984; Brooks-Gunn and Kirsh, 1984; Hunter and Sundel, 1989;
Wainrib, 1992; Lachman and James, 1997; Stewart and Ostrove, 1998;
Lachman, 2001; Hunter et al., 2002). Nevertheless, there are some
significant ideas that warrant consideration.

Reconceptualizing Women's Development

Many authors have offered new perspectives on women's development and shed light on women's unique strengths and difficulties
throughout the life cycle. From a general theoretical perspective,
Nancy Chodorow (1978) and Carol Gilligan (1982) are early feminist pioneers who have challenged the male bias in traditional
psychodynamic theories. They argue that females have an individuation process different from that of males because of women's initial
primary and close attachment to a same-sex rather than opposite-sex
parent. Those authors describe girls, in contrast to boys, as sharing a
greater sense of identification and merger with one another. The authors believe, too, that the consolidation of girls' psychological
growth does not require distancing from or rejection of their mothers. Chodorow and Gilligan suggest that girls, rather than separating
from their mothers, experience a prolonged closeness and diffuse individuation process. Moreover, girls' ego strengths develop through
connection rather than separation and autonomy. Alternatively,
boys go through a process of defensive autonomy and denial of their
identification with the mother. These two writers also observe that
female, unlike male, self-development involves permeable rather
than rigid boundaries and a greater capacity for empathy, caring, and
intuition.

Like Chodorow and Gilligan, members of the Stone Center for Developmental Services and Studies at Wellesley College in Massachusetts,

including Jean Baker Miller (1977), Alexandra Kaplan and Janet Surrey (1984), Judith Jordan (1990), and Irene Stiver (1991), also have noted the importance of connection and "mutual empathy" in women's "self in relation" development. They argue that women, unlike men, thrive on enhanced connection rather than increased selfobject differentiation and separateness. These authors also believe that unresponsive relationships and disconnection rather than problems in separation-individuation are at the root of psychopathology in women. Contemporary relational theorist Jessica Benjamin (1988) has put forth a different view. She sees women's optimal development as involving self-assertion and mutuality, separateness and sharing. She argues that a woman's inability to reconcile dependence and independence leads to problematic patterns of domination and submission. Constructivist thinkers have argued that gender itself is a social construction, that cultural conditions restrict self-expression and prevent women and men from discovering and expressing themselves in different ways depending on a person's relational and environmental contexts (Butler, 1990).

Women's Diverse Midlife Paths

There is a variety of midlife women today. They came of age during different historical times and differ considerably in their internalized attitudes about themselves and their ideas of femininity. The dramatic changes in society and the expansion of opportunities for women also may account, in part, for the fact that the negative impact of both the empty-nest syndrome and menopause itself in midlife women may be more of a myth than a reality today (Krystal and Chiraboga, 1979; Hunter and Sundel, 1989; McGrath, 1992). Nevertheless women still experience the effects of ageism and sexism (McQuaide, 1998b).

Generally, midlife women expect to be healthier and more active than those of earlier generations. Brunell (1992) and Stewart and Ostrove (1998) have noted that the vast majority of women who were raised during and after the post–World War II baby boom and who came of age in the decades of the 1960s and 1970s have been shown to have high levels of psychological adjustment and low levels of depression by their late 40s. Rather than constituting a crisis, midlife appears to have offered many of these women the opportunity for a midcourse correction. Their lives reflected different and sometimes multiple paths and showed that some women excelled in some rather than other stages or "seasons," which appeared to stimulate their generativity. For example:

> Young motherhood, like the early years of career building, may indeed be a period in which women long to be effective and responsible contributors to society and the next generation . . . but it is in middle age that they are much more likely to feel that they are actually able to do that and only in even later middle age that they feel they have actually done it [Stewart and Ostrove, 1998, p. 1191].

The theme of diversity of midlife paths is important also in understanding the experiences of women across culture and class (Baruch and Brooks-Gunn, 1984, p. 2).

Some midlife women today may still be quite traditional. They continue to view strength, power, and restricted emotionality as male characteristics and warmth, dependence, and passivity as women's traits. They look to men to help them feel worthy. Others may want to break out of old patterns but do not know how to do this, or they fear the consequences (O'Neil and Egan, 1992, pp. 112–118). Person (1982) and Ruderman (2003) have described the prevalence and reasons for women's lingering fears of success despite societal changes in the attitudes toward women today. Echoing the view that women's work inhibitions relate to their fear that success will lead to a loss of affiliative ties, Ruderman (2003) writes that women's blocks in actively pursuing their careers stem from their anxiety about ambition, assertiveness, and achievement, which they link to their deepest fears of object loss:

> Internally, a part of them still exists within a more traditional value set. They often feel compromised by it, and are unable to break out of the yoke imposed by messages inculcated from their earliest infant–caregiver relationships and throughout their early development [p. 11].

There are other differences among midlife women. In contrast to those who had a traditional upbringing, younger women may have attained a greater degree of personal freedom, confidence, and power. Often marrying and having children at a later age, after pursuing careers, they sought husbands who would value their wives' careers and independence and who were more egalitarian, sensitive, and expressive than previous generations. Nevertheless, many of these women paid or are still paying the price of stress overload, burnout, and a deep sense of guilt for not spending sufficient time with their families. Moreover, those who became the major breadwinner had to struggle with the responsibilities, stress, constraints, and discomfort of this position and its impact on their marriage.

The youngest and least traditional group of midlife women who came of age in the 1980s were raised to be more self-confident, assertive, and competent than those who were reared earlier. This 1980s group also felt entitled to actualize themselves and to have successful lives in many areas. Often seeing their own mothers pursue educational and career opportunities, they were raised with heightened expectations about being able to have both a career and family life and thought that they would find men who would be good husbands and fathers. Most important, they expected to have choices.

Many encountered unpleasant surprises as the realities of life clashed with their expectations that they could have it all. Those who wanted careers had to work extremely long hours and more was expected of them. Little time was left for anything else. Marrying and having children seemed to be passing them by. When they awoke to this fact, they sometimes became desperate to find a suitable partner. On marrying, they expected to be able to stop working in order to raise their children and did not expect that they would have to continue to work so as not to lose their place on the career ladder or to maintain their lifestyle. Having children often had to be postponed and fertility problems increased. Time for sexual intimacy and companionship barely existed. When children were born, there was little time to spend with them. Although some husbands became more involved in parenting and sharing household responsibilities, women generally carried the burden of tasks as well as their work responsibilities. Some had superhuman standards for their own performance. Often working to the point of exhaustion, many felt constantly guilty, inadequate, disappointed, and resentful.

The women of these different generations with the least sense of well-being in midlife were those who had regrets about the traditional choices they had made but were unable to make meaningful changes. Many internalized the values of their parents and society regarding the primacy of their roles as devoted mother, dutiful, dependent, and submissive wife, and passive sexual partner. If they wanted a different kind of life, they often experienced conflict about liberating themselves. Frequently lacking positive role models for more autonomous, assertive, and risk-taking behavior, they felt guilty and selfish. They lacked confidence and a sense of mastery and competence and feared being labeled as unfeminine or too masculine. Wanting their husbands to be more communicative, better sexual partners and companions, and more willing to share decision-making responsibilities and power, they felt frustrated and did not always know how to make their needs known or how to negotiate. They also bore the brunt of their husbands' disapproval or anger if they tried to move out of their customary roles.

A growing number of midlife women remained single or became single again (Hunter et al., 2002, pp. 87–106). One study (Dalton, 1992) placed choice of singleness on a continuum and showed that, while some women chose to remain single to pursue education and careers, others attributed their never marrying to unfavorable circumstances, such as not finding the right person or having to manage caretaking responsibilities. Some clearly said they would rather remain single than compromise too much. Many women who never married found their own niche and built a network of supports. Sometimes they had serial romantic relationships with men or became single parents. Others may have enjoyed their autonomy but experienced loneliness, a depreciated personal identity, and social stigma. They had a sense of failure, regrets, and rootlessness (Spira and Richards, 2003). Divorced women had to deal with their own emotional, economic, social, and parenting challenges, not the least of which was the need to let go of an old identity and develop a new self-concept and life structure.

The Impact of Multiple Roles

Women in midlife perform multiple roles that either can be enriching and result in a sense of mastery and well-being or can lead to overload, strain, and conflict. Despite their continuing involvement in work, women retain many of their traditional family responsibilities. Although often receiving help from others in fulfilling some of their parental-role obligations, they feel caught between their work and family roles (Long and Porter, 1984; Polasky and Holahan, 1998, p. 399).

The theories about and research findings on the effects of carrying multiple roles are contradictory and lend support to opposite conclusions (Goode, 1960; Sieber, 1974; Marks, 1977). On one hand, many women seem to benefit from carrying multiple roles, and lack of significant social roles is associated with distress (Baruch and Barnett, 1986; Barnett and Marshall, 1991). Work plays an important role in the lives of many midlife women (Sterns and Huyck, 2001). For example, Rodin and Ickovics (1990, pp. 1023–1024) noted that employed women show better physical and mental health than unemployed women in most studies, that unemployment is a risk factor for women's health, and that higher status jobs and adequacy of employment are associated with better health outcomes.

Alternatively, role strain and role conflict have psychological and physical costs, particularly when the maternal role is involved. Such stress has been associated with depression (Barnett and Baruch, 1985; Greenglass, 1985; Krause and Geyer-Pestello, 1985; Tiedje et al., 1990). Moreover, women's use of cigarettes and alcohol has increased dramatically. They continue to be at greater risk than men for generalized poor health and acute illnesses and symptoms, and their mortality advantage over men has decreased in recent years (Rodin and Ickovics, 1990; Hunter et al., 2002, pp. 135–168).

Although some of the role strain involved in caring for young children may ease in midlife, those women who had children in their mid- to late 30s continue to face the stress of carrying multiple roles at a later age. In addition, midlife women are likely to have to take on the caregiver role for their aging parents; these women sometimes are sandwiched between their children and their parents. Here, too, however, the research on caregiver burden in midlife shows both its psychological costs on one had and its positive significance on the other (Parks and Pilisuk, 1990; Dautzenberg et al., 1999; Hunter et al., 2002, pp. 59–86).

Revisiting the Experiences of Men in Midlife

A controversial question is whether the societal changes that have widened women's roles and opportunities have affected midlife men positively or negatively. Have men evolved beyond the traditional, narrow expectations of their gender roles in a corresponding or complementary fashion, or have they held on to their usual ways of seeing themselves and relating to women personally and professionally? Another important question is how the changes that have taken place in American society in the occupational environment are influencing men's choices in midlife.

Gay Men and Lesbians in Midlife

The special developmental issues that midlife poses for gays and lesbians and the nature of their life course are relatively new areas of investigation. Until recently, research into adult development has been based on studies of heterosexual men and women (Cornett and Hudson, 1987). There is little data to counteract the negative bias toward and stereotypes regarding homosexuals on the part of members of the professional and lay communities. This state of affairs is compounded by the gay and lesbian literature's preoccupation with the coming-out experiences and relationships of gay and lesbian adolescents and young adults.

There is considerable diversity among gay men and lesbians, and there are important similarities and differences between gays and lesbians, on one hand, and between those who identify as gay and those who identify as heterosexual, on the other (Kimmel and Sang, 1995; Kertzner and Sved, 1996; Goldstein and Horowitz, 2002). These authors have emphasized certain features of midlife gays and lesbians.

They note that—in contrast to the stereotypical view that being gay or lesbian in later life means that one is alone, depressed, and alcoholic—white middle-class gays and lesbians generally describe midlife as the best period in their lives and this sense may stem from some special features of their personal struggle. For example, although some gays and lesbians come out for the first time in midlife, many of those who have been out for most of their adult lives feel that they have "paid their dues." They are more self-accepting and feel less concerned about others' disapproval. They have developed coping mechanisms that help them manage the lingering effects of discrimination and oppression. They come to midlife with a greater sense of freedom and power than they had previously and want to enjoy their lives.

Likewise, lesbians usually have greater continuity in their work identities than do heterosexual women who follow more traditional paths. Because lesbians usually have had to deal with the pressures of the work world, many have developed a sense of mastery and self-confidence in this area of their lives. Usually having coped with becoming economically self-sufficient since early adulthood rather than with performing the role of housewife or parent, they do not necessarily experience the empty-nest syndrome or the need to reenter the world of work after a long absence as they enter their 40s and 50s. Nor do they experience menopause as being as much of a threat as do their heterosexual counterparts.

Gay men appear to perceive midlife as beginning earlier and may place a greater importance on sexuality and being attractive than do men who identify as heterosexual. They tend to be better educated and more affluent than is true of the general population but experience a less desirable career ladder than heterosexual men because of discrimination. In contrast, lesbians tend to lack financial security despite their many years of gainful employment, and they often do not receive adequate health care.

A majority of gays and lesbians are in committed, long-term relationships, derive satisfactions from their friendship networks, and are involved in the community. Although part of couple relationships, they are much more likely to be living alone than are their heterosexual counterparts and look to their friends rather than family for support and concrete assistance. Balancing work and relationships is a major theme of midlife for gay men and lesbians alike. Because many gays and lesbians are deciding to become parents, often later than is the case for their heterosexual counterparts, they have to balance the demands of childrearing during the midlife period.

Despite increasing attention paid to gays and lesbians in midlife, we are at a beginning stage in understanding their particular psychological challenges and the factors that support or obstruct their navigation of midlife. This observation pertains to an even greater degree when we consider the life course of people of color and ethnic minorities.

3
MIDLIFE EVENTS
The Impact of Loss and Change

As we note throughout this book, midlife dynamics and the events of midlife bring about both objective and subjective losses and the need for change. Experiences of loss result in acute and sometimes prolonged grief reactions. Making significant changes often requires that people let go of what has been familiar. Both loss and change may necessitate a modification or expansion of one's self-concept and life structure. Change and loss create challenges to self-esteem and self-cohesion. Whether the impetus is self-imposed or externally caused, change makes most people feel unsettled. It is not easy to give up what is known. It is difficult to relinquish emotionally charged expectations and develop new identities and environmental supports. The personal qualities of resilience and flexibility and a firm sense of self seem to be associated with successful coping, but these characteristics do not operate in isolation from the surrounding environment. When life events drastically alter the essential supports that have sustained the self or compensated for its weakness, even seemingly resilient persons may encounter serious difficulties. This chapter considers the impact of ten common midlife events or situations on the self and the consequent treatment implications.

Remaining Single

Whether out of choice or circumstance, increasing numbers of midlife women have remained single or never became involved in committed long-term relationships. Many of these women enjoy their autonomy and build relationships, support systems, and life-styles that are enjoyable and nourishing. Some even have become single parents, a circumstance that has its own rewards and challenges. Nevertheless, many single midlife women experience feelings of loneliness, lack of intimacy, a sense of rootlessness, and an acute awareness of the lingering social stigma attached to being unmarried. Some develop more disabling emotional reactions when they face the reality that they may remain single and childless.

There are many possible reasons that women remain single. Sometimes deep-seated personal conflicts and dynamics have contributed to their difficulties in attracting and sustaining romantic partnerships with men. Or they have become absorbed in building their careers or, perhaps, taking care of their parents. They may not have found the "right" man. And they do not want to "settle" or compromise in choosing a mate (Dalton, 1992; Hunter et al., 2002, pp. 95–97; Spira and Richards, 2003). Or they may have had bad experiences with men that they did not want to repeat.

Whether or not midlife single women continue to try to find a life partner, it is necessary for them to readjust their self-concept, establish a new basis for their self-esteem, and develop a satisfying life structure. Troubling feelings and attitudes, however, may obstruct their ability to move on with their lives. For example, it is not unusual for more traditionally raised single women, who believed that marrying and having children was the most important measure of their success as a woman, to experience their singles status as a sign of failure. Feelings of inadequacy and self-blame even may exist alongside significant success in other areas of their lives. Additionally, these women may feel a deep sense of sadness and regret for having lost out. They may harbor feelings of anger at and envy of others who seem to have what they think they lack.

In contrast, many younger midlife women were reared with a greater belief in their own rights to self-actualization and equality with men and enjoy more opportunities and encouragement to pursue their interests and talents than did women of earlier generations. They expected to pursue their education and successful careers, to have families of their own, and to have husbands whom they could admire and who would value their abilities and achievements. They never anticipated that they would remain single in midlife or have to settle for a life partner who did not live up to their standards. Consequently, many experience a blow to their feelings of entitlement, competence, and sense of fairness, along with feelings of loss and deprivation when they realize that they may remain single, childless, or both.

Here are two examples illustrating the different issues that two single midlife women experienced.

A Deep Sense of Failure

Ellen was a youthful-looking, well-dressed, unmarried schoolteacher when she entered treatment just prior to her 55th birthday. She said she was becoming more acutely aware that she was going to grow old by herself. She felt alone, depressed, and hopeless about the future. She hated her job and felt like a failure in both her personal life and her work life. She described life as passing her by and both envied and resented her younger brother and sisters, all of whom were married and had successful careers. Although they showed an interest in Ellen, she felt that they were patronizing. She wanted a family connection but dreaded going to family events because of her feelings of humiliation that she was still single, did not have children to brag about, and lacked a really fantastic job about which she could feel proud. Although she was a size 14, she felt fat and quite certain that a man who was worth anything would not be interested in her. She was tired of being involved with self-centered men who were focused on themselves.

Ellen was the eldest child of third-generation American-born parents, who were quite traditional in their values and attitudes. Although her father was in medical training when she was born, he eventually became successful and prominent in the community. Her mother, an attractive and intelligent woman, remained a housewife throughout the marriage despite seeming stifled. Ellen admired her parents and wanted their approval but felt quite lonely during her childhood. Involved in career building, her father paid little attention to her, and her mother was often depressed or involved with her own siblings. Her mother catered to her husband and took a backseat to him. Moreover, she had an alcohol problem that no one ever addressed directly.

Ellen said that her parents placed considerable importance on appearances. She recalled her mother's efforts to bring her up as a proper young lady, and she seemed to have internalized her mother's values about how girls were to behave.

When Ellen was six years old, her brother was born, and her father became more attentive to him than he had ever been to Ellen, who at this point was shy, quiet, and fearful. Soon after her brother was born, her mother gave birth to two daughters in quick succession. They also seemed to enjoy a different relationship with both parents than Ellen did. Ellen felt that she could never measure up to her father's standards. She was older than her siblings by six to 10 years but always felt that they were more outgoing, intelligent, and confident than she was.

She felt lost in high school but began to find her own niche when she attended college in the 1960s. She made some close friends but dated infrequently. She felt uncomfortable in the presence of men and out of sync with her peers, who seemed to be more assertive and adventuresome and less sexually inhibited than she was. Nevertheless, she assumed she would get married right after college as her mother had done. She described herself as waiting to be discovered.

During her college years, Ellen became more invested in doing something with her life. She would have liked to enter the Peace Corps but was too frightened to do so. Her father died just before Ellen graduated from college, and his death had a devastating impact on her mother, who became more dependent on her adult children. A dutiful daughter, Ellen returned home to live with her mother right after graduation. "Can you believe that I became a teacher? As if I wasn't boring enough. I could have found something else to do. It's not as if I'm stupid," she said. As a young adult, Ellen became aware of the world changing around her but she did not change with it. Eventually Ellen did try to change careers. She went into catering and had a modicum of success until there was an economic downturn. Rather than persevering, she returned to teaching.

Ellen did have relationships with men who she felt were narcissistic. She deeply resented their expecting her "to stroke their egos" and subordinate her needs to theirs but did not know how to make her own needs known. "I was a total wimp," she said. "I see that, but I didn't know how not to be. I would have been a good 19th-century woman except that I don't know how to flirt and make small talk." Eventually, her relationships would peter out: "I don't know if I became tired of them or they became tired of me. It probably was mutual. I got tired of being a sieve but I was far from your interesting person. I didn't think I had to be." In the five years before entering treatment, Ellen had an off-and-on relationship with "another narcissist," as she put it. "There has to be someone who is not self-centered, but who am I kidding? I wouldn't know what to do with someone who was really interested in me. I've just messed everything up."

A Blow to Feelings of Entitlement

Stephanie was 39 years old when she entered treatment because she did not know what to do with herself. An intelligent, nice-looking, highly competent attorney, who had just been made a partner in her firm, she felt a sense of urgency about her biological clock running out. She knew she had to make some kind of change but did not feel clear about her direction. She also described feeling sorry for herself and being angry all the time. "I just never thought I would be here." Stephanie explained that she thought she would be married with three children, have household help, and work part-time. "Don't misunderstand. I don't feel desperate about getting married at this point. I went through my frantic period earlier. I realized I was going to wind up alone if I didn't stop working all the time and make room

for a personal life. I dated like crazy for a while, but I never found Mr.
Right and now all the good ones are taken or are interested in younger women. Men all have radar. If you're in your 30s, they avoid you
like the plague, except for the ones you don't want anyway. I've dated
those too. I have to be with a guy who interests me in some way. I'm
just not going to settle for anyone, but I don't want to live my life
alone. I don't think I should have to compromise.

"My parents have a great marriage, and they love and respect each
other. It's not about my mom's catering to my father's ego. I've been
told all my life that I should make the best of who I am and that someone who's good will love me for that. It shouldn't be so hard to find a
good companion. It makes me furious. Men don't really want to have
a strong, independent woman who makes demands on them. They
want us to work so they can have a good life, but they still want to be
catered to. My friends are in the same boat. . . . I'm not sorry that I put
my career first for a while. I just think it's hard to find a guy who's
evolved but who's also going to be faithful. Where are they? I don't
think that I'm being unreasonable. The problem is I can be right but
alone. I don't think I'm asking for that much."

Stephanie was the eldest of three girls in a New England family.
Her parents met when they were in their early 30s and had been married for 40 years. Stephanie's father, an attorney, age 73, was the senior partner in his law firm and still worked. Her mother, age 72,
recently retired from her job as an office manager in a small medical
office. Stephanie described her parents as a team and their relationship as caring and respectful. She said she grew up admiring them and
imagining that she would have a similar kind of marriage. She felt
that the family was close and preferred to spend time with one another rather than with outsiders. Stephanie described her parents as
highly successful. Both valued intelligence and achievement and
were critical of those who did not work hard or make something of
their lives. She acknowledged that they tended to set themselves
apart from others in their town. Stephanie felt that they encouraged
and supported her and her sisters to make the most of their abilities.
She described her father as having doted on her, often confiding his
professional concerns to her. She grew up taking pride in her abilities, drive, and self-discipline and tended to view those who had less
ambition and "smarts" as weak.

Stephanie attended an all-girls' high school and college. She was an honors student and excelled in sports. Although she got along well socially, she had few close friends and confided in her sisters. Focusing on her studies, she dated infrequently and did not have much contact with male peers until she went to law school. She found the atmosphere there highly competitive and demeaning of the women students. She felt that she had to be better than her male classmates if she was to be taken seriously. Although she dated, she found the more intelligent men to be totally self-involved, desirous of admiration, and insensitive to her; she experienced those who seemed interested in her as needy and uninteresting.

After graduation, she obtained a position in a prestigious law firm and worked long hours. She dated and had some serious relationships that did not work out because the men just were not "right" for her. When she was in her late 20s, she almost became engaged but broke off the relationship because she did not want to give up her job, where she was on a partner track, to move with her potential husband to another state because of his career. She began to feel pressured about getting married when she turned 35.

Discussion. Ellen and Stephanie were at opposite ends of the midlife spectrum with respect to their chronological age. They had been reared with different attitudes toward marriage and women's roles, and each possessed a distinctive self-concept and sense of self-esteem and competence. Ellen felt that her mother had been stifled in her marriage and that her mother was highly dependent on and admiring of her husband. Ellen identified with her mother and subscribed to the traditional view of women as being passive caretakers who subordinated themselves to their husbands' needs. From her earliest years, Ellen believed that marriage would just happen when she came of age. Although she recognized that her father was very self-centered and self-involved, Ellen nevertheless blamed herself for not being able to attract his positive attention when she was younger and for not being able to get her teachers to notice and encourage her.

She did not understand why her stance had not led her to marry and blamed herself for her deficits as a woman. She viewed her single status as evidence of her inability to attract a man. Ellen felt extremely alone and was angry and envious of others who did not seem better than she was on the surface but who had been able to marry and have children. Suffering from chronically low self-esteem and a negative self-concept, she did not feel good enough about herself to attract and sustain a relationship with a man, on one hand, or to find a satisfying life structure without a male partner, on the other.

In contrast to Ellen, Stephanie saw her parents as having a collaborative and egalitarian marriage in which both partners developed themselves. She had been taught to value a woman's assertiveness and accomplishments and to expect that a man would love and value her for herself. At the same time, Stephanie's parents seemed to be intolerant of those who did not live up to their standards. They encouraged Stephanie and her sisters to look to the family for support to the exclusion of others. Having been taught to value achievement, self-reliance, and hard work, Stephanie appeared to identify with and internalize these values. Having grown up without much experience in developing close ties outside the family and with men other than her father, Stephanie may not have been able to develop or learn to negotiate close relationships with men.

In some respects, Stephanie's expectations about the type of male partner that she wanted were reasonable. She had a high level of self-esteem and appeared to possess a strong sense of self as a competent, assertive, and successful woman who deserved a male partner who would have similar characteristics and value her. At the same time she seemed to have a rigid, idealized self-concept and a one-dimensional view of men. She lacked empathy for and acceptance of some of her own and others' needs and traits that she regarded as weak. It made her angry to think that she would not have the kind of relationship with a man that she wanted. Having to compromise was not only absent from her experience, the very idea of having to make do made her feel that she would be going against her values. She could not understand her life's not working out as she thought it would.

Men, as well as women, may remain single in midlife for a variety of reasons. Sometimes, problems in making a commitment to another person are involved. Although there are different causes for this situation, issues related to the self are almost always among them.

The following example illustrates some of the factors that contributed to a man's continuing single status in early midlife.

A Search for the Perfect Woman

Mark was 42 years old when he entered treatment. A tall, handsome, articulate man, he spoke in a matter-of-fact and intellectualized manner that seemed more appropriate to a job interview than to a first therapy session. He said that since his 40th birthday he had been concerned that he was unable to find the "right" woman to marry. He thought that it was time for him to commit to a long-term relationship and settle down. He explained that most of his male friends were married or engaged, even the ones who had been the most anti-marriage. They had always looked up to him but now teased him about his "holding out." He also said that he felt guilty that he was disappointing his parents, who had given up on his sister's providing them with grandchildren. He had begun to feel uncomfortable in his single status on his job, particularly when he brought new girlfriends to work-related social events. Employed as a midlevel manager, Mark felt that his employers expected him to have a wife, family, house in the suburbs, and a dog.

Mark reported that since his college days he had always been successful in attracting women and seldom was without a significant relationship. Nevertheless, he had not found someone with whom he wanted "to close the deal." He was beginning to question whether he just had not found the "right" woman or something else was involved. He revealed that he was contemplating breaking off with a woman he had been seeing for about five months because she wanted a commitment and he did not feel ready. He felt conflicted about ending the relationship because he initially thought she would "be the one."

Despite his stated desire to be in a committed relationship, Mark's record for staying with a woman was six months. He related that he seemed to have relationships with two very different types of women: those whom he felt attracted to physically and emotionally but who lacked certain values, intellect, education, or achievement, and those who were great women on their resumes and whom he cared about but who did not "do it for" him. He placed Karen, the woman he was currently seeing, in the first category. Although he said he was "crazy about" her, he could not see himself marrying her. He knew that his parents would think she was not up to his intellectual or cultural level and that they would be greatly disappointed. He often found himself irritated with her when she revealed her lack of sophistication, general knowledge, and immaturity.

Mark described himself as a "pretty sensitive guy" as men go and as a "good" boyfriend who always tried to be thoughtful and attentive. He revealed, however, that his previous girlfriends had accused him of being too controlling of his emotions, lacking openness about his feelings, and being hypercritical and condescending. He acknowledged that their criticisms had some basis, but he thought that it was their behavior that provoked his reactions. He became defensive and withdrawn if they pushed him and would become "turned off" if they cried or showed their anger.

Mark also mentioned that he was experiencing some increasing frustration in his work life. He felt that he had been a rising star in his company until recently. A project manager, he was not able to get his team to deliver the positive financial results that his employers desired. Although they seemed to recognize that this outcome was not his fault, Mark felt that he had fallen from his pedestal in their eyes. For the first time, he did not receive a good bonus and was not being considered for promotion. He said he did not want to leave the firm, for he had many years' service, but he did not know how to get what he wanted. He adopted a "wait and see" attitude but described feeling a lack of motivation about his work.

Mark was the younger of two children born to Jewish parents. He described his mother as having a strong sense of values and high expectations of him, yet as extremely loving, affectionate, and admiring, if not sometimes overwhelming in her emotional displays and accolades. He also depicted her as very needy and insecure. Mark felt that she put all her hopes on him and that he always has been able to live up to her expectations. He was clearly favored over his sister, who rebelled against and fought with her mother from an early age. Mark recalled siding with his mother against his sister when the mother criticized her daughter's attitudes and behavior. He added that it was only recently that he had distanced himself from his mother, became closer to his sister, and saw her point of view more clearly.

Mark described his father as a businessman who earned a good but not great income and who tended to leave jobs and make sideways moves frequently for interpersonal reasons and who retired early in order to avoid stress. Although a loving and dedicated father, he appeared to be a compulsive, if not out-of-control, collector of certain household items and could be explosive when frustrated. Although Mark thought that his parents were ill-suited to each other, having fought throughout their marriage, he was amazed that they had stayed together over 45 years.

Almost apologetically, Mark described having had a "charmed life." He never felt pressure about time until he turned 40, when he began to realize that he should be moving on. There was not much that Mark could say about himself at a deeper level. He eventually disclosed that he did not understand why he was often anxious, suffered from headaches at times, and had trouble making decisions.

Discussion. It appeared that Mark's entering psychotherapy was triggered by his feeling that he was not moving on or living up to his own and others' expectations in his personal and work life. He viewed getting married as a measure of success at his age, and he was discouraged by no longer being treated as a rising star, or even appreciated, on the job. In his relationships with women, Mark seemed to seek out those who showered him with love, affection, and positive mirroring but who he felt were not up to his family's or his own standards. Or he took to women who had the right credentials but who were clearer about what they wanted and demanded more of him than he could give. Although he had cultivated the ability to be the "perfect" boyfriend in the early stages of his relationships so that the women he dated thought he was a "good catch," he never delivered emotionally. Treating them well superficially, he seemed unable truly to depend on or allow himself to need or love anyone. Used to living by himself, making his own decisions, and fitting others into his schedule and routines, Mark was accustomed to being in control of his time and relationships and was often critical of others' "annoying" habits or "stupid" ways of doing things. Mark often seem devoid of intense feelings and intolerant of others' emotional displays.

In Mark's work life, he was a "good soldier" but was cautious and did not take risks. He tended to be compliant and politic rather than direct in saying what he thought and advocating for himself. Although these qualities may have worked well for him at an earlier point in his career, when he was regarded as "up and coming," Mark seemed to be losing ground in the face of increasing competition and demands for more creativity and leadership.

Pressures from Multiple Roles

Although remaining single is a problem for increasing numbers of women, being married is not always a panacea. A major source of difficulty that many of the younger midlife working or professional women experience results from their carrying multiple roles (Long and Porter, 1984; Tiedje et al., 1990; Polasky and Holahan, 1998). Having grown up believing that they would have choices, some feel trapped in a life that is filled with overwhelming pressures from which they can cannot escape. Wanting to pursue both a career and a family life, many married later than did women of earlier generations. They believed that they would be able to stop working, at least for a time, in order to be "hands-on" mothers and imagined that they would have husbands who shared the responsibilities of child rearing. They did not expect to be the major wage-earners in their families, to have to continue to work full-time so as not to lose their place in the career hierarchy, or to have to give up the comfortable lifestyle afforded by two incomes.

Trying to conceive at a later age, many women discovered that they had fertility problems. They frequently engaged in multiple grueling attempts at conception through in vitro or in vivo fertilization or made plans for adoption. When children did arrive on the scene, husbands were not always eager to share parenting and household responsibilities. Even when they were supportive, women generally carried the burden of the child rearing along with their continuing work responsibilities, household help notwithstanding. They felt compelled to become a superwoman, someone who could have it all if she did it all by herself (Hayes, 1986). Because of their perfectionist standards for their own performance or what they perceived as others' expectations of them or financial necessity, they often worked themselves to the point of exhaustion, often feeling guilty, inadequate, disappointed, and resentful.

The following case example shows a married midlifer for whom the demands of multiple roles and the contrast between her expectations and reality demands were causing severe stress and stirring up an underlying vulnerability in the self.

Life on a Treadmill

A successful art director in the advertising field, Jessica was 43 years old when she entered treatment. She suffered from severe back pains for which there was no diagnosable physical cause and worried about having missed time at work. She was medicating herself with alcohol and was aware that this made her more tired. On her most recent medical visit, she broke down and cried in her doctor's office. He suggested that she either take antidepressants or seek psychotherapeutic treatment or do both.

Jessica had been married for seven years to Greg, age 48. They had two children, a six-year-old girl and a four-year-old boy. A high school teacher who earned a stable but relatively small income, Greg had considerable flexibility in his schedule, which allowed him to be home in the afternoon to help in looking after the children. In contrast, Jessica held a high-powered and stressful position and earned a sizable salary, which was necessary to support the couple's lifestyle. Although she worked in New York City, she and Greg purchased a small starter home in northern Westchester, where Greg worked. The couple hoped they would eventually be able to purchase a larger "dream" house. With the help of Greg and a part-time nanny, Jessica worked continuously except for very brief periods just before and after giving birth to each of the children. Despite having enjoyed many aspects of her career, Jessica found it hard to return to work after each child was born. She worried constantly about them when she was at the office and perpetually felt that she was depriving them and herself of being with them. She cried on Sunday nights before the start of her work week. She spent as much time with them as she could in the evenings and on weekends, but she had to leave the

house at 7 a.m. and usually did not arrive home until 7 p.m. Her job
also made demands on her for additional preparation at home, and
she was often exhausted.

When Jessica was home, she placed priority on being with her
children. Although she and Greg slept in the same bed, they would
go for prolonged periods without sexual intimacy or even close companionship because of stress and time pressures. Moreover, Jessica
had no time for herself or for friends. Recently, her agency had
merged with another, and she now faced increased work demands.
She felt frustrated and ungratified and wanted to leave but felt that
she could not do so because of the financial responsibility on her. She
counted on Greg and was grateful that he was a good father to the
children, but she resented the time he had with the children and the
financial load she had to carry. She was disappointed that Greg was
not more ambitious professionally and financially and angry that he
did not seem to be concerned about the pressures on her.

Jessica was the eldest of three siblings and had two younger brothers. When she was a small child, her father left his well-paying job as
a salesman to become a writer. Although he had some initial critical
and financial success, his erratic income forced Jessica's mother to resume her career reluctantly as a commercial interior designer when
Jessica was nine years old. Her mother had been content to leave the
world of work behind when she married. Jessica said she could remember frequent fights and ongoing tension about money. Because
of her mother's income, the family maintained a comfortable but not
extravagant lifestyle, but her mother frequently expressed her resentment about having to work so hard; she hated not being able to
be home more and enjoy the life that she wanted. Jessica recalled that
she used to comfort herself by overeating and by playing with her
dollhouse. She used to draw pictures of clothes and furniture for her
dolls and care for them lovingly, imagining that she had the perfect
family. Later she devoted herself to her schoolwork and her drawing.
She described her mother as caring but strict, harried, and irritable
and as seldom available to her. Nevertheless, she admired her mother
for holding everything together. She recalled her father as more loving and easygoing but as childish and irresponsible. She thought that
her father had had numerous affairs despite his remaining married to
her mother.

Having attended private schools and college, Jessica had been given the essentials (clothes, food, books) but had been unable to be as free with money as were most of her classmates, who came from more affluent families. She confessed that she had never learned to balance her checkbook and often overspent as a result. She was not part of the most popular crowd but did have many friends. She was a good but not stellar student. Talented in art, Jessica received encouragement from her teachers for her drawing and painting. She had never felt confident of her abilities, though. She dated infrequently and usually went out with men she thought were "nerds." She was slightly overweight and lacked the confidence to be able to attract men she thought she could really like.

Obtaining a job in advertising after college, Jessica planned to build her career and then settle down. She married briefly when she was 27 in spite of her mother's advice not to do so. Her first husband was exciting and made her feel pretty. Unfortunately, he was an alcoholic who lived on the trust fund that his grandparents had established for him and who had no desire to work for a living. After the divorce, it took Jessica a long time before she met Greg, when she was 35. By this time she was becoming panicky that she was getting older. She was attracted to Greg because he seemed mature and stable and she thought he would be a supportive and loyal husband.

Discussion. The clash between the realities of Jessica's life and her expectations both challenged her self-concept and expectations and reactivated highly stressful experiences from her childhood that she had never addressed. Despite her mother's having been the primary wage-earner out of necessity, and with considerable ongoing resentment, Jessica was reared to believe that women should pursue a career in order to fulfill themselves rather than because of financial necessity or expectation. She also wished to have a husband and children and thought it important to be a mostly stay-at-home mom for a time. Perhaps as a result of how she had coped with the reality of the financial pressures in her family, Jessica imagined that she would always have enough money when she married and that she would be able to afford the lifestyle that her mother wanted. Consciously, she did not think that she, like her mother, would also become the main breadwinner. Nor did Jessica imagine that she would have to leave her young children with substitute caretakers, as she had been left when she was a child.

After her first, disastrous marriage, she decided that it was crucial to marry a man who would be supportive, loyal, and stable, unlike her first husband and her father. Jessica did not contemplate that Greg, while fitting the bill, might not be a good enough provider to support the family and a comfortable lifestyle. It seemed likely that Jessica had repressed or disassociated the many disturbing feelings connected to her earlier family and school experiences. Although she appeared to have made a good choice in marrying Greg because of his positive qualities, she was replicating in her marriage many of the problems that her parents had encountered, and she was reliving some of the highly stressful experiences from her childhood and adolescence. Moreover, she could not fulfill the ideal dream for her married life because of the financial and time pressures on her and the felt need to do everything well. Not being able to live up to her image of her mother's strength and her own standards for herself left Jessica highly vulnerable to the painful emotions she had experienced when she was younger.

Infidelity in Marriage

Many different factors contribute to unhappy or disappointing marriages. Often the inability that either or both members of a couple demonstrate in meeting each other's needs and in coming together as a team or in their parenting roles is a major factor in marital disharmony. It is not unusual for spouses or partners to carry their archaic selfobject needs or other dysfunctional relational patterns or scripts from the past into the couple relationship.

Marital infidelity plays a major role in marriages today. Whether it is a cause or an outcome of serious difficulties that couples experience or is best understood as an outgrowth of a person's need for an outside relationship, the unfaithfulness of a spouse or life partner, when discovered, usually wreaks havoc for the couple. It has different causes and its frequency and intensity vary. It can result from a deliberate choice or belief system or be accidental, opportunistic, or situational.

Some people seek treatment after having learned that a spouse has strayed, so to speak. Others seek help because of their strong urges to engage in conflicts that arise because of their active involvement in extramarital relationships. In the former instance, feelings of betrayal, anger, and continued distrust may become overwhelming even if the spouse or partner renounces the affair and expresses the desire to maintain the marriage. This may be true especially when the infidelity triggers the injured spouse's feelings of low self-esteem or threatens his or her self-concept. Confidence in one's sense of reality may be shaken or feelings of shame and humiliation triggered. For those who are tempted to have an affair or who actually become involved in one, sometimes frustrated or conflicting self-needs may be at play that make it difficult for them to contain their desire to pursue a new relationship or to choose between one relationship and another.

An affair may signal an attempt to leave an unhappy marriage, but it also may occur in a committed relationship. Although some people are secretly unfaithful to their spouses episodically or even chronically, infidelity sometimes must be understood as a means of coping with the stresses of aging and mortality or changing or frustrated selfobject needs. Infidelity may be a way of dealing with the fears associated with closeness, stability, and dependency.

The following two case examples show the effect of infidelity as well as the impetus to an affair and its resultant stresses.

The Undermining of Trust and Confidence

Joanne, a 48-year-old mother of two young adults, entered treatment several weeks after learning that her husband, Nathan, age 51, was having an extramarital relationship with a 25-year-old female graduate student at the university at which he was a professor. Joanne had become aware of the affair when she received a note from one of Nathan's colleagues and a long-standing academic rival. Joanne confronted her husband, who at first denied the involvement and then finally admitted it when she told him that she needed to know and would feel more betrayed if he kept lying to her. When he did confess,

Joanne became hysterical, and the couple fought for what seemed like days. Although Nathan professed his love for Joanne, proclaimed that the student did not mean anything to him, and agreed to end the affair, Joanne learned that it had been going on for nine months. She was totally shocked, not only because Nathan had been unfaithful to her but also that he would lie to her.

Joanne obsessed about the length of time Nathan had been involved with the young woman and questioned him endlessly about the exact details and times of his meetings with her. She wanted to ascertain if she could match up what he was doing behind her back with what was occurring in the marital relationship. Concurrently, Joanne became hypervigilant about Nathan's whereabouts and activities. She showed a marked distrust of everything he said and checked his answering machine and e-mail by surreptitiously locating his security codes and passwords. She developed severe headaches and ruminated about whether or not to leave the marriage, and, although she decided not to do anything hasty, Joanne blamed herself for being "weak" and a "fool." She did not believe that Nathan would keep his word, and she did not know how she was going to live with him if she could not trust him.

Significant in Joanne's history was that her father, whom she described as greatly admiring and loving and whom she said she regarded as her best friend, left the family for another woman when Joanne was 11 years old. Not only did his sudden departure leave Joanne, her mother, and her two younger sisters in a financially impoverished state for a time until her mother returned to work, but it also was a profound shock to Joanne. She missed her father terribly, although she did see him once or twice a month and spent some vacation time with him. She felt that an enormous hole had been created in her family. At first she could not understand how her father could just walk, but she soon began to blame her mother, whom her father openly criticized for her coldness.

Joanne did not recall much about her high school years, but it seemed likely that she had been quite depressed. As a teenager, she isolated herself from her peers and also had to work to earn money. She lacked confidence and felt that she was not as attractive or bright as her classmates. She did not date until she went to a local city college.

She met Nathan when she was studying for her M.A. in education. He was a teaching assistant in a class that she was taking. He made her feel attractive and special, and she thought he was intelligent and interesting. She loved talking to him. They had many common interests and were able to have serious conversations about a host of subjects. Although they pursued more or less independent lives during their marriage, Joanne totally trusted Nathan, who she felt loved her and was a good and involved father to the children. Joanne went back to work when the children attended school and became a principal in a high school near their home around the same time that her youngest son went to college. She loved her work. Joanne was aware that, as a result of a change of leadership, Nathan was having a difficult time at the university where he taught. He had difficulty identifying with the new thrust of the school. Nathan also missed the children now that they were both out of the house, and he often complained about feeling pushed aside.

A Need to Feel Vital, Special, and Carefree

Stanley was a 52-year-old married father of three children when he sought treatment. He was an attorney in a small boutique law office firm that had just been bought by a larger firm. He had been extremely anxious for a few months and recently became frightened by having experienced what the doctor in the emergency room that he visited diagnosed as a panic attack. He was driving home from work and had to pull over to the side of the road because he thought he was having a heart attack. After his visit to the local hospital, Stanley went to his own doctor, who checked him out thoroughly and questioned Stanley about whether he was under any unusual stress. Although Stanley denied that he was, he later acknowledged to himself that he had been feeling mounting tension and conflict in his personal life.

He revealed to the therapist that he had been having an extramarital affair with Nicky, a 35-year-old woman in his office, for almost a year. He described the affair as having begun innocently enough when he was traveling on business to a conference and he went out to dinner with Nicky and several others from their group. After dinner, she invited him for a drink and acted in a highly seductive manner. One thing led to another. He said that they had great sex and that he surprised himself by his sexual energy and endurance. Although Stanley later went over the evening's events repeatedly, he considered it to have been a one-night affair. On returning to the city, he continued to think about Nicky, and, when she actively pursued him, he eagerly agreed to meet her. She had an apartment near the office, and they would often leave work a little early in order to be alone for a while before Stanley returned home, somewhat later than usual. Their meetings increased in frequency so that they were seeing each other at least twice a week. He described their time together as completely different from the humdrum routines and burdens of his usual life.

When the affair began, Stanley recalled feeling like a new man—alive, important, and free of worries. He exercised more than previously, bought some new clothes, became more focused at work, and was more cheerful. He told his wife, Anne, that he was likely to get a promotion and had some new clients at work with whom he needed to spend more time. He thought this was a credible explanation for his lateness and behavior. He and Anne had a strong, 25-year marriage and three children, one of whom was in college and two were in high school. Anne, age 51, was a real estate agent, having returned to work several years earlier when she wanted to do more with her life. She had many friends and outside interests and seemed to be blossoming. As the affair continued, Nicky placed more pressure on Stanley to leave his wife. He felt conflicted because he did not want to give Nicky up but also did not want "to abandon" Anne, who had been a loyal and supportive wife, and his children, who he felt still needed him.

Before beginning the affair, Stanley had been feeling lost. Turning 50 was difficult for him and he ruminated about it for an entire year before his birthday. He began to worry about his health and had visions of having a heart attack at an early age. Some of these thoughts seemed to be triggered by the sudden death of a friend whom Stanley had known since law school. Around the same time, Stanley learned that his law firm, at which he was a partner and for which he had worked for 25 years, was going to merge with another, larger firm. Although this change did not threaten his actual position, it soon became clear that he was going to have more pressure on him. At the same time, he would become one of many attorneys who specialized in the same legal area rather than have the special status that he enjoyed previously. To make matters worse, Stanley was acutely aware that his children no longer needed him as much as they had, nor did they look up to him as they had previously. Moreover, although he felt good that Anne was blossoming and enjoyed her work, he also was aware of feeling envious of her and less important in her life.

Stanley was an only child. Significant in his history was that his parents, who were devoted to each other, had both died in their late 50s in an automobile accident when he was in law school. They never saw him graduate. He recalled the family as close. He had received a lot of positive attention from them when he was a child and adolescent. He described them as his cheerleaders and felt that he could do no wrong in their eyes. Although they encouraged his studies, he did not experience a lot of pressure from them and described himself as not being the most ambitious or hardworking student. He did competently in law school but did not stand out among his peers. In the years after his parents died, Stanley's work environment was like a family. He was well liked and received considerable positive recognition. An average-looking and somewhat needy man who lacked confidence, Stanley had never been highly successful with women. He was attracted to Anne because she seemed sensitive and loving. Somewhat shy, Anne looked up to Stanley and made him feel strong. Their marriage and his relationships with his children also made him feel special—admired, loved, and respected—and provided him with a sense of security.

Discussion. The cases of Joanne and Stanley illustrate two different aspects of marital infidelity. Joanne was the spouse who felt betrayed when she learned about her trusted husband's affair with a much younger woman. Her sense of betrayal and acute feelings of distrust seemed to stem not only from the shock of her husband's infidelity, but also from the shattering of the major ways she had coped with the earlier childhood and adolescent experience of her father's having left the family for another woman. Her self-esteem, self-cohesion, and defenses had been bolstered by her belief in her marriage, in Nathan's love for and honesty with her, and in her belief in his loyalty to her. Learning of the affair completely undermined her self-structures and stripped her of her defenses against her anger at and having been betrayed by her father.

In contrast, Stanley developed panic attacks after having succumbed to an extramarital affair with a woman who mirrored his need to feel special at a time when he was feeling frightened and insignificant. At the same time, her demands threatened his security and evoked fears of abandonment, loss, and guilt. His vulnerability at midlife likely was exacerbated by his getting closer to the age his parents were when they died. He was also affected by the death of a longtime friend. Moreover, his wife and children were becoming increasingly autonomous and successful, which he equated with their not needing or looking up to him as much as they had previously. Then, too, there were the drastic changes in his firm that led to the loss of his close work environment and of his special niche.

One consequence of the prevalence of marital infidelity is the likelihood that some single women engage in sexual affairs with married men. Even when these relationships are ongoing, they often have their own disappointments and frustrations. When they end, however, they may not only result in feelings of loss but also may trigger other types of intense emotional reactions.

Here is an example that shows the many-layered effects of the breakup of a single woman's affair with a married man.

The Crushing of Hope

Sheila was 51 years old when she entered treatment. A seemingly highly intelligent, slightly overweight but attractive, well-dressed woman with a hard edge and a sharp tongue, Sheila recounted that, three months earlier, Roy, a man whom she had been seeing for a year and hoped to marry, broke off their relationship suddenly and refused to talk to her when she tried to get him to explain. She was devastated by this unilateral action on his part and by being shut out and became quite depressed and immobilized. Prior to seeking help she had become overcome with anger and could not stop obsessing about

Roy and what he did to her. Although she was not as depressed as she was initially, she was having trouble concentrating on the job and was irritable with her staff. An employee had complained about her, and her immediate boss had to call her into his office to reprimand her for how she had conducted herself with the staff member. "I know he's worried about her filing a grievance because it will make him look bad, the poor thing. He doesn't care about me and what I've been going through. He doesn't want to acknowledge what a disaster this employee is because then he'll have to do something about it. The jerk! He actually had the nerve to tell me that I was too tough on people and had to get myself together."

In exploring Sheila's feelings about the breakup with Roy, the therapist learned that Sheila had felt frustrated in her relationship with him and had almost ended the relationship herself. In retrospect, she thought that she had talked herself into loving him despite finding some of his behavior to be disagreeable. "It's not like he was God's gift to women. He had some pretty disgusting habits." She kept trying to make the relationship work because she realized that she was not getting any younger. "Who am I to be so choosy? I don't want to be alone but my age is not on my side. I believed him when he said that I was the first woman that he really loved and that he wanted to get married and be with me. I was shocked when I found out that he had returned to live with his wife. I tried to call him and his phone was disconnected. I looked up his wife's number and called and a man answered who sounded like Roy. I hung up. I'd like to kill him or devise some kind of slow torture."

Sheila blamed herself for doing something wrong and always coming up empty when it came to her relationships with men. "Other women my age have husbands and grown children, not that having children is so great. They go off to the far ends of the world and never call. Maybe they e-mail if you're lucky. At least those women have had a chance." Sheila said that before she had met Roy, she had dated and had some brief sexual relationships but not been involved with anyone for many years and had become resigned to not meeting anyone. When she and Roy seemed "to hit it off," she thought that maybe she had one more chance. "What a fool I was." Since the breakup, Sheila described feeling that she did not have it in her to try again. She launched into a tirade about the men in her life, including her two ex-husbands, who had lied to her and became Mr. Jekyl instead of the Mr. Hyde that they pretended to be. "I must have a sign on me that says, 'I'm stupid, go ahead and kick me.' I'm not going to go through this again."

In describing Roy, Sheila said that he, too, was not who she thought he was. An early retiree who appeared to have left his marriage of 20 years, Roy seemed eager to start a new life and told Sheila that he wished he had met her earlier in his life. Continuing to live in a nearby state, Roy frequently visited New York. "Not only did he stay in my apartment but he never wanted to leave, not when I was working and not when I was home. I don't know what he did with himself except sit and watch TV. He didn't even try to learn the computer. He just sat. First, I thought he was fearful of the city but he lives in Philadelphia. Then I thought he didn't want to spend any money. He is a little cheap even though he calls it thrifty. I had to buy him a new jacket and tie to go out to dinner. I do think they have nice restaurants in Philadelphia. I thought he had more life. Maybe I was just too much for him."

In talking about her background, Sheila spoke of growing up in Chicago as one of five children in a Roman Catholic Irish American family in which she and her four younger sisters and brothers fended for themselves to a considerable degree. Describing her parents as old-school, strict disciplinarians who believed in physical punishment, she later described some quite disturbing and sadistic incidents that had taken place when she was a child. She said that her parents fought a lot, usually about her father's drinking, spendthrift habits, and poor income. After a few months of treatment, Sheila revealed that her uncle, who lived next door, had sexually molested her on several occasions when she was 11. He threatened to have her sent away if she ever told anyone and doesn't know why he suddenly stopped. Sheila remembered changing around this time. When she entered high school, she spent her time with a tough group of girls, much to her parents' chagrin, and she became less intimidated by her parents' attempts to punish her or restrict her freedom and activities. Despite all this, Sheila was a reasonably good student and liked school. When she was 16, she was raped by an older boy whom she dated, and when her parents found out, they made her leave the house. She temporarily moved in with one of her friends and eventually her parents relented and let her come home. As soon as Sheila graduated from high school and turned 18, she enlisted in the armed services and by the time she was discharged, she had decided to go to college and complete her education. Quite self-reliant, she worked as a waitress and focused on her studies. Upon graduation, she was able to get a good position in the personnel department of a company that believed in supporting its employees. Sheila was promoted on numerous occasions, and, although she moved frequently from position to position because of interpersonal conflicts after leaving her original company when it merged with a larger firm, Sheila worked her way up in her field and earned an income that afforded her a nice lifestyle. Since her army days, Sheila had numerous short-lived affairs with men whom she was never interested in marrying. "I didn't want to take care of anyone." She had just turned 30 when she met her first husband and thought it was time to get married. "He was good-looking, came from an affluent family, always seemed to have money to spend, and swept me off my feet. What a mistake that was! I knew it soon after the wedding. I thought he was going to work every day but he was really going to the track. He loved the ponies. He had this great habit of slipping out of the apartment before we went to sleep and coming back with liquor on his breath." They soon divorced. After 10 years had elapsed, Sheila met her second husband, a recent widower who lived in a wealthy suburban town with his two school-age children, a dog, and three cats. "I thought he wanted me but what he really wanted was a housekeeper, babysitter, and animal feeder. Then I found out that he was using my credit cards because his were maxed out. It turned out that his business was going down the tubes and he wanted to borrow money from me. We didn't last too long either."

Sheila's parents had passed away 10 years earlier. Estranged from most of her family members, except for one brother, she initially said that she had many good friends. The therapist later learned, however, that Sheila felt that the relationships were superficial. "I don't think they get me. They think that I'm successful, independent, and have no worries. They don't realize that I have needs too and I can't always be smiling and happy."

Discussion. It seemed that the sudden termination of Sheila's relationship with Roy not only caused her to feel rejected, injured, and powerless but also represented the destruction of her chance to have an ongoing relationship with a man. It also stimulated her life-long anger at those people in her life, particularly men, who had hurt, disappointed, lied to, exploited, and abused her. Moreover, it triggered underlying feelings of being unlovable and nonexistent. Having been mistreated as a child and adolescent, Sheila's tough-minded approach to life, self-sufficiency, sarcasm, and difficulty allowing herself to need and depend on others seemed to help her make something of her life. It is likely that these characteristics also protected her vulnerable self from disappointment and emotional pain. This adaptation left Sheila lonely and without a true companion, however, and she episodically reached for men without any real ability to let herself get close to them or belief that they would be there for her. Needing to feel that she could make the relationships work, she chose men for superficial reasons, often without really knowing them, and then either selectively denied their true qualities or became overly critical. Sheila also seemed to have difficulty letting her friends see her needs and consequently ended up feeling unappreciated and resentful. Moreover, Sheila's difficulties with her staff on the job and her feelings of lack of support from her immediate boss suggested that her frustrated personal needs were spilling over into the workplace and creating problematic interactions with and expectations of others.

Contemplating Divorce

Even marriages of some duration may dissolve in midlife. Some marriages end because of serious and long-standing problems or because one or both members of a couple yearn to have a different or more gratifying kind of life (Aldwin and Levenson, 2001; Hunter et al., 2002). Despite the prevalence of divorce, the decision to end a marriage is a difficult one that often takes considerable time even when a marriage is riddled by anger and blaming, acrimonious arguments, ongoing disappointments and frustrations, and continuous obstacles to creating more harmony. At the most manifest level, divorce brings

about numerous actual and potential losses, including loss of a partner, lifestyle, economic well-being, and security. Friends and family
display changed attitudes. There may be a loss of status, and dreams
and plans for the future must be abandoned. The decision to divorce
commonly engenders feelings of guilt, particularly when children are
involved, and feelings of personal failure. At a deeper level, ending a
marriage may assault one's self-concept and challenge one's values
and identifications. At the same time, divorce creates the potential
for positive changes, which may also seem frightening and for which
a person may feel unprepared.

The next example illustrates a woman's difficulty coming to terms
with the deterioration of her marriage and her awareness that she
needs to separate from her husband.

A Blow to the Self-Concept

Becky was 43 years old when she entered treatment after realizing
that she felt totally hopeless about her marriage. She was considering
separation and divorce but did not feel ready to take this step. Crying
throughout the first session, she repeatedly asked, "Why can't he
change? Why doesn't he realize that he's hurting himself and us?"
Married for eight years to Andrew, a 45-year-old attorney, Becky had
given birth to three girls, now aged seven, five, and three. She continued working full-time with the help of a daytime nanny, whose
salary amounted to over half of Becky's income. The family lived in a
modest house in an affluent suburb, and the couple had a sizable
mortgage.

Becky acknowledged that Andrew had always used alcohol and
marijuana too much, even prior to their marriage. But she did not
consider it to be a huge problem. Becky herself had a drink or two
only on social occasions. Although she became upset at times when
Andrew's substance use seemed out of control, it had escalated in the
past six months, since the World Trade Center attack on 9/11. Andrew had then become increasingly fearful of being in New York City
and took every opportunity to leave his office early. He was losing clients and income and giving her less money to run the household. He
was secretive about his financial affairs when Becky inquired or tried

to offer advice. Consequently, their debt was mounting. Becky regarded Andrew as a good father who loved his children, but she became fearful of leaving them with him or letting him drive them anywhere after he had a minor but potentially serious automobile accident. She worried about his impaired judgment and volatility.

What seemed worse to her was the lack of intimacy in their relationship, a lack that Andrew blamed on Becky's having gained 15 pounds and no longer being a size 10. She berated herself for not being a good enough wife and for letting herself go. "I don't have any time to exercise. When can I do that? I get up at 6 a.m. as it is, and I don't put the kids to bed until 8 or 8:30 p.m. I'm exhausted by then, and all I want to do is go to sleep but I have lots of chores to do in order to get ready for the next day. It's bad enough that I don't get a chance to spend much time with my children. I don't know what I'm supposed to do. . . . If only Andrew would get help. I love him. I don't want a divorce. I don't even care that much about the financial part. We could sell our house. He could give up his office and work from home. He doesn't take any responsibility for his drinking and he's always angry at me."

The theme of having failed at making Andrew happy and helping him recurred in early sessions. "If he would just let me help him. We can do anything if he wants to but I can't reach him. . . . I can't bear the loneliness I feel. I don't want to live like this the rest of my life. Why isn't my loving him enough for him? He's turning my love for him into hate."

Becky was the firstborn of two children and had a younger brother. She described her parents' 45-year marriage as dedicated but not really happy. Her father ran a family business, and her mother worked as a teacher. She recalled being her father's favorite while her brother was favored by her mother. From an early age, her father had taken her to his office and taught her the business. As she got older, he would actually seek her advice. Her mother was frequently depressed, irritable, and withdrawn. She also had an intermittent alcohol problem that she tried to hide. It did not seem to affect her work, but she relied on Becky to organize the household and take care of Becky's brother. Even as a child, Becky saw herself as more competent than her mother and prided herself on her intelligence and good judgment. She also remembered feeling angry that her mother did not help herself and catered to Becky's brother, who could "do no wrong" despite his never "raising a finger" to help out in any way.

Even as a preadolescent, Becky was a tall girl with a large frame; she felt self-conscious about her appearance. She was a good student and made close friends but rarely dated until she graduated from college. At the company where she was employed, she was promoted consistently because of her business savvy, single-mindedness of purpose, and hard work. She had some long-term relationships with men who made her feel attractive but who were "opportunistic and immature." She wanted to settle down and have a family.

She was 35 when she met Andrew. He liked to go out to clubs and parties, and they had a lot of fun together. He was the first man she had been with who earned a reasonable income and who treated her with respect. She was aware that he was self-centered and placed a high value on appearances. He lacked ambition. He needed a great deal of attention and was easily stressed, but she felt that she should overcome her tendency to be hypercritical for she was not getting any younger. Moreover, she felt that she would be able to make Andrew happy. The difficulties in the marriage increased after her children were born. Andrew seemed overwhelmed by the family responsibilities and felt pressured to earn more income. He was resentful of the attention the children received and felt angry because of the constraints on the couple's social life.

Discussion. It appeared that Becky's self-esteem and self-concept were organized around being strong, independent, intelligent, and capable of doing anything. From the time she was very young, both parents placed her in a position of authority in the family. Her father encouraged her abilities and made her feel competent and important, and her mother looked to her to help her take care of the household. At the same time, Becky lacked nurturing from her mother and did not feel that her mother showed her much love. She also felt fat and unattractive. She seemed to take pride in her intellectual abilities and sense of competence but lacked self-esteem as an attractive and lovable woman. Always wanting to marry and have a family, when Becky met Andrew, she saw him as a last chance and tried to make him into the ideal husband and father who would also make her feel loved. She ignored the clues that Andrew had some serious difficulties that might have an impact on the marriage. Whatever role Becky may have played in the deterioration of their relationship and the marriage, Andrew's criticism of and blaming of Becky and his refusal to stop drinking shattered her belief that he loved her. His inability to face up to their financial problems, his refusal to seek help, and his rejection of Becky's attempts to help him frustrated her and made her deidealize him. She felt a sense of profound helplessness and powerlessness. Becky's loss of belief in her own powers to make Andrew happy and to fix him, left her feeling like a failure. This sense of failure likely stirred up earlier feelings related to her inability to help her mother overcome her depression and stop her drinking and to make her father happy.

Involuntary Unemployment

The economic impact of being fired or let go because of cutbacks, downsizing, or reengineering can be staggering, necessitating drastic changes in lifestyle. Savings and pension are eroded, necessitating borrowing money and extending credit. Health insurance is lost, and dislocation may be forced. When the period of unemployment is prolonged and there is little opportunity for finding work or a job at a reasonable salary, the impact may be more catastrophic and may necessitate changes that many people do not feel able to make. In addition to these material losses, however, involuntary unemployment, whether short-term or prolonged, may have a marked affect on self-esteem and self-concept and trigger feelings of hopelessness (Sterns and Huyck, 2001).

In the next example, the loss of work, which was the mainstay of the patient's life, had a disastrous impact on his self-esteem and self-concept.

A Deep Sense of Worthlessness and Failure

Alan, age 48, had worked in developing communications technology for many years when a recent and prolonged economic downturn led to drastic job losses in his field. Alan took some small measure of comfort initially in the fact that he was one of literally thousands who were in the same boat and that he did have a cushion of about $20,000 in savings. After 14 months of seeking work but having little success in obtaining an interview, let alone a viable offer, he became increasingly panicked and had intermittent suicidal thoughts. His unemployment insurance had ended after six months, and another eight months later most of his savings had been depleted. To add to his desperation, his Cobra health benefits, for which he had continued to pay, were going to end in another four months. During this 14-month period of forced unemployment, Alan put himself on a bare-bones budget and seldom spent any money on nonessentials. Fortunately, he paid a relatively low rent for his small apartment in downtown New York City, which he had to vacate for a period of time after the collapse of the World Trade Center on 9/11 because of the toxic air quality. His gratitude for being alive and no longer working near the site of the attack only temporarily lessened his terror at continuing to be unemployed.

Alan's fears about his economic survival were only one part of the problem that he presented to the therapist, a member of the network that managed his precarious health benefits. He had started seeing her just prior to losing his job for help in dealing with the breakup of a long-standing relationship with a woman. He wanted to move forward in his personal life. He was feeling somewhat better about his future prospects when his job was terminated. He continued in treatment only sporadically during the first year of his unemployment but then increased his visits after 9/11, when he became increasingly frantic. "It's ironic. All those people who lost their lives in the towers were working and I'm still alive but I'm unemployed. It doesn't seem fair. They were just doing what they were supposed to be doing. What am I doing? Not much of anything. I'm of no use to anyone." This statement reflected the tip of the iceberg with respect to the emotional impact of Alan's unemployment. He described feeling rudderless and had a profound sense of his own failure in life, having never been able to please his father or earn his respect.

Alan was the youngest of three sons in a high-achieving family that he described as austere, hypercritical, and conformist. Closer to his mother than to his father, he was devastated by her death when he was 11 years old after which his father married a woman who had her own children. Alan recalled that as a child he had never felt that he could please his father or get his positive attention, whereas Alan's brothers and their father seemed to get along fairly well. Alan attributed this discrepancy in relationships to his father's being disappointed in him because Alan was not a good student like his brothers. Alan tended to daydream and attract negative attention by acting up in class.

Although it took Alan six years to finish college, he was accepted to law school because of his high scores on the LSATs and his improved academic performance in his last two years of college. Interested in computers, which had become a hobby, he did not particularly want to be a lawyer but felt that this was the career that his father expected him to pursue. Unable to pass his bar examination, despite two attempts, Alan never practiced law. Instead he moved away from the small upstate New York town where he had grown up and came to New York City to be free of his family and to be his own person. He loved the city for its energy, diversity, and cultural and sports activities. He became a true Yankees fan. He avidly attended as many events as his salary would allow. He worked at odd jobs and as a part-time college instructor and then entered the technology field, where he eventually began to earn a stable and adequate income that allowed him to enjoy the city and even save some money, in addition to his 401(k) contributions.

The work challenged and energized him and he did well, enjoying the respect of his boss and colleagues. Alan had a few close male and female friends and episodic long-term relationships with women but never married. Considering himself a loner, he valued his autonomy and did not mind being by himself. Alan had a more or less estranged relationship with his father and brothers, who did not share his politics or sensibilities and who viewed him as a renegade and did not respect his lifestyle. He saw them only occasionally and usually came away from his visits home rather let down and sad but happy to be back in New York City.

Discussion. Alan's main sources of pride were his work, his love for New York City and his enjoyment of its life and activities, his sense of autonomy, and the Yankees. He had struggled to become his own person but did so at the expense of his relationship with his family. The niche he had carved out for himself enabled him to feel a sense of competence and to experience the regard of his colleagues and employers. His salary enabled him to pursue his interests and feel that he was getting something out of life and working toward building up some financial security. The loss of his job, thorough no fault of his own, and his prolonged period of unemployment robbed him of the life structure that had provided Alan with a sense of self-esteem, supported his positive self-concept, and provided him with the means for enjoying his city, which at the same time, had also been attacked by terrorists and was "not the same." These events invoked Alan's long-standing and underlying feelings of having been a disappointment to his father and his self-blame for past failures and for who he was.

Marriage of an Offspring

In a different vein, an event that parents usually look forward to, the marriage of an adult child, is supposed to be a time of great joy. Yet it, too, can be an event that is fraught with overwhelming feelings of sadness and loss, disappointment and guilt, envy and jealousy, anger, and outright rejection (Benatar, 1989). Although these intense reactions do not always crowd out other more positive feelings, in some cases they do, making it difficult for parents and their adult children to make this important event a mutually satisfying experience. These reactions result from far more than a parent's feeling disappointed that a son or daughter has not selected the perfect or ideal partner. Even when parents feel that their adult children are making good choices for themselves, the marriage of an offspring may recall unfulfilled yearnings of their own or rob the parents of selfobject experiences that have been the mainstay of their lives. When parents feel that their adult children are making a mistake, going against the family's values or wishes, or embarking on a course that will cause prolonged geographic separation, their reactions can be expected to be more problematic for them to overcome. Some parents are unable to make the internal and external changes necessary to creating a different type of relationship with their adult children and to encouraging them to live their own lives, as is suggested by the following example.

Loss of a Dream

Janice was an American-born, 58-year-old, Jewish married mother of two children, when her older daughter, Ruth, age 23, a second-year doctoral student in economics, announced her intention to move in with and then become engaged to Lee. Lee was a 26-year-old man she had been seeing for a year while he was completing his medical training at a northeastern university. They planned to marry in a year, when Ruth completed her course work and Lee finished his residency. They wanted to have a large wedding. Janice and her husband, Jerry, knew that their daughter had been romantically involved with Lee since Janice asked if she could bring him home with her at holiday time, but they did not imagine that she felt ready to get married. Although they wanted to be happy for Janice, who was excited and overjoyed, they were stunned by the news of her engagement and impending marriage. Their hearts sank when they further learned that the couple planned to live on the West Coast for a few years because Lee's parents were in ill health and he wanted to spend some time with them before they died.

Almost immediately after learning about Janice's plans, Ruth became depressed, was unable to work at her job as a speech therapist, and spent a week in bed because of severe back pain. Meanwhile, Jerry withdrew, as he did periodically in their 25-year marriage, and was uncommunicative and unreceptive to Janice's concerns. Although her back eventually improved, her depression did not and Janice sought help at the urging of one of her close friends.

In her early sessions, Janice spoke about her wrenching sense of loss at the prospect of Ruth's marrying and going to the West Coast even though Ruth had been living at school in another northeastern city for several years. She also thought her husband was experiencing similar emotions but was unable to talk about them and was even more uncommunicative than usual. "I have no one to talk to about what I'm feeling. I haven't felt this alone since I was a child." Janice described feeling not only that she was losing the accessibility of Ruth as a companion but also that her dream always revolved around the idea of the girls' marrying and having children and living close by. She could not imagine what it would be like to be so far from Ruth and her grandchildren and could not imagine that she and Jerry would be able to visit frequently because of their work schedules. "Visiting is not the same anyway."

Janice said that she felt pushed aside as Ruth did not seem to value her ideas and opinions any longer and appeared tense with her. Moreover, Janice felt angry at and betrayed by Ruth, who was not making her case with Lee for their staying on the East Coast. "Lee is a new person on the block. I've been the one who has been there for her for years." Janice believed that Ruth should consider Janice's needs and not just cater to Lee. She did not like feeling angry at her own daughter. "She's just forgetting us. She's happy to accept our paying for the wedding but she and Lee want to decide everything. Maybe it's our fault that she's taking us for granted. I've tried so hard to put her needs first." At the same time, Janice also was aware that she felt some envy of Ruth's excitement because she herself had been feeling uncertain about her own plans for the future. She had an acute awareness of getting older and no longer being at the center of things.

Janice was the eldest of three children born to immigrant parents. She described her parents as having a tight marital bond at the expense of their relationships with their children, who received little emotional nurturance and were expected to fend for themselves. Janice recalled that, in addition to her father's lack of positive involvement with his children, he dominated her mother, was controlling of her outside involvements, and was highly critical of her friends and family. She remembered his explosive outbursts and mean-spirited nature. She said she had grown up feeling very alone and frightened and unable to talk to her mother about what she was experiencing. She envied her friends who seemed to have more loving and close families and vowed that one day she would be a different kind of parent to her children.

A good student, Janice thrived at school, where her teachers gave her positive attention. Attending college on scholarship in the 1960s, she developed a strong sense of social consciousness. Imbued with traditional values from her parents, who never encouraged her educational or career pursuits, Janice embraced the feminist movement in the 1970s. At the age of 30, she married a passive, serious, and somewhat noncommunicative man who was trained as an engineer and had a stable job. They had a very small wedding for only immediate family. Born and raised outside the United States, his family members remained in their country of origin. She and her husband got along reasonably well and worked together as a team with respect to their parenting, but Janice was frequently frustrated by their lack of intimacy as a couple. She suffered from a low-level depression most of her adult life. From the time the girls were born and continuing through their graduations from high school, family life was centered on them, and both Janice and her husband seemed to have close relationships with both daughters.

Janice returned to work on a part-time basis when the girls went to school, but she always placed a high priority on her family responsibilities. Although she received gratification from her job, she derived greater satisfaction from her parenting role and felt good about herself as a mother, taking pride in both daughters. She enjoyed an especially close connection to Ruth, in particular, whom she regarded as more like her in temperament than was her younger daughter, Sarah, an affectionate but less communicative child who demanded less attention than her sister did. Janice experienced some depressions and feelings of loss in anticipation of Ruth's going away to a nearby university, but, even during her daughters' college years, they frequently came home for weekends and Janice and Jerry were actively involved in their lives. This pattern recently began to change, though, and caused some tension in Janice's relationship with Jerry.

Discussion. Fulfilling her vow that she would be a better parent to her children than her parents were to her became a major force in Janice's life, and that she felt successful in having done so was an important source of self-esteem. Giving to her two children, especially Ruth, also provided her with, and in major ways made up for, the nurturing and closeness that she did not have with her parents, particularly her mother. She thrived on being the center of her daughters' world and imagined that this state of affairs would continue when they married and had children. She would be the grandmother who lived nearby and was involved in their lives. Janice never really thought that she would be displaced and that Ruth would move a huge distance away. It was not only the loss of Ruth's accessibility due to geography but also the loss of Janice's dream and her feelings of being "numero uno" that so shook her. Her distress was all the more severe because of her growing feelings of vulnerability as she recognized that "our time has past." She was feeling at a loss about her own life.

Parental Caretaking

Assuming the role of caretaker to an elderly parent can impose serious burdens on any adult son or daughter, but it can also have its rewards. Knowing that one is giving back to a loving parent whom one loves can make one feel good even if the responsibilities are taxing (Dautzenberg et al., 1999; Aldwin and Levenson, 2001). The caretaking role becomes more problematic, however, if relationships with parents or other family members have been strained, conflicted, or estranged and if there are deep emotional, and sometimes physical, injuries that the caretaker has experienced at the hands of parents. Although it is possible that there can be some repair of past wounds and some positive resolution under certain circumstances, these may not always be possible, as the next example illustrates.

Opening Old Wounds

Evelyn, age 46, was referred for treatment by an Employee Assistance Center connected to her office. Her work supervisor had become concerned about Evelyn's lowered productivity and erratic attendance. On meeting with her, Evelyn broke into tears and talked about what she was going through in her personal life. Six months earlier, her 79-year-old, physically and mentally active father died suddenly, leaving her mother, Harriet, age 76, to fend for herself. Harriet lived in a Massachusetts town that was four hours away from New York City by automobile. Having been highly dependent on her husband to manage their financial and household responsibilities, Harriet became depressed and agitated in her grief and also seemed to be somewhat disorganized and forgetful. Evelyn's older sister, June, who lived near the mother, looked in on her daily and took her to doctors. Shortly after their father died, June demanded that Evelyn come back to Massachusetts regularly to help her to take care of Harriet. Feeling guilty about June's burden and confused about what her role should be, Evelyn agreed and visited on weekends. Sometimes she stayed overnight, leaving her 13-year-old and 10-year-old with her female partner, Sheila, who was out of work on disability as a result of a taxi accident that injured her back. Sheila had only recently become more able to move around and Evelyn felt upset about leaving her and the children.

Despite Evelyn's attempts to participate in the caretaking of her mother, June resented the infrequency of her visits and portrayed herself as the "good" daughter and Evelyn as the "bad" daughter. Both Harriet and June berated Evelyn for her "selfishness and irresponsibility" and refused to consider any other plan for Harriet, such as using some of her considerable assets to pay for a part-time or full-time companion or moving to an assisted-living facility. June told Evelyn that she wanted to preserve their mother's assets and that she would make sure Evelyn never inherited anything if she did not comply with her plans. She threatened to use Evelyn's lesbianism and lifestyle against her. Although Evelyn was not concerned about the inheritance because she had never had any interest in her parents' money, June's threats enraged her and stirred up the pain that she had experienced in the family as a result of her coming out as a lesbian earlier in her life. She felt torn about the right thing to do under the circumstances. This state of affairs was made worse by June's frequent telephone calls about their mother's worrisome escapades in which she would lose her jewelry, overpay for household maintenance, and invite strange men who offered to help her carry her groceries into the house. The whole situation began to feel like a nightmare, and Evelyn began to lose sleep and have frightening dreams. She experienced difficulty getting to work and had trouble concentrating.

Evelyn was born and raised in New England. Her parents were Catholic, first-generation Irish Americans. They were hardworking people, strict and old fashioned in their beliefs. Significant in Evelyn's history was that she had had a strained relationship with her parents and her sister since Evelyn was an adolescent, when it became apparent that she was a lesbian. She described that until that time she was her parents' favorite, which made her feel guilty. She and her sister, who was less attractive, intelligent, and talented than she was, had always had a difficult relationship as June felt an intense rivalry with Evelyn for their parents' attention. When Evelyn came out as a lesbian during her adolescence, the sisters' roles reversed and June became the "good" daughter. The parents gave Evelyn a choice. Either she could renounce her lesbianism or move out. On the surface, Evelyn went along with their wishes and attended a church group, but she secretly found ways of seeing other girls and moved out when she went to college, which she financed through scholarships, loans, and part-time and summer work. Evelyn remembered having a very difficult time during those years, when she felt quite alone. Although she felt she had the strength to be her own person, she payed a high emotional price for the rift; she sometimes questioned her sexual identity and blamed herself for being different. Evelyn never returned home to live and visited very infrequently for brief periods. Her father tried to reconcile with her, and they maintained telephone contact until his death, but her mother remained cold and rejecting despite Evelyn's earlier efforts to make peace with her.

Evelyn moved to New York City after college and eventually obtained a job with a promising future. As an adult, she became increasingly comfortable with and accepting of her lesbian sexual identity. She excelled in her work and had a series of monogamous romantic relationships with other women. She met her partner, Nancy, at a job-related event and they almost immediately felt that they were meant for each other. Evelyn adopted two children that she and her partner were raising together. Although their life together was pressured, particularly after Sheila's accident, Evelyn enjoyed being a mom and was happy with her children's development.

She felt crushed that her mother did not want to even see the children, let alone be part of their life. Evelyn's main regret was not having a close family who could be a part of her children's support system. At times, she would become sad and angry about this lack and felt awful that her children did not have more loving adults and cousins around them. Fortunately, Nancy's family were totally accepting of the couple and were involved with the children. On several occasions, Evelyn, Nancy, and the children stayed in a motel near Nancy's parents' home. Evelyn's father would meet them there, but these meetings were awkward for all of them. Her father tried to get his wife to relent but to no avail; she acted as if Evelyn were dead.

Evelyn maintained telephone contact with her sister, June, on special occasions but never was invited to her house.

Discussion. Evelyn struggled to make the most of her life and derived satisfaction and self-esteem from her work, parenting, and romantic partnership with another woman. Although she weathered the severe rejection that she had experienced from her mother and sister, she had a sense of underlying vulnerability about not having a place in her family of origin because of her sexual identity. She had never had the opportunity to repair the rift in her family and tried to overcome her feelings of anger, sadness, and occasional self-blame for what had transpired. When her mother's deterioration necessitated that she play a role in taking care of her mother despite her mother's and sister's ongoing resentment and rejection of her, Evelyn experienced a serious disruption of her usual functioning. Not only did her trips to Massachusetts, which separated her from her partner and children, put her under enormous strain, but they opened the wounds that had never healed properly.

Loss of Significant Others

If they have not already experienced the premature death of parents, midlife adults often must confront the illness and death of one or both parents and sometimes the loss of siblings or a life partner (Nolen-Hoeksema and Larson, 1999; Aldwin and Levenson, 2001). In addition to the grief that midlife adults experience in the event that parents, siblings, or life partners die, these events may have a far-reaching impact on their sense of self and necessitate an internal reorganization. The death of parents may signal the recognition that there is no longer another generation between the midlife adult and death, that one is alone in the sense of not having a parent to offer love and protection. The death of a parent removes the fantasy that an unloving or otherwise difficult parent will change and become the loving or appreciative parent that one has hoped for; it leaves one with the awareness of and pain connected to what one has not had from one's parents. The death of a sibling, a member of one's own generation, is a stark reminder of one's mortality. A person with whom one shared a sense of history no longer exists. One may feel that one has been left to face life alone. A sibling's death may trigger underlying issues of sibling rivalry and one's position in the family.

The death of a spouse or partner is one of the most painful experiences in human life, whether or not one is prepared for such an event and despite the possibly advanced age of the deceased. Always difficult are the tasks of accepting the reality of the death of a significant person and experiencing the feelings connected to the loss. One must become accustomed to living in a world without the loved one and learn to go on with one's life. In some instances, grieving for the loss of a partner is complicated by the fact that the partner was a significant selfobject who bolstered the survivor's self-esteem, self-concept, and self-cohesion. The bereaved person, who has been dependent on the selfobject functions that the deceased provided, may experience a loss of self.

> These losses are felt as critical injuries to the self, evoking intense pain. The pain leads to fears of fragmentation and to overpowering anxiety. The absent function results in a state of depletion in which the self experiences helplessness and hopelessness [Palombo, 1985, p. 38].

Turning to others, who often do not share their pain, grieving persons who feel depleted may also feel ashamed of being needy. They become impatient with themselves and angry at those who are able to enjoy life. For those who strive to meet the perfectionist demands of the grandiose self, such a loss also can result in the survivors' blaming and punishing themselves for not preventing the suffering or death of the loved one.

In the following case example, the patient lost a part of herself when her sister died. The patient also blamed herself for not having been powerful enough to prevent her death.

Going On Alone

Maryann, a 39-year-old Italian American married mother of three children, sought help after her sister's death from an aggressive form of cancer. Many months after the death, the patient's priest convinced her to seek help after she told him about her suicidal feelings. When she saw the therapist, Maryann described the past year as having been "nightmarish." She said that it took her six months to accept that her sister was gone: "I'm not sure that I accept it even now. I can't believe that she's not going to just come back one day and say that this has all been a big mistake. We had our fights but we were there for each other. She held my memories. We always used to talk about what it was like for us growing up. There's no one else with whom I can do that. I feel like a part of me is missing. I feel depressed all the time. I even started taking antidepressants but I don't know if they are doing anything except that I'm not crying all the time. . . . I think about what might have been different if I had made her get medical checkups on a regular basis." When the therapist commented that Maryann seemed to blame herself for not being able to prevent her sister's death, Maryann said, "I should have been able to. I've looked after her all my life. That was my job."

Maryann was the eldest of three siblings. Her younger brother died in an automobile accident when he was 16. Her parents were born in Italy but emigrated to the United States when they were children. They lived in a tight-knit community in the city and seldom ventured outside it except for the purposes of work. They expected her to assume responsibility for her siblings when she was quite young. Maryann described her relationship with her sister, Marie, as close. "We were like twins except that she was prettier and more popular than I was." In addition to being responsible for her siblings, Maryann felt it was her job to take care of her parents from the time she was a child. Her mother had married and had children at a late age, so that she was in her late 30s when Maryann was born. Both parents expected her to know what to do and to meet all their needs. Maryann remembered feeling, from an early age, that they were not able to handle things on their own and needed her help. During her adolescence, she rebelled for a time, and her parents repeatedly accused her of being selfish and self-centered. Marie knew that this was not true, and her reassurance made Maryann feel better about herself. The parents died, two years apart, when Maryann was in her late 20s. Although she missed her parents, she was relieved at not having the burden of taking care of them.

Discussion. In early sessions, several important themes emerged that served as a basis for exploration in months of later meetings. The first theme involved Maryann's feelings about being left alone now that she was the only one who remained from her family of origin. The second theme was Maryann's feeling that she no longer had anyone with whom she could share her history. This was especially difficult because she felt that her sister was the one person who had witnessed how difficult her parents had been and who helped her to feel that she was not a bad person for not always being there for them. A third theme was Maryann's anger at herself for having failed to live up to her self-concept as being the responsible one, a view that had been reinforced from the time she was a child. She was unaware that unrealistic expectations had been placed on her and that she internalized, leading to feelings that she could control life and death. This belief was shattered earlier, when her brother was killed, a trauma that she pushed aside but that was now reasserting itself. Maryann believed that she really could have prevented her siblings' deaths. Thus, for Maryann, the loss of her sister robbed her of a much-needed selfobject who bolstered her positive sense of herself. The death also undermined a mainstay of her sense of herself and challenged her unrealistic sense of power and control.

Loss of Health

Illness and disability are physically and psychologically assaultive experiences (Aldwin and Levenson, 2001). People may experience the loss of health, bodily intactness, strength, youth, and vitality. They may have feelings of vulnerability. Some feel a loss of physical attractiveness and mental and sexual functioning. Activities and roles that have been mainstays of their self-concept and self-esteem seem gone. Even minor conditions may seem traumatic. Sometimes people feel that they are being punished for past misdeeds, angry feelings, acts of independence, or for not having lived up to the unrealistic demands of their grandiose self. These onslaughts may be greater when there is a stigma attached to the condition, as is the case with HIV or cancer. The personal meaning of illness and disability plays a major role in how afflicted persons respond to and cope with their physical challenges. In many instances, people recover physically or are able to manage the sequelae of their illnesses or disability but do not recover well emotionally, as was the case in the following example.

Another Episode in an Unlucky Life

Rita was 54 years old when she returned to treatment with a therapist she had seen for a few months several years earlier. At that earlier time, she felt depressed about being divorced and childless and not having a man in her life. Although she realized that she needed to make some major changes, she was unable to mobilize herself. Despite the therapist's recommendation that she continue in treatment, Rita dropped out, saying that she was not ready to work on herself.

When she returned four years later, she had gone through a grueling period. She had been diagnosed 11 months earlier with stage II breast cancer that necessitated a lumpectomy, radiation, and chemotherapy, followed by a five-year regimen of the drug tamoxifen. The active treatment lasted seven months, causing hair loss and intermittent periods of weakness, nausea, and other flulike symptoms and a loss of red blood cells. She often took to her bed and needed occasional blood transfusions. During this time, Rita managed to keep up her spirits and commit herself to the treatment with the hope of full recovery. Her doctors told her that her prognosis for the future was excellent. After the completion of this phase of treatment, however, Rita became despondent and immobilized. She reluctantly reentered psychotherapy at the insistence of her oncologist, a sensitive woman who was worried about Rita's emotional and physical state.

In her first session, Rita railed against life. "I don't know why I am so unlucky. Whatever I do turns out badly. I think that's my fate." She cited numerous examples of bad things that had happened to her: having been physically abused as a child, losing a father at an early age, having been raped as a adolescent. In addition, she had been deprived of her only child and had a series of unhappy relationships with men, including her former husband, who was unfaithful to her and left her for another woman. She felt she was losing her looks, and, of course, she had cancer. "I can't seem to stop thinking about everything that has happened to me all my life. I must have done something to deserve all this, but I don't know what it is. I don't know why God is punishing me like this. . . . The doctors can't understand why I'm not getting back on my feet. What is there to look forward to? Sure, I'm alive and I guess that's something, but I don't feel that there's anything that I can look forward to. What's the point of it all? Everything I do turns out badly and who would want me now anyway."

Rita was the eldest of four children. Her father died when she was eight, and she described her mother in glowing terms despite the mother's alcoholism and maltreatment of her. Although many of Rita's needs were neglected, her mother took some pride in Rita's being an unusually attractive child whose appearance was a focus of positive attention. Her mother did buy her pretty clothes when she could. Popular among her peers, Rita felt that people responded to her because of her looks and that she had little else to offer. In later life, she continued to place importance on appearing fashionable and perfectly groomed.

Rita married when she was 20 to get away from home, but her husband left her when she was pregnant. A baby girl was stillborn. Her later relationships with men usually did not work out. Always able to attract men, she tended to respond to those who showed an interest in her without thinking about whether she liked them or whether they were worthy of her. She was able to support herself financially as a legal secretary, and her job at a law firm was an important and secure part of her life. Prior to her cancer diagnosis, she broke off a relationship that she had thought was her last chance for happiness. She had been seeing a married man who she thought would leave his wife for her. After two years, she decided that he would never leave his wife and children.

Discussion.   Although the seriousness of Rita's diagnosis and the physical effects on Rita's treatment were considerable and left her in a weakened physical and emotional condition, their more drastic impact was on her sense of self. They dealt a significant blow to her compensatory structures. They stimulated her rage, caused her to feel a sense of despair, and made her feel that she was being punished for past misdeeds. Rita felt that her cancer diagnosis and treatment were further evidence that she was fated to have a hard life because of some inner badness that stemmed from her childhood experiences. Rita also felt devastated that her positive feelings about body and attractiveness had been marred by her illness and treatment. Taking pride in her appearance was a mainstay of her self-esteem and her feeling that she could attract others. Her appearance seemed to compensate for a sense of inadequacy and unworthiness.

Early Retirement

Whether the decision is voluntary or forced, midlifers are retiring early and look forward to enjoying another phase of their lives, particularly when they have the economic assets to make this period comfortable and secure financially. Sometimes the planning for retirement goes on for several years. It can involve geographic changes as well as alterations in lifestyle. Despite its positive potential, early retirement also may force a drastic change in the self and one's relationship to the world. It is a more complicated choice when work has been a major support to one's self-concept and self-esteem; when making the changes necessary for successful retirement require actions that are unfamiliar or uncomfortable for the person; and when it triggers long-standing insecurities (Kim and Moen, 2001), as was true for the following patient.

Fears of Letting Go and Starting Over

Sam was 55 years old when he sought treatment at the urging of his wife, a former social worker, who was frustrated by his indecisiveness about their plans for early retirement and worried about his increasing depression. In the first therapy session, Sam looked tired and haggard. When describing himself, he quickly mentioned that he had worked in the financial field for 30 years and had had some great successes along with some major disappointments, the most recent of which was his being passed over for a major position in favor of a younger man whom Sam had mentored. Sam felt angry that he was being pushed aside and that he had nowhere left to go in the company. He obsessed about retiring early but worried that he did not have enough money to do so, particularly in the aftermath of the stock-market downturn that resulted in his losing a considerable sum.

Nonetheless, he had a sizable number of assets, which he thought would finance a comfortable retirement if he and his wife sold their suburban house, relocated to Florida for six months of the year, and maintained a small apartment in the city. His wife was eager to make such a change. He promised her that he would ask for a retirement package, but he felt conflicted about raising the subject with the head of the company. Sam acknowledged that he was tired of his job. He had to work harder just to maintain his income and was frustrated by all the changes in the company. He thought he might welcome a change. He also thought it likely that his boss would be happy if Sam retired so that his job would be freed up, but this idea made him furious. "I made a lot of money for this company and I wanted to go out on a high note not in defeat."

Since his associate's promotion, Sam felt that others in the office who sensed his diminished power were avoiding him or at least treating him differently than they had previously: "Those opportunistic SOBs. Of course, I would probably do the same thing if the tables were turned, but it doesn't feel good. Nothing feels good. Work used to be fun and exciting. Now everyone locks themselves in their offices and communicates by computer. Many of the guys that I worked with for years are gone, one way or another. I don't even travel that much anymore. Instead, we teleconference. My wife can't understand why I don't want to leave. I'm not sure I understand it either. I just know I am having trouble letting go."

As sessions continued, Sam spoke about his fears that he would no longer be important: "It's true that I don't get a lot of strokes any more for what I am doing and I miss that, but I don't want to be a 'nobody.' I can just see myself in Florida talking about the old days with other men who are trying to pump themselves up. It's not a pretty picture. . . . I've always been a workaholic. I was good at my work and knew what I was doing. I had a great reputation and I earned it. I could be pretty hard-nosed and difficult and made some great deals, but I also had integrity. I might have done a lot better if I had been willing to cut corners and been more of a wheeler-dealer. . . . If I have any regrets it's that I was too cautious. At a certain point, I stayed in a secure job and didn't push myself to take more risks. Maybe deep down I lacked real confidence in myself." Sam spoke of himself as never having had much of a need for friends. "Don't misunderstand, we've had an active social life, but my wife has been the one who has maintained it. I don't know what it would be like for me to first start making friends in Florida. That's never been my strong suit. My wife will have an easier time. She's always been the social planner in our relationship, and she seems to truly enjoy other people."

Sam was the youngest of three brothers born to a Jewish family who lived in Brooklyn. He described his childhood as dreary because of a lack of money and his parents' depressed outlook, religious practices, and lack of zest. "They cared about us, but they weren't warm and loving and didn't believe in praise. I think the only time I remember my father telling me I had done a good job was when I gave him the money I earned from odd jobs. He was a shoe salesman. He was a smart guy and had the gift of gab, but he never made any money and he always worked for people who pushed him around. I used to hate seeing him come home so tired that he could hardly talk. What a waste! He and my mother never had much fun. Both of them were always working. My dad used to tell me that I should never be ashamed of working hard. One year I made more money than he had in all his years of employment. I think he loved me in his own way. He did want me to get an education. Before they died, I was able to help them financially for a while."

In his younger years, going back as far as elementary school, Sam had never felt popular. "I never had the time. I guess I was a bit of a nerd in those days. In high school and college, the story was the same. I studied hard, worked, and didn't socialize much. . . . I was attracted to my wife because she was outgoing and warm as well as attractive. We've been married for 33 years and our three kids are out of the house now. One is married and has two little girls. The other two are involved with nice guys." He attended a city college and supported himself by working. He had a series of jobs after graduating from college and always bettered himself. He gradually worked his way up to a significant position. He married when he was in his early 20s, and, although he loved his wife and children, Sam was always more in-volved in work than with his family. He and his wife had many couple friends as a result of her social skills, but Sam did not have many male friends. He did maintain contact with some of his old college class-mates, with whom he played golf occasionally. He envied them for having been more aggressive and ambitious in their careers and having made more money than he.

Discussion. Having a successful career, making a lot of money, and earning the respect of others in the business world were driving forces in Sam's life and were the mainstays of his sense of self. Except for his wife and children, Sam never developed outside interests or friends. He took pride in his career achievements but also had regrets about not having taken more risks because of a lack of confidence. Sam became depressed when the comfortable niche in which he had operated for many years changed and he was passed over and pushed aside, robbing him of his good feelings about himself. At the same time, leaving his position was fraught with anxiety and insecurity. He was fearful of losing his core identity and of having to reach out to others in a way that he had never been able to do previously. He had no model in his family of origin for taking risks, seeking pleasurable activities, or making friends. Sam was worried that he would wind up an impoverished nonentity who had no friends—as he was when he was a child.

Implications for Psychotherapy

The current life events and situations of the midlife persons whom I have described in this chapter resulted in their experiencing signif-icant loses, stimulated the need for change, and tapped into signifi-cant areas of vulnerability that made it difficult for them to cope effectively. The elements of the psychotherapeutic process that are discussed and illustrated throughout this book provided opportuni-ties for these patients to deal with their feelings of loss and depriva-tion and blows to their self-concept and self-esteem. Their sense of failure and self-blame was reduced, and they came to value who they are and what they had achieved. A better fit between what they wanted and what they could have was achieved, and they were helped to develop and express diverse parts of themselves. These patients were able to overcome the obstacles to adapting to and making important changes in their lives and to build gratifying life structures.

4
HEALTHY AND PATHOLOGICAL NARCISSISM
Theoretical and Clinical Perspectives

The term narcissism is confusing because of its various meanings. It refers to both healthy and pathological adult character traits, a sexual perversion, a normal stage of infantile development, and a full-fledged personality disorder. It describes an immature type of object choice, a dimension of self-esteem, and a way of relating to the environment (Pulver, 1970). Calling someone narcissistic in popular parlance usually has negative connotations, implying self-involvement and feelings of entitlement to special attention and treatment. Narcissism connotes arrogance, grandiosity, exhibitionism, and a lack of empathy for others. Until recently, the psychoanalytic literature focused on the origins and manifestations of pathological narcissism and overlooked or gave only lip service to the importance of healthy narcissistic needs.

Despite the diverse ways in which writers have defined narcissism, there is general agreement today that it refers to either the normal or the pathologic regulation of self-esteem or self-regard. Healthy narcissism results in a feeling of well-being and intactness without a grandiose sense of self-importance. It is reflected in the desire to take care of one's basic needs without becoming overly obsessed, the pursuit of realistic goals and ambitions, and the enjoyment of attention and praise without being driven to attain them. It enables a person to empathize with others and refrain from exploiting them. A healthy narcissism allows one to survive criticism and rejection, disapproval and insults, failures and setbacks without becoming devastated. With a healthy narcissism, one can weather losses, physical changes, and environmental stressors without losing a basic sense of worth.

According to the *Diagnostic and Statistical Manual of Mental Disorders* (American Psychiatric Association, 1994), pathological narcissism is characterized by an overinflated sense of being special, feelings of entitlement, and excessive need for admiration and approval. The pathological narcissist is arrogant and has chronic feelings of envy of others and a disregard for others, along with tendencies to exploit them. Additionally, some narcissistic persons experience a chronic sense of emptiness and are unable to depend on others. When their excessive needs are frustrated or they or others fail to live up to their perfectionistic expectations, they may become depressed and angry, often experiencing profound feelings of shame and humiliation. Blows to their sense of self can trigger paranoid rage, violence toward others, or suicide.

Nevertheless, many narcissistic persons are intelligent, talented, and successful. They present as charming and superficially warm and related. They often place considerable importance on looking as if they lead an ideal life. Their grandiose self-concept, perfectionism, unrealistic expectations, and characteristic patterns of relating to others, however, make them extremely vulnerable to life's vicissitudes as they grow older.

The term narcissistic vulnerability encompasses the broad range of internal structural weakness in the self that is not restricted to its most overt and severe manifestations (Jacobowitz and Newton, 1999). It may appear in more subtle ways, and those with less severe forms of underlying narcissistic vulnerability may possess an ability to relate to others as separate people who have needs of their own. Nonetheless, they may exhibit chronic problems in functioning or more acute flareups at times when life events trigger the underlying weakness in their self-structures. Because they depend on others for the regulation of their self-esteem, however, they may fluctuate dramatically in their self-regard, plunging from feeling good to feeling worthless or from being strong and powerful to impotent and helpless. They may have a chronic sense of feeling inadequate, inferior, fraudulent, or bad, and underfunction in their work lives. They may show extreme sensitivity to criticism, disappointment, or seeming rejection, or be unable to tolerate difference in their close relationships. The loss of self-cohesion and tendencies toward depletion states and fragmentation can be very debilitating.

Theories of Narcissism

According to mythology, Narcissus was a handsome young man who was caused to fall in love with his own reflection in a mountain pool of water as a punishment by the gods for his indifference to and callousness toward the nymphs who loved him. Gazing enraptured at his own adored face for hours and unable to embrace the object of his love, he soon became melancholy and plunged a dagger through his heart. Numerous psychoanalytic writers have drawn on the story of Narcissus to describe a form of pathological self-love that they call narcissistic (Freud, 1914; Hartmann, 1950; Reich, 1960; Jacobson, 1964; Rosenfeld, 1964, 1971). The most recent and influential of these are Otto Kernberg and Heinz Kohut, who recommended contrasting clinical approaches to patients with narcissistic pathology.

In his seminal writings, Otto Kernberg (1970, 1974) emphasized the role of constitutional aggression and early frustration in the etiology of narcissistic disorders. He described pathological narcissism as reflecting a rigid defensive structure, which he called the grandiose self, that comes into being when an infant defensively fuses his or her ideal self-representation, ideal object representations, and actual self-representations into a fantastic structure that rigidifies and becomes walled off from reality to some degree. Thus, in Kernberg's view, the grandiose self reflects a highly idealized self-concept that the person tries to preserve by defensively projecting his or her split-off aggression, self-hatred, and other negative traits and feelings onto others. By this means, the person maintains a pathological form of self-esteem at the expense of realistic perceptions of the self and others.

In contrast to Kernberg, Heinz Kohut (1966, 1971, 1977) placed normal and pathological narcissism on a continuum, with the latter being a consequence of the caretaking environment's failure to respond adequately to the healthy narcissistic (selfobject) needs of the child. Rewarding experiences with at least one type of selfobject give the child a chance to develop a cohesive self (Wolf, 1988, pp. 50–64; Goldstein, 2001, pp. 79–85). When there are serious failures of attuned parenting, structural defects in the self result. In Kohut's (1977) schema, the child may be able to acquire compensatory structures that strengthen the self by enabling him or her to make up for or repair deficits in one aspect of the self through successful development of its other facets. It is noteworthy that Kohut also believed that even those who attain self-cohesion never outgrow their need for others' confirmation and require the presence of selfobjects all through life.

Kohut described all psychopathology as reflecting self deficits, that is, gaps, missing or underdeveloped elements in self-structure. Kohut believed that disabling self-disorders occur when the child's protracted exposure to a lack of parental empathy in at least two areas of selfobject need leaves the child unable to develop the compensatory structures essential to a cohesive sense of self. The result is pathological outcomes and lifetime vulnerability. Such malformations, deficits, and vulnerabilities are fixed and usually do not spontaneously correct themselves. Kohut and Wolf (1978) put forth a classification of self-disorders related to primary disturbances of the self.

A crucial difference between Kohut and Kernberg revolves around their ideas about the role of aggression. Rejecting the presence of an innate aggressive drive, Kohut views narcissistic rage as a reaction to or a disintegration product resulting from early selfobject failures. This rage may be remobilized later in life when a person with narcissistic vulnerability or a weak self-structure experiences disappointment, rejection, a lack of appreciation, or even minor criticisms from those on whom they depend as selfobjects. Narcissistic rage reactions later in life can be seen as understandable responses to a lack of selfobject attunement when the self-structure lacks cohesion and is weak.

The Fate of Narcissism in Midlife

From the ideas put forth about both adult development in chapter 2 and the perspectives on normal and pathological narcissism and narcissistic vulnerability that have been discussed so far in this chapter, it is possible to speculate about the impact of midlife on the adult personality and in causing serious stumbling blocks to successful adaptation. For some people, their entrenched pathology may take its toll. Midlife forces them to face unpleasant and unsettling realities about themselves and their lives:

> The eventual confrontation of the grandiose self with the frail, limited and transitory nature of human life is unavoidable. . . . For them, to accept the breakdown of the illusion of grandiosity means to accept the dangerous, lingering awareness of the depreciated self—the hungry, empty, lonely primitive self surrounded by a world of dangerous, sadistically frustrating and revengeful objects [Kernberg, 1974, p. 238].

In his pessimistic view of the fate of narcissism in midlife, Kernberg (1980) describes numerous dynamics that contribute to difficulties: the narcissist's devaluation of others and of his or her own past achievements; a lack of gratitude that leads to feelings of emptiness; an endless greed that results in longings for constant refueling; fears that the future will not live up to the past, coupled with a tendency to lose interest in pursuing what might have been previously desired; and envy of his or her own children, particularly as they become independent.

> The narcissistic devaluation of the past is compounded by the painful awareness that the narcissistic gratifications of youth and past triumphs are no longer available. . . . The narcissistic patient is "eternally young" not only in the sense of not being

psychologically prepared to acknowledge the passage of time but also in his lack of accumulation of an internal life that provides sustenance and compensation for later loss and failure. . . . The question "where has life gone?" is common even in normal people, but the feelings that prompt it are painfully maximized in narcissistic patients [pp. 138–139].

For those who show more extensive forms of weakness in the self, the loss of selfobjects or of experiences and opportunities that provide selfobject gratifications may contribute to acute reactions. The bursting of their bubble of omnipotence, control, and perfectionism may create chronic distress. Unfulfilled fantasies of attaining success, status, and recognition may generate ongoing problems in functioning. Sometimes any of these results in frantic efforts to regain a sense of youth, vigor, and attractiveness.

Other people, who show less extreme personality traits and reflect a broader range of underlying narcissistic vulnerability, may be unable temporarily to weather setbacks or embrace new opportunities. Kohut and Wolf (1978) drew attention to what they called secondary self-disturbances. These usually are temporary reactions to life stress from which the patient is able to recover using his or her own inner resources or available selfobjects and affirming activities. Because there is a range of self-pathology and narcissistic vulnerability, the extent to which stressful life circumstances cause a loss of self-cohesion varies. Mild to severe symptoms may develop that express a person's feeling states, such as anxiety, panic, rage, or depression, that reflect defenses against painful experiences or that represent attempts to soothe or restore the self. These symptoms may find expression in substance abuse, compulsive sexual behavior, binge eating, and the like (Baker, 1991, pp. 204–206).

Any of the following common triggers can result in serious difficulties during the midlife period:

- Blows to self-esteem.
- Awareness of the discrepancy between one's dreams and reality.
- Recognition that one cannot attain perfection or complete control of others and life.
- Envy of others who appear to have what one wants.

- Disruptions or failures of compensatory activities and characteristics.
- Loss or unavailability of vital selfobjects or a career niche that has valdidated and affirmed the self or of opportunities for self-expression.
- Profoundly tragic or catastrophic and sometimes unexplainable events that create loss or feelings of betrayal and challenge one's values.
- Awareness of chronic feelings of emptiness and aloneness.
- Recognition of having destroyed or failed to make use of opportunities.
- Need to reappraise one's goals and way of life.
- Having to take on burdensome roles and responsibilities.
- Being unprepared for new roles and life changes.
- Understanding that one has contributed to the demise of or serious problems in relationships.
- Disappointment with or anger at others for failing to gratify one's needs or expectations.
- Difficulties dealing with the limitations of time and the reality of illness and death.
- Fear of increasing dependency.
- Awareness that one cannot change the past.

These triggers result in complex emotional reactions for most people but especially for those who lack the internal self-structure to deal with them effectively. The failure to recognize and address the complexity of these reactions is the reason that some people are unable to transcend the inevitable difficulties of the midlife period.

Treatment Frameworks

Freud (1905) and most early writers were pessimistic about the psychoanalytic treatment of narcissistic personalities because of these patients' alleged inability to develop the requisite transference or involvement with the analyst, their extreme characterologic defenses, and their negative reactions to interpretations experienced as intrusions or criticisms or that do not fit with their view of themselves.

This posture sometimes led to treatment strategies aimed at the alleviation of symptoms through supportive measures, the use of medications, or both (Jacobowitz and Newton, 1999, pp. 458–459).

Although Kernberg (1970) wrote that the overall prognosis for the treatment of narcissistic personalities was guarded, he argued that psychoanalysis is the treatment of choice for certain higher functioning narcissistic patients, particularly if they show some capacity for guilty depression and mourning rather than only paranoid rage, possess basic superego integration and reasonably good impulse control and anxiety tolerance, do not show a tendency to regress to primary-process thinking, and are not involved in life circumstances that provide unusual narcissistic gratifications (pp. 235–240).

Kernberg (1984) described his overall strategy of analyzing patients with narcissistic personality as involving the "systematic analysis of the pathological grandiose self, which presents itself pervasively in the transference" (p. 197). He advised that the analyst employ consistent confrontation and interpretation of the patient's resistances to the analytic process, use of primitive defenses, denial of dependency on the analyst, and need to defeat and envy of the analyst.

> When it is possible to work through this defensive constellation, it turns out that this denial of dependency on the analyst does not represent an absence of internalized object relations or of the capacity to invest in objects, but a rigid defense against more primitive, pathological object relations centered around narcissistic rage and envy, fear and guilty because of this rage, and yet a desperate longing for a loving relationship that will not be destroyed by hatred [p. 220].

Kernberg stressed the importance of the analyst's maintaining an atmosphere of technical neutrality in interventions. He advised therapists to remain "abstinent" and refrain from giving in to the patient's demands for transference gratification and to rely heavily on the use of interpretation. He argued that detours from technical neutrality compromise the therapist's ability to confront and interpret the patient's pathological defenses and behavior (Goldstein, 1990, pp. 103–121). He did acknowledge, however, that narcissistic patients may experience the analyst's consistent attempt to deal with their primitive defenses and resistances, even if so-called technical neutrality is maintained, as assaultive. Nevertheless, he cautioned against the use of supportive techniques in these instances. Instead, he urged the analyst to continue to interpret the patient's reactions.

An important feature of Kernberg's treatment approach is the analyst's ability to monitor his or her countertransference closely in order to recognize the hidden intention of some of the patient's behavior. For example, an analyst's feelings of impotence may be reflecting the patient's attempts to make the analyst feel helpless and insignificant. Kernberg (1974) also cautioned against treating too many narcissistic patients at the same time because of the stress they cause the analyst (pp. 70–71).

Kohut's writings reflect a radically different view of the treatment process than Kernberg's. Treating patients with narcissistic difficulties in psychoanalysis, Kohut identified what he called the selfobject transferences, which reflect the revival of frustrated early mirroring, idealization, and alter-ego or twinship needs in the new, more empathic and nonjudgmental context of treatment. Wolf (1988), a close collaborator and loyal follower of Kohut, expanded the types of selfobject transferences to include the transference of creativity and the adversarial transference (pp. 124–135). The remobilization of these earlier frustrated needs offers patients a "second chance" to complete their development.

In the mirror transference, the patient seeks acceptance and confirmation of the self. This search often takes the form of wanting the therapist's validation, admiration, applause, approval, and enthusiastic participation in the patient's affect states.

In the alter-ego or twinship transference, the patient experiences the therapist as a carbon copy of, or at least someone like, himself or herself. Patients who exhibit this type of transference often assume that the therapist thinks, feels, and behaves as they do, and they are derailed if they become aware of the therapist's differences from them.

The idealizing transference shows itself in the patient's admiring or looking up to the therapist as a soothing, strong, wise, and good selfobject.

The transference of creativity is an experience of merger with a selfobject while one is engaged in a demanding creative task, such as an artistic endeavor.

The adversarial transference involves the need for a supportive relationship that the patient can oppose in order to grow.

All the selfobject transferences contain elements of merger or defenses against them. In merger, the patient experiences the therapist as an extension of himself or herself; the therapist does not have an independent center of initiative. Instead, the therapist is subject to the patient's wishes and needs and must be totally in tune with them. When patients defend against such merger experiences, they may maintain distance from the therapist to protect themselves from reexperiencing trauma at the hands of a disappointing or frustrating selfobject.

Notwithstanding that the selfobject transferences may take exaggerated and extreme forms of the patient's frustrated developmental needs, they must be viewed as understandable, albeit dysfunctional, outcomes of the patient's early caretaking experiences. Usually one dominant form of selfobject transference will emerge, although there can be shifts over time.

Empathy with the patient's subjective experience, rather than technical neutrality in the Kernbergian sense, is the cornerstone of self-psychological treatment. Because the appearance of a selfobject transference in treatment provides narcissistically vulnerable patients a significant opportunity to ameliorate the effects of their past development and to move forward, any signs of such a reaction should be allowed to flourish rather than be discouraged, confronted, or intentionally disrupted. This principle is diametrically opposed to Kernberg's admonishment that the analyst must point out and interpret primitive transference resistances.

Originally, Kohut did not advocate that analysts actually try to meet their patients' selfobject needs. Instead, he viewed the analyst's role as one of empathically understanding those needs and explaining their origins in the patient's early caretaking experiences. Later, he and others recognized that it was not always possible or even useful to distinguish between empathic understanding and empathic responsiveness and suggested a somewhat freer use of the analyst's self in treatment. For example, arguing that Kohut's early emphasis on optimal frustration as a prerequisite for the development of psychic structure was an unfortunate carryover of the instinctual emphasis in classical psychoanalysis, Bacal (1985, p. 225) suggests that the concept of optimal responsiveness be used instead. By providing optimal responsiveness, the therapist can selectively provide actual "mirroring" as well as respond in soothing or other need-fulfilling ways.

In this connection, others have noted that patients may require concrete evidence that their needs are understood. They may need demonstrations of the therapist's active caring, genuineness, and responsiveness or even the actual experience of having some of their needs met. Consequently, whether or not patients seek it out directly, selective therapist self-disclosure may play an important role in enabling some to feel that their needs are understood. They will find the courage to risk relating. Their feelings of shame and aloneness will diminish. They will be able to remember and explore traumatic experiences and feel validated in their very existence (Goldstein, 1994, 1997a).

Kohut also observed that, at the beginning of treatment, many patients with narcissistic vulnerability and early experiences of severe or repeated frustrations and disappointments in their early self–selfobject relationships show difficulty developing a selfobject transference. He believed that they try to protect themselves from exposure to disappointment or injury once again and thus erect defenses that keep them from becoming involved in treatment. Kohut urged analysts to refrain from confronting the defenses of these patients and to comment on their understandable fear of being retraumatized, disappointed, or hurt by the analyst (Wolf, 1988, p. 111). In contrast to Kernberg's (1974) admonitions that therapists should interpret such reactions as manifestations of patients' envy, denial of dependency, or wish to defeat the therapist, Kohut advised analysts to continue to interpret patients' angry behavior as the understandable outcome of the emotional injuries they experienced earlier in their lives. Interpretation or explanation within the framework of self psychology also can be used to help patients understand the links between their selfobject needs, or the defenses against them, and early parental empathic failures and their impact. Self-psychological therapists may need to refrain from explaining or using interpretation for a prolonged period with certain patients, who may experience even seemingly empathic comments as unwanted intrusions.

Once the selfobject transference is on a firmer footing, patients experience a greater sense of well-being and often are able to contain their feelings to a greater degree. Inevitable disruptions occur, however, and derail the treatment until they are overcome. These reactions commonly result from the therapist's lack of attunement to the patient's needs or failure to live up to the patient's expectations, or from the inevitable constraints of the treatment. Patients may experience turbulent emotions and setbacks or may react quite negatively to the therapist, sometimes without recognizing the triggers for their responses. It is crucial for the therapist to attempt to repair the rupture so that the selfobject transference can be restored as soon as it is noticed.

The repair of selfobject transference disruptions has both immediate and long-term benefits. It gets the treatment back on track in the short run, but repeated disruption–restoration sequences over the course of treatment strengthen selfobject connections and are the major pathway for change. The therapist's willingness to acknowledge and even apologize for his or her lack of empathic attunement and to validate the patient's perceptions of reality in a nondefensive manner provides a new type of experience for the patient that leads to transmuting internalizations of the patient's archaic needs and self-structures.

Indispensable features of therapists' ability to repair disruptions are their efforts to try to understand their patients' reactions even if they seem extreme and unwarranted and to accept the validity of patients' subjective experiences even if they are at variance with therapists' intentions or perceptions. Therapists generally should refrain from confronting patients about the seemingly distorted or overly intense nature of their responses. This does not mean that therapists cannot share their own perceptions of the situation or the probable reasons for the patients' behavior. The purpose of such explanations, however, is to clarify misunderstandings and misinterpretations rather than to try to convince a patient that the therapist is "right" and the patient is "wrong."

In addition to acknowledging their role in contributing to disruptions in the selfobject transference, it may be useful for therapists to make empathic interpretations that link such disturbances to earlier frustrations and disappointments in patients' lives, particularly with respect to their relationship with parents or significant others. Such interpretations enable patients to explore and understand the origins of their archaic selfobject needs. It is important, however, for the therapist not to move too quickly into connecting current disruptions to patients' past experience before having sufficiently acknowledged their own role in precipitating the disruption.

It is not always easy to accomplish these tasks. Well-meaning and empathic therapists may nevertheless make what are experienced by the patient as inadvertent and unintentional lapses or errors even while the therapists think they are doing the right thing or staunchly defend their point of view and actions. "There is a ubiquitous resistance to the acknowledgment that the truth we believe about ourselves is no more (though no less) real than the patient's view of us" (Schwaber, 1983, p. 389). It is not unusual for a therapist to be surprised or taken aback by what appears to be a patient's distortion, hypersensitivity, or extreme reaction to a seemingly minor incident. The therapist may fear that empathizing with the patient will be taken as approval of dysfunctional behavior. Although this risk exists, it is usually a misplaced concern. There is a difference between trying to understand patients from their point of view and approving of their behavior. Additionally, empathizing with patients' subjective experience does not prohibit therapists from sharing their own perceptions of the situation or their reasons for certain actions.

As patients develop or regain greater self-cohesion and a firmer self-structure as a part of self-psychological treatment, it is important for them to find new ways of expressing their healthy narcissistic needs and more appropriate selfobjects. Although this may occur spontaneously, some patients may require that the therapist support and validate such efforts. For example, the therapist might encourage the patient to locate a new job or return to school. Perhaps the patient can develop new interests and find creative outlets. The patient can make new friends, perhaps join social or professional organizations.

In the absence of psychotherapy outcome studies, it is not known whether either of these two quite divergent treatment strategies—Kernberg's or Kohut's—is effective or whether one is preferable to the other. Both models have their supporters and critics, and it is possible that each approach may be useful for different types of patients. The self-psychological framework appears to apply to a much broader range of difficulties and is kinder, gentler, and more flexible than the Kernbergian model. The latter model is relentless in its confrontation and interpretation of narcissistic defenses and focus on the role of aggression and envy and fear of dependence in patients with narcissistic difficulties. Although both approaches rely heavily on interpretation and insight, treatment following Kohut's recommendations occurs within a more empathic environment and places greater emphasis on the potentially reparative effects of the therapeutic relationship than does Kernberg's method. It also focuses more attention on the therapist's contribution to impasses in and derailments of the therapist–patient relationship than does a Kernbergian approach, which tends to emphasize the patient's efforts to resist engaging with the analyst or to defeat the treatment.

Whatever their relative merits, neither treatment approach explicitly deals with the interplay between midlife events and narcissistic vulnerability in treatment (Goldstein, 1990, pp. 182–202). Both map out strategies for addressing long-standing personality issues that patients present, but the events that trigger symptomatic outbreaks and acute and chronic distress occur in the current reality of people's lives. Thus, there is a here-and-now as well as a past dimension to the difficulties that patients present, and treatment must address both of them.

5
THE NATURE OF ASSESSMENT IN PSYCHOTHERAPY

When people enter psychotherapy, it is important for clinicians to consider the extent to which midlife events and stresses are playing a role in their presenting problems. If it is determined that such occurrences are frustrating patients' healthy self-needs and stimulating areas of weakness in the self, treatment should focus dually on the patients' current difficulties and their underlying narcissistic vulnerability.

Identifying Triggering Events

Although midlife patients may be aware of what has precipitated their coming for treatment, many present with symptoms or problems that they do not fully understand or know how to address. Even those who are able to identify some of the factors contributing to their discomfort may be bewildered by the intensity and duration of their reactions.

At the outset of treatment, it is useful for therapists to explore their patients' current lives and recent past so as to identify the circumstances that may have triggered or are continuing to affect their healthy self-needs, self-esteem regulation, self-concept, compensatory structures, or defenses. Although such catastrophic events as fires, floods, hurricanes, violent attacks, sudden untimely deaths, and the like may be generating disastrous effects for some people, less dramatic and more usual occurrences generally are at work. There are four significant areas of patients' lives that clinicians should investigate: life-stage marker events (e.g., birthdays, anniversaries, weddings, early retirement); interpersonal relationships; occupational and financial issues; and illness or disability.

Life-Stage Marker Events

Certain special events in midlife may cause a confrontation with unpleasant realities or point up discrepancies between a patient's dreams and reality. For example, approaching his 50th birthday, a divorced stockbroker who prided himself on his youthful appearance, good health, and vigor became preoccupied with the idea that he was losing his physical and mental edge and became obsessed with the limitations of time, lost opportunities, and the prospect of illness and death. He could not concentrate on his work, could not sleep, engaged in extensive exercise workouts, and frantically dated younger women.

The 48-year-old woman who loved her husband and children reacted to the infidelity of her husband by developing severe headaches and feelings of betrayal and rage. She felt that the whole foundation of her life had been undermined (see chapter 3).

The 57-year-old married woman whose 25-year-old daughter announced her engagement to a young man, whom the family liked, nevertheless became overwhelmed by feelings of envy of her daughter, anger at her husband, and regrets about the choices she had made in her own life (see chapter 3).

A 55-year-old man became distraught after taking early retirement and selling the successful business he had owned for 25 years.

He ruminated about having made a terrible mistake and resisted making the geographic move that he and his wife had planned for the past two years.

Interpersonal Relationships

Clinicians should also investigate whether patients have experienced changes in meaningful relationships that are leading to intense reactions. For example, the single, 42-year-old, successful businessman with a history of having had short-lived relationships with women who he felt were never good enough for him became quite upset after his latest breakup. For the first time, he began to wonder if he was making bad choices or finding ways of ruining his relationships (see chapter 3).

A 43-year-old recently divorced woman with two school-age children could not adjust to being without a husband and live-in father. She was unable to overcome a sense of shame and stigma and move on in her life despite having initiated the divorce because of feeling trapped in a frustrating relationship.

The 46-year-old lesbian mother and professional who had reluctantly assumed a caretaker role for her deteriorating mother, from whom she had been estranged, became overwhelmed not only by her burdensome responsibilities but also by having to face the never-changing reality of her mother's lifelong emotional unavailability and rejecting behavior (see chapter 3).

The death of a single 48-year-old woman's father, whom she viewed as her best friend, left her in a prolonged state of grief in which she felt lost and feared that no one else in life would ever understand and appreciate her.

Occupational and Financial Issues

Therapists should be alert to changes or problems in patients' work lives and financial conditions that may be inflicting blows to the self. For example, the 42-year-old department manager in a large corporation, who was previously regarded as a rising star, could neither accept having fallen out of favor with management nor mobilize himself to find another position (see chapter 3).

A financially insecure 42-year-old actress who viewed herself as highly talented and deserving of stardom fell into a depression, began to abuse alcohol, and could not motivate herself to pursue her career after she failed to get a major role in a promising Broadway play that she thought would bring her the recognition that she deserved.

The 48-year-old male computer programmer who had earned a good income became angry, bitter, and inconsolable after being laid off by the technology company for which he worked for eight years. He had no prospects of employment because of the downsizing in his field (see chapter 3).

The 55-year-old married man who was contemplating an early retirement after becoming demoralized at work became indecisive and despairing and questioned the value and purpose of his life. He felt angry but also blamed himself for having lost 65% of his financial assets as a result of the country's economic downturn. He had trouble letting go of his work life, unhappy as it was, because it was so central to his identity (see chapter 3).

Illness and Disability

Minor or major illnesses and disabilities and perceived changes in physical and mental capacities can have a dramatic impact. For example, an athletic 48-year-old man who excelled in tennis and marathon running began to feel worthless when he was forced to give up both of his highly valued sport activities because of problems with his knees. He became involved in numerous extramarital affairs that threatened his marriage.

The 54-year-old woman whose self-concept centered on her appearance became despondent and unable to regain her sense of well-being and zest for life one year after being diagnosed with and successfully treated by means of a mastectomy and radiation for an early stage of breast cancer (see chapter 3).

The specific triggering incidents described in these examples might be expected to produce at least temporary disturbances in many so-called healthy persons. Their presence, in themselves, does not tell a clinician whether he or she has tapped a patient's narcissistic vulnerability. Moreover, certain tragic events or highly stressful circumstances may have traumatic sequelae for the persons who experience them in the absence of underlying weakness in their self-structures. Nevertheless, not all people respond the same way to similar life situations or even devastating occurrences. Consequently, it is not always the identification of the objective events in patients' lives that help the clinicians to understand their severe reactions. Rather, it is therapists' efforts to comprehend the subjective meaning of those reactions that provide clues to their sometimes profound and long-lasting effects.

Being Attuned to the Patient's Subjective Distress

The therapist's empathy, or ability to place himself or herself "in the shoes of the patient" and to see the world through the patient's eyes, always is crucial to understanding the patient's reactions. Achieving such empathy is particularly important when patients show intense reactions that may not seem objectively warranted by their life circumstances. Therapists must try to be attuned to their patients, grasp their plight, and bear their feelings—rage, despair, bitterness, envy, loneliness, powerlessness, shame, humiliation, unrealistic expectations. Therapists must convey that they appreciate what patients think and feel. They must resist seeing some patients as being overly dramatic or underestimating the depth of patients' reactions. Being careful not to minimize their patients' pain, therapists should avoid pointing out what seem to be extreme reactions or unrealistic expectations and attitudes. Well-placed empathy will enable patients to feel less alone and, perhaps paradoxically, in many instances to feel some sense of hope. It is only within the context of this type of empathy that patients can explore themselves more deeply.

Whether or not patients' intense responses to life events seem objectively warranted, it is not always easy for therapists to stay empathically attuned to them. Palombo (1985, pp. 46–48) offered a cautionary note describing the difficulty of watching people in pain without feeling overwhelmed or having to take it away, empathizing with a patient's despair while conveying hope, and dealing with the existential dilemmas raised by patients who are questioning their lives. Among other potential sources of strong reactions in therapists, particularly those who are midlifers themselves, are their identification with and anxiety about patients' struggles that are similar to their own.

On the other hand, therapists may have difficulty relating to patients' problems that seem unfamiliar or alien, or they may be impatient with or disapprove of patients' ways of dealing with life or others. Therapists may have an unwavering belief in the correctness of their own solutions to problems. Or they may feel assaults to their own sense of self or selfobject needs. Therapists may be taxed by having to observe patients' unrealistic expectations of life or cavalier treatment of others or having to endure their feelings of entitlement. It may be extremely difficult to deal with a patient's narcissistic rage and devaluation or rejection of what the therapist has to offer. And being unable to influence a patient's deeply negative self-concept can be frustrating. Moreover, just as it is difficult for parents to establish a good enough holding environment for their children when they are surrounded by a nonnurturing and stressful environment, it is difficult for therapists to be emotionally present and to show empathy for patients when they are under siege in their own professional lives. The task of remaining emotionally available to patients has become more difficult for many clinicians as managed-care companies have created increased demands for recordkeeping, written reports, and telephone calls while intruding on the therapist–patient relationship, capping fees, and violating the rules of confidentiality.

In the following three cases, although the patients' distress about the circumstances of their current lives was palpable, the nature of their reactions challenged the therapists' empathic capacities.

A Case of Frustrated Expectations

Marge, a 53-year-old Jewish woman, worked as a school librarian and lived with her second husband, a research scientist. Marge sought help because for the past year she had been consumed with anger and regrets about not having the family life that she had expected to have by this time in her life. Recently, her anger had been escalating instead of diminishing: "I know that I'm driving my husband crazy. I'm afraid that he is getting tired of me. I'm exhausting myself. I can't stop myself from going on about my gripes. . . . I can't stand myself any more but I hate my life. I don't know what I've done to deserve all this." With a trace of humor, she asked, "Do you want to hear my list?"

Marge's chief complaint was her disappointment with and anger at her grown children. Marge alternately blamed them for what she described as their failure to live up to their potential and for making bad choices: "My daughter, Jessica, is 30 going on 15. My husband and I just finished paying for her to do graduate work in art history at an Ivy League school, no less. Now she's working part-time as a waitress, lives in a run-down, tiny apartment that has no stove, and can't even pay for health insurance or support herself financially. I never wanted her to go into art history in the first place, but at least I thought she would get a job in her field. Now she says she wants to be an artist—but no one is going to discover her in a coffee shop. If I say anything to her, she tells me to get off her case and that I've always put too much pressure on her, as if wanting your daughter to be successful in life is a bad thing. It wouldn't be so bad if she were happy, but I see that she isn't. How can she be? She has always had high aspirations but she gets frustrated easily. She's not dating either. I've given up on the idea that she will ever have children. I don't even want to be with her lately.

"I know I should keep my big mouth shut but I can't, so we fight all the time. She says I'm abusive. It makes me furious. . . . When my friends ask about her, I don't know what to say. I know I sound horrible. But when I look at her, I see an attractive, talented girl who's making a mess of her life and who's depressed. She sees my disappointment in her. I can't help it. All I want is for her to be able to support herself. That's all I ask. But I know I have to change. I don't want to lose her completely, and she is distancing from me. . . . I see my other friends enjoying their relationships with their daughters. God forgive me; I envy them and I feel like there's something wrong with me that I can't have what they have."

When the therapist inquired about Marge's son, Adam, who was 27, Marge launched into a another tirade, this time against Adam's fiancée, Sarah, whom she viewed as trying to separate him from the family: "He's a great guy but he's blind. He loves her and defends her if I say anything remotely critical of her. She wouldn't even come to dinner for the holidays and she rarely calls. When I call her, she is polite but always has an excuse to get off the phone quickly. Adam says it's just her way, but I can see that she's totally involved in her own family and wants no part of ours. That wouldn't bother me so much if she didn't try to get between Adam and me. Can you imagine that they called me from her mother's house to tell me that they are getting married? Couldn't he have called me himself first? You can be sure that her family isn't going to pay for the wedding. They don't have the money. I don't care if we have to pay for the whole thing. . . . I just don't want to lose him. All my life I thought I would have my children and their children around me as I got older. . . . I've failed somehow but I don't know what I did that was so terrible. Just look at them."

Discussing her husband, Alex, Marge said that, although he could be very frustrating and they had had their fights during their 20-year marriage, she felt that they had worked out a companionable, if not always emotionally rewarding, relationship. She admired his intelligence and easygoing temperament but often felt angry at him for needing to be the center of attention and not showing interest in and respect for her opinions.

Two other complaints appeared on Marge's list. Although she derived some satisfaction from her work, she felt plagued by regrets that she had never become a writer or a journalist or lived up to her potential because of her fears of rejection and her "laziness" when it came to her professional development. Marge also felt disappointed that she did not have more close friends but acknowledged that she had trouble reaching out to others because of her insecurity. She waited for others to approach her and often became tired of and impatient with people who "go on about themselves and need constant stroking."

Discussion. The therapist felt compelled by Marge's feelings of disappointment and engaged by her apparent neediness and sense of humor about herself, but she also felt that Marge's anger at her children seemed out of control and destructive to her relationships with them. Having herself had a critical mother who was never happy with her children's choices and having sought to be different from her family from an early age, the therapist was aware of her identification with Marge's children. Similar in age to Marge, she felt pulled between a desire to help ease her pain and an impulse to point out Marge's difficulty accepting and appreciating her children for who they were. Recognizing the contribution of her own issues, the therapist attempted to put aside her somewhat judgmental reaction to Marge and focused on trying to put herself in Marge's place. When she did this, the patient seemed to feel understood, but the therapist felt drained by Marge's intense feelings of betrayal, deep sense of being victimized, envy of others who appeared to have what she wanted, and alternating feelings of anger and self-blame.

A Case of Loss of Self-Cohesion

Life seemed to be going well for Richard. At age 43, he occupied a management position in a good company, lived in an apartment in New York City with his male partner of 12 years, and had a weekend home in the country. They had an active social life with a small circle of friends. Prior to the past year, Richard had prided himself on his resilience in dealing with life's vicissitudes.

Born in New England to an Irish American family, Richard was the eldest of five male siblings, who looked to him for advice and support. From an early age, he became accustomed to being in charge and in control. As an adult, he was driven in his work life but did not view this as a problem, for he saw himself as having high standards. He was exacting of those who worked for him and was intolerant of their mistakes. His live-in partner, Roger, was a few years younger than he and also had a good job. Roger was less ambitious than Richard and more fun-loving, spontaneous, and easygoing. Richard's only complaint about Roger was his expectation that Richard be responsible for everything in their lives. Richard recognized, however, that he preferred to do many tasks himself because he did not like his partner's careless approach. Richard tended to hold his feelings in and would withdraw and sulk rather than confront difficult situations. He took good care of himself physically and worked out with a vengeance. At times when his frustrations mounted, he would have an explosive outburst. Recently, Richard felt that he was "losing it" more frequently as work pressures were escalating and veering "out of control." He sought refuge in his house, which felt like a sanctuary, away from the stresses of the world. He loved the house and devoted considerable time and money to making it look beautiful.

So why did Richard seek treatment? In a routine visit to his doctor, he learned that he had slightly elevated blood pressure and high cholesterol despite his being physically fit. These findings frightened him because of his family history of heart problems. His doctor, who knew him quite well, suggested that Richard try to reduce the stress he placed on himself and learn to slow down, in addition to taking medication. Soon after, Richard's neighbor in the country cut down a large number of trees on his property in order to build a barn. Those trees screened Richard's house. Richard was devastated and beside himself with anger. He tried unsuccessfully to get the town to intervene on his behalf and learned that the neighbor had not obtained a proper building permit. Richard then hired an attorney to obtain a financial settlement to replant. He felt that his property had been violated (although no one else seemed to notice the missing trees). He became moody and did not want to socialize with friends. He worried about his health, had difficulty concentrating, and burst into tears when frustrated. He was irritable with Roger, who was urging him to "get over it already" and "to get on with his life." At his doctor's urging, Richard sought therapy in August 2001.

By the time Richard entered psychotherapy, he realized that there was something "screwy" about the intensity of his reactions even though he could make himself feel better. Indicating that he had been having suicidal thoughts that frightened him, he said, "No one commits suicide because his trees have been cut down." His only explanation for his reactions was that he did not tolerate change very well especially when it was thrust on him. Nevertheless, he was still in a rage at his neighbor for ruining the property and wanted to sell his house, which he felt would never be the same. Within a few weeks of beginning treatment, the September 11 terrorist attacks on the World Trade Center and the Pentagon took place. Although Richard did not lose anyone and was never in actual danger, he worked in a building in New Jersey from which he could see the burning towers and their collapse. Stunned, he was able to make his way home on the last boat across the Hudson River that went to Manhattan and by walking the rest of the short distance to his apartment. He and his partner drove to their house in the country. Richard felt as though he were going to explode. In early therapy sessions, Richard cried as he talked about the fall of the towers. "I just can't believe they went down. I looked at them every day. They were so majestic. I don't know what to do. It feels like I can't go on."

Discussion. When he began treatment before September 11, Richard knew that his health issues were mild and treatable and had some awareness that his reaction to the cutting down of the trees was extreme. He was not able to use this knowledge, however, to help him take a step back form his intense responses. For example, he readily agreed that recent events had tapped into deeper concerns but quickly returned to his preoccupation with the loss of his trees and perfect house. He was totally wrapped up in his intense feelings, and, initially, the therapist felt at a loss to help him other than to allow him to vent.

Like Richard, the therapist was taking medication for mild high blood pressure and cholesterol and also had a weekend house in which she took pride. It was not difficult to understand that Richard's work situation was taxing his need for control, that learning about his health issues surprised and worried him, and that he was upset that his refuge had been marred in some way. Nevertheless, these events by themselves did not seem to account for Richard's fragmentation, loss of self-cohesion, rage, and traumatic reaction. Richard himself acknowledged that he knew that he was basically in good health and that it was only he who felt that the damage to the house was serious. Likewise, although most New Yorkers, as well as people elsewhere, were devastated at least temporarily, if not traumatized long after, by the World Trade Center attack, Richard's feeling that he could not go on and his suicidal thoughts suggested that the meaning of the towers' collapse was highly personal and reflected a complex form of acute stress disorder. Although it generated anxiety in the therapist, the fact that she, like Richard, was greatly affected by the events of September 11 helped her to stay connected to Richard's painful state.

A Case of Loss of Self-Esteem and Paralysis

Carol was a 45-year-old former college professor who was working as a word processor when she entered treatment after a year of feeling depressed, withdrawn, and paralyzed in her work life. She felt desperate and hopeless about the future, questioned all her past choices, and berated herself for her inertia and weakness. Carol's main initial concerns were her career and her financial condition and, to a lesser degree, her relationships with a married man and her family of origin. "I'm barely managing and I'm not getting any younger. I don't know what I have been working for all my life. I can't see what's ahead for me. I don't know what to do. I feel lost but I'm not doing anything to help myself. . . . I know that no one can do it for me. I'm just vegetating. I don't know what I'm waiting for. . . . I'm also not doing anything about the relationship with a man I've been seeing. I know I should break it off because it's not going anywhere and is totally frustrating. I don't even want to be with him any more but I'm afraid of being alone. I have to get myself together. I can't waste any more time."

One year earlier, Carol's application for tenure at the college she had taught at for six years was not approved. As was customary, she was given a terminal 12-month contract, which had just run out. In addition to losing her job, she had to move out of her university-subsidized apartment. "I should have looked for another teaching position but I couldn't make myself do it. I felt ashamed and was afraid of being rejected. I'm not sure I want to go back into academia. I don't know if I can make it there. It feels too hard. But I don't know what else to do. I always wanted to be a professor."

Carol said that, although she was stunned when her application for tenure was not approved, she was not really surprised because she had been warned three years earlier that her publication record was not up to par. In fact, at that time she had decided to find a different teaching position that would have less rigorous requirements and a more supportive environment, but she stayed on, only half-heartedly invested in her writing. She published a few articles, but, when others that she had completed were not initially accepted for publication, she did not make the revisions and resubmit them in a timely fashion. She felt it was not fair that her position depended on her publishing. "I'm a good teacher. I relate well to my students. I can tell when they are responding to me. . . . I don't know why I held myself back in my writing, not that anyone ever tried to help me. I know I shouldn't have expected that. I've done this to myself. I'm so stupid!"

When Carol had to leave her position and her apartment, she moved in with some graduate students in order to save money on rent. With the help of the husband of a colleague, she took a job as a word processor on the night shift in a law firm. "The new academic year is going to start in September, and this is the time I have to apply for another teaching position if that's what I want to do. I can't go on being a word processor. I hate it and I don't make enough, not that a teaching salary is so great. . . . I could teach part-time at my school and make a little extra, but I have to let them know and I don't really want to be there. I'm so mad that I have boxed myself in."

Describing her relationship with the man she was seeing, Carol said that she knew from the beginning of their relationship that it was not going to work. "I guess I should tell you that he's married and has no intention of leaving his wife. I don't even care that we don't live together or see each other that often. I'm not able to be that present myself right now. . . . I just don't feel good about his cheating on his wife. I never thought I would be the other woman. . . . I haven't had the greatest track record with men. He used to make me feel important and special, and I knew he was there even if I didn't see him. Now, it's just not working but I can't bring myself to break it off completely. I sound pathetic, don't I?"

A third area of conflict for Carol was her relationship with her parents, churchgoing Methodists, who lived on a farm in a small Midwestern town that could be considered to be part of the "Bible Belt." Her parents were in their 70s and were retired, and her four siblings (three older brothers and one younger sister) and their families lived close by. "They're great people and they love us. I left when I went to college and I go back for visits, but it's not the same. I'm not a part of their daily lives, and I don't really have the life here that I thought I would have at this point. It makes me feel very sad. Maybe it would have been better if I never left. What do I have to show for my years away from them? I've wasted so much time."

Discussion. Carol's distress evoked a sympathetic response in the therapist, who felt drawn to helping her. Having for many years been in academia herself, the therapist had no difficulty empathizing with what it might be like for the patient not to obtain tenure and to lose her job and financial livelihood. But the therapist also had witnessed others in similar situations mobilize themselves and move on after a period of depression and anger. For Carol, her losses appeared to have undermined her sense of self drastically, so that she was unable to pursue her career and questioned her future path.

Yet it also appeared that Carol's self-needs and self-esteem regulation had been shaky for a long time before she was denied tenure. She had not been taking good care of herself in her teaching position: she neither did what she needed to do to be successful nor did she leave to go elsewhere when she saw the "writing on the wall." Carol's self-disparaging and self-blaming comments were striking. In fact, the therapist was aware of feeling distressed that Carol may have brought the current state of affairs on herself through her inaction. Thus, it seemed likely that successfully moving toward her goals and ambitions had been seriously compromised early on. The reasons behind this required exploration.

Although it was not difficult to understand Carol's reluctance to break off her relationship with the married man, it also seemed apparent that here, too, she found herself unable to leave a situation that she knew was not good for her. Likewise, Carol's comments about her parents and siblings, whom she did leave behind at least geographically, suggested unfinished business that also might be blocking her pursuit of her career and a committed relationship.

Eliciting the Patient's Narrative

In the beginning of treatment, it always is advisable for a therapist to create a safe therapeutic environment in which the patient can talk freely. Creating such a climate should take precedence over prematurely delving into the patient's deeper struggles or confronting and interpreting the patient's defenses and character traits. The clinician must strike a balance in focusing on both the here and now and the there and then of the patient's life. To set the stage for a collaborative

exploration of the patient's background and past life experiences, often it is useful for the clinician to help the patient develop a framework
for understanding his or her discomfort and pain by discussing the potential link between the past and the present.

An empathic exploration fosters patients' ability to share their
personal stories or narratives and to reveal themes that help therapists to understand the patients' personal strivings and views of
themselves and others. As therapy proceeds, therapists may feel free
to identify significant themes and to explore more charged material.
Patients can be helpful to develop a fresh perspective on their lives.
Therapists can interpret the possible connection between the patients' self-needs and self-concept and their current distress.

Assessing the Mainstays of a Patient's Self-Esteem, Self-Concept, Compensatory Structures, and Defenses

Hand in hand with the exploration of patients' personal stories, clinicians make a beginning assessment of the patients' self-needs, the
mainstays of their self-concept and self-esteem regulation, compensatory structures, and major defenses. This exploration is accomplished through the examination of the patients' views of themselves
in different contexts. What are the patients' understandings of what
contributes to their feeling good or bad? What contributes to their
optimal or problematic functioning? What do they take pride in and
use to bolster themselves? How do they relate to others? How do they
cope with anxiety or threats to their self-esteem? How do they relate
to the therapist? Understanding patients' self-structures will enable
the therapist to formulate an idea about the intensity and impact of
the patients' current life circumstances. These early formulations
help to guide the therapeutic process and may evolve and change as
new information emerges and the therapist experiences how the patients relate in treatment.

In the previously discussed cases of Marge, Richard, and Carol,
the therapist gleaned the following information in early sessions that
formed the basis of her understanding of their responses to current
events.

Making Up for Feelings of Deprivation, Inadequacy, Loneliness, and Failed Ambition

The younger of two daughters, Marge was born when her mother, a European immigrant, was 40. According to Marge, the family was poor and her mother was a "plain, old-fashioned" woman who did not wear makeup or dress well. She often seemed depressed and burdened, kept to herself, and was both fearful and critical of outsiders. Marge described herself as a blonde, blue-eyed child who was unusually attractive and stood out among her dark-haired cousins. Although her mother took pride in dressing her every morning, she rarely spent other time with her, seemed uncaring about Marge's feelings, and was overprotective and highly critical of her. Marge viewed her father as a financially unsuccessful, unassuming, and depressed man who worked as a presser in the garment industry. The parents fought frequently. Marge remembered their small apartment as dark and cold and lacking in joy. She recalled feeling guilty when her mother bought clothes for her and deprived herself. She felt ashamed that her mother did not speak English well and did not wear makeup or take good care of herself; Marge wished that her mother were more modern and happier. Marge longed to be part of a different family, and some of her friends' parents "adopted" her. The only really positive memories of home that she has are of the smell of bread baking in the oven and her father sometimes bringing her pretty dresses from the company where he was employed.

Marge described herself as shy and fearful at school but as having temper tantrums at home to get her way. She thought that her mother wanted her to be a good student, attend college, and make something of herself, but Marge felt that she was not smart and never tried to excel. Marge did attend a local college and soon married in order to get out of the house. Despite feeling that her lack of ambition to pursue a career disappointed her mother, in retrospect she realized that no one in her family was a role model for success, took an interest in what she did, or helped her to negotiate the world. She was attracted to her husband's worldliness and thought he would provide a secure income, but he quickly became involved with other women and was emotionally and physically absent all through her pregnancies. She had a miscarriage just before she conceived Jessica, who was a replacement child.

Marge recalled feeling extremely alone and frightened when the children were born. She experienced her mother as mostly unavailable and had no one else to help her. Although Marge desperately wanted children, she was an anxious mother, particularly with Jessica, not an easy child and extremely willful. Marge regretfully said she was very structured, if not rigid, in her parenting but did not know any better. She felt frustrated when Jessica did not go along with her routines. Marge acknowledged that she had been too controlling and perfectionistic with Jessica. "I wanted her to use her talents and make something of herself. I know I pushed her too hard, but she could have done it if she wanted to. I tried to encourage her and be there for her in ways my mother never could have imagined."

As a child and adolescent, Jessica took voice and drama lessons and was praised by her teachers for her talent. "I attended every recital she had. She wanted to pursue a career as an entertainer but was always high strung and sensitive to criticism," Marge said. According to Marge, when Jessica encountered more serious competition in her college years and was no longer the "fair-haired child," she became highly stressed, seemed to lose her motivation, and has struggled to find a place for herself ever since.

Adam was a more easygoing child, who became self-reliant quickly. He was a sensitive boy with whom Marge always felt she could talk. He was a good student who excelled in whatever he did and had recently found a promising position in the publishing field. Marge felt very close to his former girlfriend and was greatly disappointed when they broke off their relationship. She was never able to warm up to Adam's current fiancée, "who is a cold fish and totally self-involved."

Marge and her first husband divorced when the children were young. She felt that she and the children had been close, especially after her divorce, but that their relationship with her suffered when she remarried. Recently, Marge realized that Jessica blamed her for the divorce. Jessica idealizes her biological father and does not see his "bad" side and destructive behavior. When the children were in elementary school, Marge did graduate work and became a librarian, which she regarded as a "nothing" career but one that got her out of the house. "I didn't have the guts to go after the career I would have liked, and I was too old anyway."

Also significant in Marge's history was her relationship with her older sister, from whom she had been estranged for many years. She felt bitter about this, for she recalled looking up to her sister when they were younger. The sister, however, seemed to be indifferent to, if not envious of, Marge. After the mother's death 10 years earlier, Marge and her sister had a major falling out after an argument about who had been the mother's favorite, and the sister has rebuffed Marge's efforts to reconcile. This breach left Marge feeling that she has no family. She resents her husband's involvement with his large extended family, who are welcoming of Marge but who "are not my real family."

Discussion. From the exploration of Marge's background, it was possible to begin to formulate an understanding or the subjective meaning of her current reactions, which later sessions confirmed. Marge's current life seemed to be out of step with her long-standing hopes and dreams and her belief that she was going to be a better parent than her own parents had been and that she would have a better life than they did. She was angry that Jessica was not living up to Marge's expectations that she have a successful career, that both her children were depriving her of the idealized family life that she imagined "good" mothers enjoy, and that she lacked a loving sister and friends with whom she could feel close. Moreover, she felt frustrated that she had never pursued her ambitions for herself and regretful about her passivity and fearfulness. She alternated between seeing herself as a victim of life's injustices and blaming herself. It is noteworthy that Marge was angry at her daughter, Jessica, for possessing the same traits that she disliked in herself—Jessica, like Marge, did not seem to be making the most of her life and was waiting to be discovered rather than actively pursuing her ambitions. Jessica's lack of career and interpersonal success and her intermittently rejecting attitudes and behavior were crushing Marge's main means of compensating for her low self-esteem and negative self-concept, that is, being a good mother. On one hand, Marge continued to feel that she, unlike her own mother, had done everything for Jessica, who was ungrateful and stubborn. At the same time, she was like a "bad" mother because of Jessica's "failure" and rejecting behavior.

Adam was overtly more successful in his career and interpersonal relationships than was his sister and Marge's expectations of him in this area were not as highly charged as those for her daughter. In Marge's eyes, Adam's engagement and impending marriage to a woman who did not make Marge feel important, who did not seem to want to be close to her, and who was possessive of Adam burst Marge's fantasies about the kind of future relationship she would have with them and their children. It also deprived her of her continuing dependence on Adam for his ability to nurture her.

Although Marge's wishes for a close family were normal and understandable, it seemed likely that they reflected, in part, a need to repair her early emotional deprivation, feelings of aloneness, need for mirroring, and sense of inadequacy. Consequently, the frustration of this need was exposing Marge's underlying vulnerability. Her intense anger may also have protected her from experiencing a deep sense of sadness. Marge also associated family closeness with being successful as a parent, something she had always strived for. The paths her children were taking made her feel that she was a failure. At the same time, their lives felt like a punishment for her feeling ashamed of her parents' impoverished life, as well as for her anger at her mother.

Although Marge had developed some healthy self-esteem around her appearance and ability to attract others, believed that her husband loved her in his way, even if he did not respect her opinions, and felt that she had come a long way from the Brooklyn tenement where she was raised, she also had developed some grandiose defenses to cover her profound feelings of inadequacy and badness. In addition to her attractive appearance, Marge dressed, spoke, and behaved in an impeccable manner. From an early age, she cultivated an air of superiority and aloofness in her dealings with others to cover her neediness and feelings of vulnerability. Likewise, she had a sense of entitlement that others should approach and do for her, which reflected her need to have others prove that she was a desirable person. When she failed to get the attention or mirroring that she craved from her husband, sister, and friends, she became angry and withdrawn. She lacked empathy for what others were experiencing and tended to blame them for their shortcomings. Her defenses had protected her fragile sense of self but they were no longer working well, resulting in enormous self-blame, a deep sense of regret, and painful feelings of guilt.

A Reliance on Being Perfect and in Control

Richard's family had lived a financially secure lifestyle until his father lost all his money, became ill, and died of a heart attack when Richard was 16 years old. Prior to his father's death, Richard had tried to be the "perfect son," having been told repeatedly by his mother that he had to set a standard of good behavior for his brothers. A compulsive and highly energetic person who was always involved in a project, his mother was stoical and did not encourage expression of feelings. She looked to Richard to help manage the family after her husband's death, when the family's financial and social status changed for the worst. Richard was shocked to learn of his father's poor management of his business and financial affairs. He felt responsible for the family and also felt deprived of the material things he had taken for granted.

An above-average student, Richard never felt that he was smart or could compete with others. Moreover, from childhood, he struggled with the knowledge that he was attracted to other boys and tried to conceal this from family and friends. Although he thought that his father may have suspected that Richard was gay, he never revealed his sexual identity to him and tried to suppress his sexual interests for many years. He focused on his studies and attempted to be good at anything he did so as to appear above reproach. Richard graduated from college and obtained interesting and well-paying jobs but was a "workaholic" and had a sense of foreboding that he would lose everything. He was hypervigilant for any sign of potential threat to his well-being and was meticulous in everything he did so as to ensure that he did not fail. After years of being in the closet as a gay man and trying to act as if he were straight, he decided he could not do this anymore and eventually met his partner. They were open about their relationship to a small group of mostly straight friends and to their families but tended to set themselves part from other gays.

In his work life and friendships, Richard's unrealistic expectations of himself and others, sensitivity to criticism, and disappointment if anyone fell short caused him difficulties. He withdrew from people who had "undesirable" characteristics. He often experienced a loss of self-esteem if his employers were not sufficiently appreciative of his efforts. On many of these latter occasions, he would seek a different position elsewhere rather than stick it out where he was. He had one episode of "feeling unstrung" when he was informed that he and his partner would have to move from their sublet apartment because the owner planned to reclaim it. Despite their finding another place to live that was quite nice, Richard felt enraged at the need to relocate. He was unable to sleep, could not concentrate, felt panicky, and ruminated about whether or not he could have avoided the move. Soon after the move, he learned that the company he worked for was going to be sold and that his future there was uncertain. He sought another position but became convinced that his career was about to deteriorate. He eventually sought help and, after a course of short-term treatment, felt significantly better.

Discussion. From important information Richard revealed about his early life, it was possible to create a picture of his personality strengths and vulnerabilities and to develop some hypotheses about his intense response to recent life events. Despite his many successes, Richard's self-concept and self-esteem regulation made him narcissistically vulnerable. The mainstays of his adaptation were his sense of control and perfection, which enabled him both to compensate for and to defend against underlying feelings of inadequacy, feelings of difference related to his sexual identity, fear of disapproval, and anxieties about the of loss of material possessions and financial security. The stage was set for this adaptation early in his relationship with his perfectionist, rigid, and critical mother but was reinforced by his sudden deidealization of a benign but unavailable father, after the father's business and finances deteriorated and he died, leaving the family in difficult circumstances.

The therapist believed that recent events had disrupted the major underpinnings of Richard's self-concept and defenses and also triggered the original traumatic events around his father's death. Learning that he had high blood pressure and high cholesterol appeared to signal that his body was betraying him. The destruction of the trees around his house signified that his house was no longer perfect. He was losing control of his body and his environment. The 9/11 attack also struck at the core of his belief that he could control life and death and left him feeling unsafe. In addition to the tragic reality of the attack, the towers were symbols of power and security. If they could crumble, there was no protection and he was vulnerable and could lose everything, once again. Thus, one could say that Richard's defensive structure itself was also attacked.

Lack of Self-Esteem and Guilt about Pursuing Ambitions

The fourth of five children and the first girl in the family, Carol from an early age remembered wanting to have the privileges of her older brothers and rebelled against helping out on the farm in the ways in which her parents expected. She described her parents as loving but busy, and as strict and austere, not believing in praise or displays of affection. They worked long hours but had little to show for it monetarily. They were very disparaging of those who sought material possessions or who were ambitious in their careers. They tended to be suspicious of those who became educated or moved away, particularly if they adopted an air of superiority, showed off, or looked down at others.

In elementary school, Carol looked to her teachers for affection and attention and received it. She was an excellent student and enjoyed doing her homework, much to her parents' dismay since they would have preferred that she do chores. She loved to read and watch the television news and was teased by her brothers for having "her head in her books." As she got older, Carol described their attempts to "put me down" if she spoke about a subject or used words that were unfamiliar to them. Although her parents did not actively discourage her from pursuing her studies, they did not try to understand or encourage her.

Carol continued to do well in high school, and her counselors encouraged her to apply for a scholarship to a university in a city some distance away. She was afraid to tell her parents because she knew they assumed she would live at home and attend a local college. Although she wanted to have a different kind of life from that of her family and to make something of herself, she also felt that she was going against her parents' wishes and values. From that time on, she said, she learned to keep her interests and ambitions separate from her interactions with her family.

Carol did obtain a scholarship and went away to college, where she also worked long hours to earn enough for her room and board. She was too busy to have much of a social life although she did make a few good friends. She visited her family frequently but began to feel that they were treating her like a stranger. This treatment worsened when she moved to the East Coast to do graduate work in political science. The move was exciting but difficult as Carol encountered a highly competitive and uncaring environment to which she was unaccustomed. "I felt like I stood out like a sore thumb." By this she meant that "they probably were thinking that I was a hick and had no business being there." It took Carol a long time to obtain her advanced degrees. What she found most difficult was writing by herself. Her doctoral dissertation experience was a "nightmare." She completed it only with the help of a faculty advisor who felt sorry for her and took her under his wing and friends who allowed her to use their spare bedroom for her writing so that she did not feel so isolated. None of her family attended her graduation, nor did they ever visit her in New York.

Carol had been working as a high school teacher and did not immediately seek a college position after receiving her doctoral degree. She felt sure that she would not compete well with the other candidates. When she finally began to teach part-time at a local university, she loved her contact with the students, received stellar course evaluations, and eventually obtained a full-time position. When Carol joined the faculty, she could not believe that she actually had the job. She immediately began to feel inadequate and frightened that "I had bitten off more than I could chew." When Carol moved into a university-subsidized apartment, she was unable to make it seem like a home. "I couldn't even hang pictures. I don't know why." She also began to feel very much alone and had difficulty reaching out for help for fear that she would be seen as weak. "After everything

I had done to get there, I just fizzled. I felt like I did not belong there except when I was with my students. . . . I knew I was expected to publish and I managed to push out a few articles but it was torture. . . . I always second guess myself and think that I have nothing to say that hasn't already been written about. I lose my focus. I'm different in the classroom."

Meanwhile, Carol had little experience with dating until she came to New York. She felt that she was "physically okay" as far as looks were concerned, but she never felt that a man could be interested in her and was not comfortable showing her interest in them. She engaged in short-lived relationships with men who made her feel special but who were interested mainly in sex rather than in a committed relationship. She often felt lonely but also acknowledged that she was fearful that her need to be with someone would make her vulnerable to domination.

Discussion. From an exploration of her life history and ways of viewing herself, it seems that Carol had not ever received any positive recognition and encouragement of her abilities by her family. She also was made to feel that involving herself in her studies, wishing to moving away, and pursuing a career constituted a betrayal of the family's values and needs. Concurrently, she discovered a more attuned and responsive environment outside her home through her teachers and counselors. She appeared able to thrive when others outside the family encouraged her. Nevertheless it is likely that she lacked a strong sense of her own worth and healthy entitlement to the kind of future she desired but also felt guilty about betraying her family. She learned to keep the undesirable and alien part of herself separate from her family and became dependent on others to help her live her own life and to feel good about herself. She had no emotional money in the bank, so to speak, and thus was highly vulnerable to feelings of inadequacy and guilt when left on her own.

It seems likely that, although Carol was able to move to New York to enter graduate school, she nevertheless did not feel completely entitled to be there and held herself back from truly establishing a satisfying life for herself. In turn, she felt alone in her new life but was also unable to feel good when she returned home, where she was a "stranger." Carol's relationships with men also seemed to reflect a need for someone to make her feel good about herself at the same time that she felt worthless and felt a lack of entitlement to being treated well. Moreover, the seemingly uncaring and competitive environment of New York forced her to rely on her own inner resources without the validation and encouragement of others. This lack of selfobjects, alongside her lack of entitlement and her feelings of guilt, which resulted in self-defeating behavior, undoubtedly contributed to difficulties completing her course work, pursuing a teaching position, and devoting herself to her writing when she did attain an academic appointment. It is noteworthy that Carol was able to mobilize herself when her dissertation advisor and others helped her, but she was "running on empty" in the absence of such supports. In this context, Carol's failure to obtain tenure, something to which she did contribute, nevertheless must have represented an official and just verdict about her lack of ability and her guilt for betraying her family. How could she move forward when she felt so inadequate and undeserving?

6
THE FOCUS AND PROCESS
OF PSYCHOTHERAPY
Part 1

The psychotherapy of patients who are struggling with midlife events that are frustrating their healthy narcissistic needs or triggering underlying narcissistic vulnerability should embody a number of significant foci. These include helping patients to understand what is thwarting their self-needs and inflicting blows to their self-esteem and self-concept, to temper the demands of the grandiose self, and to mourn their losses. Patients need help to overcome feelings of guilt, shame, and fraudulence; to reshape and strengthen their self-concept; and to improve their self-esteem regulation. They need to expand their capacity for empathy and find good selfobjects and outlets for self-expression. Of course, not all these goals may be necessary with a particular patient. Moreover, it is not only what therapists say to patients but also the nature of the therapist–patient relationship itself that facilitates change.

Understanding Self-Needs and
Blows to the Self

When patients are experiencing either acute or chronic distress, it is useful for therapists to help them consider the deeper significance of their reactions. Gaining this understanding will broaden their awareness of what is troubling them or causing them to feel stuck. It also will open up new avenues of exploration that can shed light on their difficulties and identify the work that needs to be done in treatment. Helping patients to acquire new ways of looking at their current concerns should stem from therapists' empathic exploration of patients' reactions and life experiences.

Therapists should begin by conveying that patients' feelings and reactions are understandable. Then therapists should identify the impact of current events on the patients' sense of self and the ways in which they have characteristically maintained their self-esteem and self-concept. The therapist employs explanations or interpretations to help patients understand the links between their past experiences and current feelings and behavior. The focus of interpretation varies greatly, depending on the nature of patients' difficulties, defenses, and background. It is advisable for therapists to be tentative rather than definitive in what they say to patients when they make interpretations of any kind.

In the following excerpt, which was drawn from the treatment of Marge (described in chapter 5), the therapist was listening to Marge's angry account of a recent encounter with her daughter, Jessica, whom Marge believed to be a failure. The therapist attempted to help Marge deepen her understanding of the reasons for her unhappiness.

P: Jess called me to complain about being cold. It's winter. What does she expect? Her shitty apartment hardly has any heat. Forget the landlord! He's a creep. So you think she would go out a buy a small heater! Not my daughter! So I offered to buy it for her. Well, you'd think that I hit her. She said that it was too bad that I couldn't accept her lifestyle but that I shouldn't impose what I wanted on her. That little ingrate! All I was trying to do was make her more comfortable.

T: I can see why that upset you. It's very frustrating when she re-
     jects your help and accuses you of trying to control her. You feel
     very unappreciated and blamed. How did you react?
P: I got angry. I couldn't help it. I told her that she didn't get it.
     She said I screamed at her. I don't think I was screaming. I may
     have raised my voice. I was excited. She thinks I'm screaming if
     I disagree with her. . . . She called her brother and told him I was
     abusive. Can you imagine? Then Adam called me and told me
     to "cool it" with her. He always tries to be the peace keeper even
     if he doesn't know what he is talking about. . . . I just want what
     every mother wants for her daughter. I want her to be able to
     take care of herself and make something of her life.
T: His taking her side must have really upset you.
P: It did. I tried to tell him what had happened, and he just said,
     "Mom, you know who she is. Stop trying to change her." That's
     like telling me to stop loving her.
T: You have tried so hard to give her the things and the opportuni-
     ties that you never had growing up.
P: She's so ungrateful. I never had any of the advantages that she
     has had.
T: No, you didn't. Making sure that Jessica was not deprived and
     had every opportunity to make something of herself has been a
     driving force in your life.
P: Yes, I guess it has been. Where has it gotten me? She's not even
     trying.
T: I know you feel that way, but I'm not sure it's that black and white.
P: I suppose she does try in her way, but I think she indulges herself
     and isn't realistic. She's barely supporting herself. She keeps
     telling me that she wants to do her own thing, but she's not be-
     yond accepting money to help her out.

In the next few months, the therapist continued to listen to Marge's
present woes and also probed her history. Sometimes she tried to help
Marge reflect on the link between her own childhood experiences
and her current reactions.

P: I'm so disappointed in both of my children. I think Adam will
     be all right even though I don't like what he is doing, but Jessica

is another matter. I just can't bear it. I can't seem to fix her. The more I try, the worse it gets. I wish I could stop feeling this way.

P: It's true that they are frustrating you right now. Have you ever thought that your own past experiences are contributing to why you feel so disappointed by and angry at Jessica? It's possible that being a good mother to her and helping her to succeed in life have been crucial to making up for your own painful child-hood and your feeling that you never realized your potential.

P: Isn't it natural for a parent to want her daughter to do well?

T: Of course it is, but your feelings of worth seem totally depend-ent on how well she does. She has the power to make you feel terrible about yourself. Perhaps your reaction to her is not only about who she is but also about what you feel to be your own lack of success. She was your chance for repair.

P: I hear what you are saying but it doesn't change anything. I don't know how to ignore how she is living her life.

T: I don't know if it's a matter of ignoring her life or of our exploring together what has led you to feel that you need her to be a success in order to feel good about yourself as a person and as a mother. Her frustrating you seems to be striking a deep chord in you.

In a session shortly after that one, Marge was depressed and angry about the disruption of her plans for the upcoming Jewish holiday.

P: I feel like killing Pam [Adam's fiancée]. I can't believe that she is not coming to our Passover Seder. "I have other plans," she said when I invited her. "Besides, my family never celebrates the holidays. It's not that important to us. I'll ask Adam if he wants to come by himself." Of course, Adam is not going to come without her, and he won't stand up to her and insist that she come with him.

T: What she said made you feel that what you want is not impor-tant to her, and she's frustrating your wish to have a close family holiday celebration.

P: I can just see what's going to happen in the future. She's not go-ing to do anything to be part of our family. . . . It makes me feel like I don't even want to make a holiday dinner. I don't know why she doesn't want to be with us. You'd think she would do it for Adam if she didn't want to do it for me. She's selfish. Adam doesn't see it. He makes excuses for her. . . . I don't know where I failed. He should know better.

T: It's quite a disappointment for you that Pam and Adam may not come for Passover, but you seem to equate your success as a mother with whether or not they come for the holidays.

P: I cried all day yesterday.

T: What were you feeling?

P: Alone and that I had done something wrong. I must be doing something to make Pam react this way. I have been nice to her and have tried to include her. One of my friends said that maybe my relationship with Adam is a threat to her. I think she's just selfish and thinks only of herself. She's very tied in to her own family and doesn't care about us. But I don't know why Adam doesn't tell her what is important to him. It makes me feel that he doesn't care either. I think he does and that he's just being a wimp. I wish he were stronger.

T: It's very hard for you when your children act in ways that make you feel like you have not succeeded as a mother.

Later in the session, the therapist linked Marge's current sense of aloneness and failure to her past.

T: You have wanted to have a close and loving family all your life, and for a time you believed you were making that happen. Perhaps some of that wish has understandably been related to how alone and disconnected you felt as a child. Maybe you even blamed yourself for feeling so alone. If something seems to disrupt that closeness now, even temporarily, it feels catastrophic and you blame yourself.

P: I feel powerless.

T: I suspect that you felt powerless as a child too and that those feelings are influencing your reactions now.

In the initial work with Richard, who had an intense reaction to the cutting down of the trees on his property (as described in chapter 4), the therapist tried to identify his need for control in order to feel safe.

P: I'm going to have the trees replaced, but I know it's not going to help. I can't explain it. The house is just ruined. I'm just going through the motions. It will never be the same.

T: You still seem very despairing about it all.

P: I am. [Tearfully] I don't know what I am going to do.

T: We've talked about how important a refuge the house has been to you. The tree incident seems to have made you feel that the house is no longer safe.

P: It isn't. Do you think that's crazy?

T: I don't think it's crazy, but I do think it's possible that being in control and having things perfect have been terribly important to you in your life. Your ability to achieve that has been impressive and has helped you survive and made you feel less vulnerable.

In the next session, the therapist continued in the same manner.

P: I don't know what's the matter with me.

T: A number of things have happened recently that have been out of your control. This may be making you feel very vulnerable.

P: I'm not myself. [Tearfully] I burst into tears at a moment's notice. Look at me now.

T: Has it occurred to you that it's not just the cutting down of the trees that is causing you to feel so awful, but that you were no longer in control and instead were at the mercy of life's forces? Other things, too, may be contributing to that feeling—what has been happening at work and with your health?

P: I do feel very vulnerable.

T: Have you wondered why?

P: Nothing seems to be working right. I can't take it.

T: Making things work right has been a motivating force in everything you do, and you have been able to achieve a lot. It's hard to keep everything around you under control. Sometimes life has other plans. And even if you always seem able to make things come out right, you pay a price for that effort.

P: I've been able to make things work. Now I can't.

T: It seems that not being able to do that has undermined your whole sense of yourself. Perhaps we need to think about how to restore your self, not just the trees.

A month after the World Trade Center attack, Richard was distraught as he talked about his experience going to work across the river from the site.

P: I'm not really frightened of another terrorist attack. I figure they will give us a break and strike somewhere else.
T: You're still pretty shook up from the whole thing. Is there something in particular that comes up for you?
P: I can't bear it that the towers are not there. [Becomes tearful] I keep seeing them collapse.
T: When they show their collapse over and over on TV, it's pretty hard to take.
P: Yes. It makes me feel so vulnerable.
T: A lot of people feel that way. What do you think it means to you?
P: I just felt better knowing that they were there, ugly though they were. But they were powerful.
T: Perhaps they signify strength to you. Maybe you fear that if they could collapse, so can you.
P: That sounds right. What do I do?
T: We have to help you feel stronger and more in control again. I think there are some concrete actions you can take that might help in the short run. Then we have to find ways of enabling you to feel not so devastated if things around you don't work right or are not perfect.

In early sessions with Carol (also introduced in chapter 5), when she said that after being denied tenure she had not applied for another academic position because of her fear that she lacked the ability to publish enough to be a successful academic, the therapist attempted to help her think about her writing problems in a new light.

P: Maybe I don't have what it takes to be an academic. I've tried but I haven't succeeded. If it were just about teaching, it would be different. My students love me. Teaching comes easily. When I start writing, I just stare at the page even when I have an idea before I start. I go blank. I feel so stupid when that happens. I can't stand the feeling.

T: It sounds pretty awful for you. Has it ever been different? You have told me that you were able to complete your dissertation and do some articles. What helped you?

P: I couldn't write the dissertation proposal in the beginning. Then my advisor finally helped me. He would meet with me every week, and I would bring him things to read and tell him what I was going to do next. He was very supportive. I felt like such an idiot.

T: It was your ideas and you did the work.

P: I was grateful that he offered to help me but I shouldn't have needed him. I should have been able to do it myself.

T: You seem to feel that was a sign of weakness. Have you considered that he was not helping you with your writing per se but was providing encouragement and validation?

P: I used to feel better after I met with him. Now that I think about it, I used to meet with a few other junior faculty members when I first came to the college and I was able to do some writing then. That was a good experience, but everyone got so busy that we stopped meeting.

In the next session, the therapist and patient again discussed Carol's writing block.

T: Last time we were talking about your experiences when some of the junior faculty used to talk about your ideas for articles and support one another. It's possible that your writing block has more to do with a lack of confidence rather than inability. Given what you have told me about your family's paucity of encouragement of and interest in your studies and their disapproval of your choices, it seems understandable that you would look to others for encouragement. Fortunately, there seemed to be many people in your early life outside the family who provided validation and support. Perhaps when you don't have that positive feedback you fall back on the old feelings you had about yourself in your family.

P: It makes me feel ashamed. I should be able to do these things myself.

In the following session, Carol brought up the fact that she gained a lot of satisfaction from teaching.

P: It's strange. I feel confident when I'm in the classroom. I know that I can do it.

T: Perhaps the presence of your students helps you to feel less alone and you get a lot of positive feedback. Writing requires more alone time, and there's no one there to cheer you on or tell you that you are doing a good job.

P: I can't always have someone to cheer me on at my side.

T: I guess that one task we have is to help you develop an internal cheerleader.

In the initial part of treatment, the therapist identified another underlying issue that might be affecting Carol.

P: Sometimes I think I should pack up and go home to my family. I left to make something of myself and have a different kind of life from them. What do I have here? I've lost my job and my apartment; I have a lousy relationship; I don't know what I'm doing in the future. My family members are having a good time with one another and I'm out in the cold.

T: You feel sad about that.

P: I do but I also blame myself.

T: It sounds as if you feel that you are being punished for wanting more from life and leaving them behind. I wonder if they ever accused you of acting "too big for your britches" or admonished you that "God will punish you."

P: Not in so many words, but they let me know that was how they felt in other ways.

T: It seems possible that, although you pursued your ambitions and moved to New York, a part of you never left home. You may hear your parents' voices internally, and they may cause you to feel that you are not deserving of success, since it means going against their expectations of you.

P: I left home so long ago. Do you think that all that is still affecting me?

T: What are your thoughts about that?

P: Sometimes I do feel like I'm choosing between my career and
     my family. . . .

T: It seems that you equate success in your career with being dis-
     loyal and alone.

P: I do feel like a traitor at times and that I'm being punished some-
     how.

Tempering the Grandiose Self

A major focus of psychotherapy with many midlife patients is to help
them temper the demands of the grandiose self. When people have
unrealistic, grandiose, omnipotent, or perfectionist expectations of
themselves and what they should accomplish in life, it is likely that
they cannot always, if ever, live up to their own demands and be con-
tented with their actual achievements. This state of affairs is made
worse when certain events intrude on their lives that are literally beyond their control or that assault their compensatory structures and
defenses. Believing that they should be able to control life, prevent
death and illness, and be strong and self-sufficient, persons with severe narcissistic vulnerability do not allow for human limitations or
life's vicissitudes. Problems that others might regard as part of the human condition are experienced as assaults or signs of failure.

Patients who have a grandiose self-structure or who employ narcissistic defenses that are failing may not always present as superior,
perfect, or entitled. Instead, they may manifest acute or chronic feelings of inadequacy, failure, badness, or shame. In some instances,
narcissistic rage may result in suicidal attempts or acts of revenge or
violence against others.

Because of their human limitations as well as their pathology,
many patients have played a role in bringing about their failures, destroying opportunities, or hurting others. The recognition that they
are imperfect and may have caused harm to themselves or others may
result in their relentlessly attacking themselves and they are unable
to forgive themselves for their actions or inactions. They often become overtaken by their mistakes and limitations and see themselves
as all "bad." Sometimes life's blows confirm a person's underlying

feelings of deserving bad treatment. The therapeutic goals are to help such patients to accept their human limitations and failings without letting these define their entire sense of themselves and to understand the origins of, and reshape, their deep-seated views of themselves.

To accomplish these tasks, it is important for clinicians first to help patients identify both their conscious and the more covert expectations of themselves and to explore the origins and evolution of these expectations throughout the patients' early lives. Then therapists may begin to question the patients' major assumptions about themselves. Therapists can help these patients to connect to, rediscover, and express different parts of their personality. They come to accept their human limitations and past mistakes and value their actual strengths and achievements. Patients can then come to terms with what is or is not possible for them to achieve in the future.

When therapists begin to identify and question the assumptions that constitute patients' grandiosity and entitlement, it is important to do so without challenging them. Thus, it is important to avoid confronting the grandiose self, particularly early in treatment. The use of confrontation may be experienced as an attack because it draws attention to the patients' contradictory, unrealistic, or extreme reactions and behavior. It may provoke patients to become more defensive or to feel misunderstood.

Instead, therapists might comment on the patients' expectations without seeming to judge them and try to relate empathically to their underlying anxiety, desperation, low self-esteem, fears of abandonment, and hopelessness.

There may be instances when therapists feel it is necessary to confront more vigorously patients' grandiosity and narcissistic rage. There is no hard-and-fast rule that guides when to do this, and it is likely that therapists will differ in their judgments about the timing of such interventions. They usually are employed when therapists find it difficult to tolerate patients' attacking, self-defeating, and destructive behavior. When one is moved to use confrontation at such times, it is important to do so in ways that show an understanding of the patients' intense and seemingly urgent needs and feeling states.

Because the grandiose self-structure is so crucial to the patient's internal life, despite its negative effects, the process of tempering its demands is complex and lengthy. It does not usually begin until the therapeutic relationship is firmly established and therapist and patient may focus on certain themes or dynamics repeatedly.

The following excerpts, drawn, again, from the treatment of Marge, illustrate some aspects of this process.

After several months of treatment, Marge began a session by talking about her long-standing disappointment in herself for not having had a more successful professional life and her envy of other women who had pursued their careers earlier in their lives.

P: I don't hate my work. I'm just bored with it, and I certainly can't talk about what I do with my friends. Who wants to hear about a librarian's day? I can just hear them leave the room if I start talking about the books I've catalogued.
T: You would like to have a more exciting and important job.
P: I envy my friends who have done something with their lives. Sometimes it is difficult to be with them. I feel like such a dolt.
T: That must be hard for you.

In the next few sessions, Marge reflected on her mother's expectations of her.

P: I wanted to make something of myself that I could be proud of and that my mother would be able to brag about to her friends. She hated my getting married right after I graduated from college and never pursuing a career. She died before I went back to school but would never have been very impressed with my becoming a librarian. [Referring to the title of a play] I was my mother's "great white hope."
T: That's a heavy expectation to put on a child. What did she want you to do?
P: She would have liked me to become a doctor or a lawyer. How was I supposed to do that? I don't think she had any idea of what it would take. But I don't think the exact profession mattered so much as my excelling. She used to tell me that I could do anything but she never helped me. Neither of my parents did. They were never interested in anything I actually did. A lot of parents of their generation were like that. They wanted

their children to become successful and famous but were involved in their own survival and didn't understand what children needed.

After this interaction, the therapist commented on Marge's actual accomplishments, which she was unable to appreciate.

T: It took a lot for you to go back to school when your kids were young.
P: I guess it did, but I should have taken more of a risk and tried something other than library school. I always loved to write when I was younger, and I even won a award for a story I wrote. I wanted to be a journalist at one time.
T: What stopped you?
P: I got married. What a mistake—not the children, of course. When I went back to school, I thought I was too old to try to break into journalism. I think I just didn't have the confidence. I was a wimp. I'm still a wimp and I'm lazy. I could try to write but I don't. . . . I'm never going to amount to anything. I think that's one of the reasons I don't try to make new friends. I want to be with successful women, but I envy them too much and feel too inadequate when I am with someone who is really accomplished.
T: You don't seem to place any value on what you have accomplished. You keep measuring yourself against a very high standard.
P: I could have attained more if I had tried. [Using a line spoken by the actor Marlon Brando in the film *On the Waterfront*] "I coulda been a contender."
T: You feel that you never realized your potential and disappointed her. It's sad, but it's also sad that you don't give yourself credit for what you have been able to accomplish on your own.

In another session around the same time, Marge returned to her favorite subject—her complaints about her daughter, Jessica.

P: She's just throwing her life away. I can't stand watching her.
T: I can understand your feeling that way. You wanted more for her and for yourself. Yet Jessica seems to feel that she's getting her life together, and she is less depressed than she was a few months ago.

P: She seems content with so little. She could be so much more. She says she can't stand being with me because she knows I don't accept where she is. She's right.

T: Well, what if she were more successful in your eyes? What do you think that would do for her and for you?

P: I think she and I would both be happier. . . . I'd feel I had at least been a really great mother and not wasted my life.

T: From what you are saying, it sounds as if you feel that your life is a failure if Jessica does not achieve the success that you think you should have been able to attain—that this would make up for what you feel to be your own failure.

P: I wanted her to be different from me.

T: It's hard for you to accept and appreciate the choices that you both have made. You have very high standards for yourself and Jessica.

P: I guess I do feel that way. You think that I am putting too much on her?

T: I think that we need to explore why being a star became so vital to you that it does not allow you to value who you are. It is likely that this has something to do with your feelings about Jessica.

After we discussed Marge's background a few months later in treatment, the following dialogue occurred.

P: I had a bad dream about my mother last night. I've been out of sorts since I got up this morning. Mom was in the bedroom of the apartment I grew up in. When I came in from school, I wanted to show her something, but she was sleeping even though it was in the afternoon. I yelled at her to wake up, but she kept sleeping so I went out to play. Later she was making dinner, and, when I came into the kitchen, she screamed at me for spending time with my friends. I think she said something like, "You'll never make anything of yourself." I started crying and said that I'd show her she was wrong about me but she wouldn't listen.

T: That's an awful dream.

P: It looked and sounded just like her.

T: In the dream, it seemed that you could not get her positive at-
     tention but she was quick to let you know if she thought you
     were doing something wrong.
P: She was very critical of me sometimes. I never seemed able to
     please her. I had to look perfect and act perfect. She would
     get upset if got an A-minus instead of an A in a course at
     school or got a smudge on a dress. She would always tell me to
     lower my voice and stop fidgeting. [Laughing] Can you believe
     that she used to have me march up and down the stairs of our
     apartment house with a book on my head so that I would have
     good posture?
T: That was a lot of pressure on you.

In the same session, Marge became more reflective about what she
felt as a child.

P: I felt frightened a lot.
T: Perhaps you felt scared that you would make a mistake and that
     your mother would know it.
P: Well, she did seem to know everything I did. That's what she
     was like.
T: You mean you felt her presence even if she was not physically
     there.
P: That's a good way of putting it. She also was frightened about
     everything. She wouldn't even let us have roller skates. The
     idea made her too nervous.
T: So, on one hand, you grew up feeling that you really had to be a
     star to get her attention and love, and, on the other, you were
     never encouraged to take any risks or helped to be out in the
     world.
P: I used to want her to do more. I didn't like that she stayed home
     all the time.
T: Have you ever thought that her expectations of you were too
     great and caused too much pressure?
P: I don't know if I ever thought that. I do know that when I was
     an adolescent I thought I had to get out of the house, get away
     from her.

T: You don't seem to have much compassion for the child you
      were. You seem to feel that she should have grown up without
      any help.

Six months later, after going over the same type of material on many
occasions, Marge spoke about a recent day she had spent with Jessica.

P: We had a reasonably good time together—for us. I called her to
      ask her if she wanted to go shopping and have lunch with me.
      To my surprise, she agreed. She looked terrible but I bit my
      tongue and didn't say anything. We chattered away. I realized
      that she really wants my approval, the poor kid. I was very upset
      when I came home.
T: What were you feeling?
P: [Tearfully] I've been very destructive to her. I didn't mean to be
      but I have been.
T: What do you think you have done that is so destructive?
P: I was way too controlling of her when she was younger. I was im-
      patient and maybe I've not recognized her neediness and sensi-
      tivity to pressure. I thought she was so talented, but I didn't see
      all of her. No wonder she fights me. I've made it hard for her to
      be herself. I don't know if she will ever forgive me or be able to
      be comfortable with me. I didn't mean to hurt her. I wanted
      what I thought was best for her.
T: That's a heavy realization.
P: I've been very destructive. I can see it now. I guess I've done the
      same thing to her that my mother did to me. The weird thing is
      that I don't know if I can change.

In fact, despite her efforts to do so, Marge did not change her behavior toward Jessica right away. She went through a period of castigat-
ing herself for both her past and ongoing destructive impact on
Jessica. On one occasion, after Marge had a very angry interaction
with Jessica, the therapist uncharacteristically confronted Marge
when she threatened to send an attacking letter to her daughter.

P: [Looking devastated] I have been a mess all week. My daughter
      had the nerve to curse at me on the phone and hang up on me. I

don't know how she could have said what she did. I'm ashamed
to even tell you what she said. [Pause] She called me an abusive
bitch! I can't let that pass. I've written her a letter. I haven't
sent it yet but I'm going to. I brought it in to show you. I think
I'll read it out loud. . . .

T: That's quite a letter. You really are letting her have it. You must
feel really injured.

P: She can't talk to me that way! Who does she think she is? I'm
not dirt under her feet.

T: Your letter certainly expresses how you feel. It's quite devastating.

P: I want her to feel the pain she causes me. I want her to apologize.

T: Don't you think the letter my have the opposite effect?

P: I don't care. I have to tell her what's on my mind.

T: I have to share with you that I am worried about your sending the
letter to Jessica. It's true that what she said was hurtful and she
shouldn't have said it, but your reaction may make the situation
worse. You have been trying to deal with your feeling that you
have been destructive to her in the past, and now you are planning to engage in the same behavior that you feel guilty about.

P: What do you want me do? Do yo think I should just grin and
bear it?

T: I guess it feels as though that's what I'm saying. Is it possible for
you to call her and arrange to meet and talk over what happened
on the phone? That might be less hurtful to both of you.

P: I don't know if I can do that without tearing in to her.

T: You can control yourself. You have to if you want to have a
better relationship with her. Let's talk about how you can do
that.

The following excerpts, taken from the Richard's treatment, occurred not long after he regained his equilibrium. They show the
therapist's efforts to help Richard get in touch with and modify the
excessive and unrealistic demands he placed himself. Prior to under-
taking this process, Richard had sought the help of a dietician to ad-
vise him on ways to lower his blood pressure and cholesterol. He had
discovered a new relaxing and uplifting water route to work that enabled him to avoid the anxiety-inducing experience of being on a
train in a tunnel under the Hudson River.

He put his house on the market and was looking for a better one in a more upscale area. This quest was fraught with peril as Richard became obsessed with finding the perfect house in a location that would protect his financial investment, ensure him total privacy and security, and serve as a proper symbol of his success. Initially, this search seemed reasonable enough. It soon became apparent, though, that Richard's needs for total control and his perfectionism were working overtime. Every house he looked at had major flaws. When he decided to have a house custom-built, he found that each parcel of land on which he might locate the house was deficient. On one occasion, he spent the entire day and evening sitting on a folding chair on a land parcel he was considering for purchase; he wanted to make sure that there were no intrusive noises that would bother him. He did not fully trust any builder with whom he consulted to do the kind of job he wanted.

P: I'm very discouraged. I just don't think I'm going to be able to find what I want.

T: That prospect seems to be upsetting you quite a lot.

P: I have to find what I want! I don't want to make a mistake again.

T: If you are referring to the tree incident at your house, I'm not sure why you feel it was the result of your error. How could you have prevented that?

P: I shouldn't have bought a house that was so close to someone else's property. I won't make that mistake again.

T: You seem to feel that you should be able to anticipate every conceivable eventuality.

P: Well, why not? That's what I do at work when I plan an event or project. I'm supposed to be on top of everything.

T: Apparently you have been terrific at doing that, although you often have worked yourself to the point of exhaustion. Don't you think that life is more complicated? How can you be expected to control everything? You couldn't have prevented the World Trade Center attack.

P: I suppose I couldn't.

T: You sound as if you have thought about whether you should have been able to.

P: [Laughs] You think I'm getting carried away with my house hunting. Roger [Richard's partner] thinks I'm crazy. He's washed his hands of the whole thing and says he will be happy with whatever I decide.

T: What do you think about that?

P: He's just mouthing off. He likes to look too. He won't be able to help himself. I don't know if there's anything out there that's good enough. I don't want to compromise.

T: I know you won't like my saying this, but we have talked a bit about the likelihood that the house represents much more to you emotionally than a wonderful place to live and a great investment.

P: What do you have in mind?

T: It's possible that your need to have a house that is perfect in all respects may be a way of making you feel safe and in control of a life that is unpredictable and frightening and in which you feel powerless and worthless. You can't accept the idea that there are things you can't control. You really believe that you should be able to attain perfection and don't seem to question why you have set such a high standard or consider that it is an impossible one to achieve all the time.

P: It's not like me to think any other way.

T: Do you ever wonder about why that is so?

P: It's just who I am.

T: You experienced some very upsetting events when you were younger that may have influenced the way you felt you had to be in order to survive. You often seem reluctant to talk about your past, but it could be having a greater effect on you than you think.

In subsequent sessions, Richard talked about his background in more detail and with more feeling than previously. Although he had discussed his mother's need for him to be perfect and to set a standard of behavior for his brothers to emulate, he never spoke in depth about how he felt about his sexual interests or about the period when his father lost his money and died when Richard was an adolescent. These sessions revealed his profound sense of shame at being different from his peers and his efforts to hide who he was both to himself and to others. This state of affairs undoubtedly was partly responsible for his feeling that he had to be perfect in the eyes of the world, so much so that Richard did not come out as a gay man until he was 29 years old. He had never experimented much sexually with other men or participated actively in certain elements of the gay male bar scene.

Although he described having felt the loss of his father, when Richard was 15, the more traumatic impact of his father's death was on his mother and on the family finances and lifestyle. Richard's mother became more helpless and turned to him for companionship and to take charge of the family. With some emotion, he recalled having to move from their traditional house on a prominent corner lot in a good neighborhood into a smaller rental house in a nearby, less affluent community. Richard was able to continue at the same high school but had to go to work after class. He felt ashamed, was too busy, and lacked the money to keep up with his friends.

P: I thought my world had collapsed.
T: Like the World Trade Center?
P: In a way, the feeling was the same. I never thought about that.
T: Perhaps your father's death and the loss of your house and place with your friends made you feel that the world was out of control and unsafe and that the only one you could count on was yourself. Maybe your need for control has been a way of protecting yourself from ever being devastated again.
P: I felt that my mother expected me to take over and make everything all right for her. I thought that was my job as the oldest.

In the next session, Richard surprised the therapist by beginning with a reflective comment.

P: I was thinking about what we talked about last time. It's hard for me to recall the events after my father's death, but I do remember the day that we had to move out of our house. My mother cried. It shook me up because she had seemed so strong until my father died. I don't remember her crying at his funeral. Later I realized that she was furious at him for leaving her without enough money to keep up the house.

T: Do you remember being angry too?

P: I don't think I felt angry as much as I felt lost. I knew I had to act strong.

Later in the same session, the therapist explored the link between the loss of his childhood home to Richard's quest for a new house.

T: Do you think there's a connection between what we've been talking about and your feelings about the damage to your current house and your quest to find an even better replacement?

P: I can see that there may be something going on, but I'm not sure exactly what it is.

T: I'm not sure either, but it does strike me that, in both instances, you felt quite devastated. When your father died, you lost a lot that you never were able to get back. Perhaps your reaction to the tree damage to your current house somehow stirred up your earlier losses. If that were true, maybe it puts your quest for a perfect house in a new light. It's possible that you are trying to find a house that not only will be safe from all intrusions but will restore the feelings of security and status that you and your family lost when your father died.

P: You think that's why I am having trouble finding what I want?

T: That's a thought.

It is noteworthy that, within weeks of these sessions, Richard found a run-down house on a large parcel of land in an affluent community that closely resembled the style of his childhood home, and he and his partner decided to purchase and restore it. After moving in, Richard developed a friendship with his male landscaper, Peter, whom he looked to not only for help in making the grounds look beautiful but also for companionship when Roger was working. Richard looked forward to talking to Peter, and they often had dinner together along with Peter's wife. Months after this friendship began, Richard came to a session upset and angry. On learning about what happened, the therapist responded in an unusual manner by confronting what seemed to be Richard's out-of-control narcissistic rage.

P: This has been quite a week. I'm still not over it. I'm beside myself.

T: What happened?

P: [Speaking excitedly and angrily] You know that I bought some expensive shrubs for the front of the property with Peter's help, and he was supposed to see that they were planted properly. Guess what? When I got to the house on Friday, the trees were dying. They looked dreadful. They're ruined. They'll never look the same even if they come back. They're right in front of the house for everyone to see. I can't believe it! I called Peter and screamed at him to get over to the house right away. He showed up on Saturday morning and just stared at the shrubs. He said he should have made sure that they were getting enough water. He thought that the nursery had put enough hoses in the sprinkler system, but he didn't check. I can't believe his incompetence! I told him that I had trusted him and that I couldn't understand how he could have let me down. He looked sheepish and apologized and suggested I call the nursery where I bought the trees. I could have thought of that. I was so mad. I still can't get over it. I don't think I can continue being friends with him.

T: Richard, I know how important it is for you to have a perfect house and that you were counting on Peter to help you, but you have to get a grip. Peter is your friend, not just your employee. Yelling at him like that is really over the top! The shrubs' not being perfect is not a life-or-death issue.

P: I don't know how he could have been so careless.

T: Obviously he made a mistake. People do. It doesn't mean he is a terrible person. We've talked so much about what underlies your need for perfection and control and here you go again.

P: [Calmer] You're right. I just looked at the shrubs and I lost it.

T: I guess it was a déjà vu.

P: I'm going to call Peter and tell him I'm sorry. But I do think he should try to make good for what happened.

T: Given what you have said about him, he probably will. We need to talk more about what your counting on him has meant to you.

In contrast to Marge and Richard, Carol did not present with anger and control issues. Instead, her problems seemed related to a lack of confidence in her abilities, coupled with guilt over her ambitions and fears of being alone. As treatment proceeded, however, it became apparent that Carol also had developed s strong wish for others to meet her needs without her having to say what they were. She had a need for help, on one hand, and unrealistically high and perfectionist expectations of herself, on the other. Her feelings of entitlement and need for perfectionism may have protected her from the feelings of deprivation, unworthiness, and inadequacy that arose early in life.

A few months into the treatment, Carol was discussing her difficulties mobilizing herself. Her words expressed a theme that she had repeated many times previously.

P: I wasn't able to do any research on prospective academic positions or get my CV together. I'm not doing anything to help myself. I just can't seem to do anything.

T: You seem very frustrated.

P: I don't know what I'm waiting for. I know no one is going to do this for me.

T: You have used those words before. It would be understandable if you wished that someone could do it for you. Perhaps you are waiting for someone to help you.

P: Well, it's not going to happen. I know that.

T: That doesn't mean you don't want it to happen. You look as though you are thinking about something. What's coming up for you?

P: I was remembering something from my childhood. I was sitting at the kitchen table when I was a kid. We had pork chops for supper. There were seven of us, and we each got one pork chop. I was a slow eater. I guess I used to day dream. Anyhow, someone took my pork chop when I wasn't paying attention.

T: What did you do?

P: Nothing. I never fought for myself. I just figured that if they were going to be that way and not let me eat, then I didn't care. They should have known I was hungry too. I shouldn't have had to say anything. Why should I fight for what I should have had in the first place?

T: What did your parents do? They didn't let you go without dinner, did they?

P: No. I'm sure my mother must have fixed me a peanut butter and jelly sandwich or something like that. I always ate something.

T: It sounds as if that kind of thing happened more than once. Did you learn to eat faster?

P: I didn't want to change who I was for them.

T: Why do you think your parents let it happen?

P: I think they wanted peace at all costs. They couldn't control my siblings.

T: What do you think made you think about this incident?

P: I guess I've always waited. Even with friends, I think that if they know me and care about me, they should know what I want. One of my friends keeps telling me that she can't read my mind. I don't know what's so difficult about thinking about what people need if you're close to them.

T: It sounds as though you are disappointed a lot. What happens if someone doesn't come through? Do you talk about it?

P: Not usually. I hold it in. I probably create distance.

T: So you remembered the pork chop incident when we were talking about whether you were waiting for someone to help you in your job search.

P: I don't see why the college doesn't keep a list of available faculty positions at other schools. It just feels like a lot of work. Maybe I do expect someone to help me. I feel upset that I'm in this position. I shouldn't have to be looking for a job at my age.

A few sessions later, Carol talked about her previous academic position.

P: I sort of knew what was expected of me, but I didn't want to believe it. I thought that my being a strong teacher should have counted for more. I gave a lot to my students, and I was good at what I did. The powers that be didn't seem to care about that.

T: I guess you thought that the decision about tenure would go in your favor?

P: I hoped it would. I hoped that they would see that I was making a contribution.

T: Did you think of appealing the decision?

P: No. I wouldn't do that. They didn't want me, and I didn't have enough of a publication record to make a good case. That's what counts. I do resent their not helping me with my writing.

T: Was it possible to have a mentor?

P: I shouldn't have had to ask. They knew I was inexperienced. I guess I was lucky in the past that my teachers knew that I needed their encouragement and support. I didn't have to ask.

P: You know, what we're talking about seems connected to the pork chop incident. You didn't want to fight for or protect yourself, and you felt that you wanted your family to be sensitive to you, which they should have been. It seems that you felt the same way in your job. I'm wondering if your feeling that people should know what you need and come to your assistance without your having to ask for help has something to do with how neglected you felt as a child. It does seem that your needs and wants did not get a high priority in your family. Perhaps it has become especially important for you that people show you that they care and that they provide what you need.

P: Are you saying that I want others to make up for what I didn't get?

T: Yes. It must have been hard for you to feel so alone.

P: I think my parents tried, but they were so busy and preoccupied trying to make ends meet. I don't think they thought about kids having emotional needs. It wasn't who they were. That's still true today. My brothers still treat me as if I am their baby sister. They don't recognize anything that I have done. They tease me. They have no concept of what my life is like, and they act as though they know everything and I know nothing. But they're home and I'm not. So mom and dad defend them and I'm the outsider.

In this same period, Carol also brought up her feelings of futility about ever having a successful career, and her unrealistic expectations of herself became evident.

P: I just don't think that I'm good enough to get what I want. I'm just fooling myself.

T: Did something happen to make you feel so bad?

P: I was looking at something I wrote that I submitted for publication some time ago. The editor wanted me to make some revisions and I put it aside. It felt too overwhelming at the time. I thought it might be good if I finished it and sent it in to the journal. I don't know if they still want it, but it would be good for me to have another publication. But when I started to work on it, I felt stupid. I just couldn't do it.

T: Can you say a little more about what it was like for you?

P: I reread the editor's critique and thought I knew what she wanted, but the words wouldn't come. I got frustrated and shut down the computer.

T: How long were you working at it?

P: About 15 minutes.

T: Do you think that you should have been able to start writing in so short a time and after you had been away from the subject for over a year?

P: Yes. If the ideas are there, it shouldn't be hard to write them down.

T: [Having written extensively] It's not that simple. Sometimes it takes a while and some false starts before one knows that one is on the right track. It's a process. There are times I'm not happy with anything I write.

P: I wouldn't have thought that of you. You seem so confident. I imagine that when you write it comes easily.

T: Have you always had the expectation that the writing should come easily?

P: Well, shouldn't it if I'm really as able as I think I am? If one is a writer, then one writes. Even when I get something down on paper, it needs a lot of editing.

T: You seem to feel that there is something wrong about that. Most writing needs editing. It's not unusual to do several drafts of an article before it is ready for submission.

P: [Looks surprised] I always think that having to do another draft means that I'm not really good at what I do. When I have difficulty, I begin to question myself.

T: You seem to be judging yourself by a very high standard that few people can reach.

P: Other people have told me that and I felt better when they did, but I also thought they were just feeling sorry for me and being kind.

T: I wonder how you got this idea that your written words have to come out quickly and perfectly.

P: I've always thought that either you have talent or you don't.

T: Do you mean that if your writing doesn't come naturally and you have to work at it, then you don't have talent?

P: Something like that.

T: I wonder where you got that idea?
P: I don't know. I don't think I got it from my family. My mother
     did have her standards. When I did chores around the house, I
     remember hearing her say, "If you can't do it right, you should-
     n't do it at all." She never thought I did anything right.
T: It would be understandable if you have carried her words with
     you and measure yourself against them.

Facilitating Mourning

Modifying major self-structures, such as the grandiose self, usually
involves helping patients to face and mourn many different types of
losses. These can include failed expectations—the childhood that
never was and the future that never will be; the road not taken, the
life not led; relationships that never were or that have been lost
(Pollock, 1987). For some patients, it also may involve dealing with
the loss of the means by which they have compensated for weakness
in the self. Often, it is the failure to accept their losses that blocks forward movement.

   When they enter psychotherapy, some people are acutely aware
of, but have not come to terms with, lost opportunities and the constraints of time. Others may engage in frantic efforts to maintain
their concept of themselves or to avoid recognizing or dealing with
unpleasant realities. Enabling them to modify and let go of the mainstays of their self-concept or obstructive means of regulating their
self-esteem and face their past, present, and future more realistically
may be painful and take a long time. It occurs only when the patient
has developed a deeper relationship with the therapist and is more
emotionally involved in the treatment. When the patient is actively grieving, the therapist must balance the need to remain attuned to the patient's feelings of sadness, anger, despair, or fear
while believing in the patient's ability to reach a better place.

   Midway through Marge's treatment, she began to deal with what
it would mean to her if she were unable to repair her own sense of failure with Jessica and have the close family that she craved all her life.
This phase seemed to be ushered in by an argument between Marge
and Jessica that resulted in a month's silence between them.

P: I'm not going to call her. I don't want to speak to her until she apologizes to me. Call it pride but I just don't care any more.

T: It seems that you care a lot.

P: She had some nerve telling me that I was interested in her only because I wanted her to make up for my own lack of achievement. How dare she say that to me! I know that I give her a hard time, but I really love her. I thought she knew that. It makes me feel terrible to think that she believes what she said.

T: I can see that your not talking is causing you pain. What do you hope will happen if you don't speak to her?

P: I imagine that she will call and tell me that she loves me and that she's sorry she said what she did.

T: Understandably that would make you feel better, but would it make a difference in how you react to her doing things that aggravate you? You still seem to have trouble accepting who she is.

P: I know. She'll never call me to apologize anyway. She's too stubborn, like me.

T: We have spoken quite a bit about your feelings of failure and your wish that Jessica would become a successful career woman. Do you think that what she said to you stung so much because deep down you felt there was some truth in it—not the part about your not loving her, but about your wanting her to make up for what you were unable to do? Giving up on her is like giving up your own dream for yourself.

P: It's too late for me. I don't want to think that it's too late for her.

T: Why is it too late for you?

P: I just think it is. My family has meant everything to me.

T: What if Jessica is not able to fulfill your dream?

P: I don't think she is going to get there. It's hard to face.

T: Perhaps facing that forces you to give up the feeling that you can repair your own life.

P: I feel that I botched my chances. I was too frightened. No one else saw my fear. They thought I could do anything I wanted.

T: But there was a lot you never had. You had a very sad childhood.

P: [Becoming tearful] I feel I wasted my life. I wasn't true to myself.

T: No one helped you. It's impressive how far you have come.

P: You have said that before but I don't see that. Sometimes I do but it doesn't stick.

T: I guess you keep hearing your mother's voice and listening to her expectations of you.

In the next few sessions, Marge spoke about the life she would have liked to have had.

P: I used to imagine that when I walked into a room, people would talk about my accomplishments. I even thought that one of my books would be made into a movie and I would make a lot of money. It's stupid, isn't it?

T: I don't think it's stupid at all. Most of us want to be recognized and appreciated. Your mother said you could be anything you wanted, but, from everything you have told me, it seems clear that she was not able to help you to you feel good about yourself.

Later in the same session, Marge spoke about her childhood.

P: It's painful when I remember what it was like to be in the apartment where I grew up. I felt very alone. Everything seemed so lifeless. We never went anywhere, and I was ashamed to invite any of my friends there. I had to get away. My friends' parents used to feel sorry for me and let me stay for dinner.

T: They adopted you in a way. You seemed to feel less alone when your kids were growing up.

P: Not in the beginning but later, particularly when they brought their friends home and we used to go on outings as a family. I always imagined that they would get married, live nearby, and bring their children to the house on weekends and holidays. . . . I thought that would happen for sure if I raised them differently than the ways in which I was brought up. I tried, but look at what has happened. Jessica will be lucky if she ever finds a man to marry her, and God knows if Adam's wife will ever let him be close to us. I get sick thinking about it.

T: It'd be quite a loss for you if it turns out the way you imagine.

Marge continued on this subject for a while. She spoke bitterly about her feeling that others were luckier than she was and about her fantasies of having her children and grandchildren around her as she got older.

P: I know I'm just feeling sorry for myself.

T: Is that so bad? It's hard to give up what feels so important. There's no way of ensuring that kids will turn out the way you want even if one is a super parent.

P: [Sighs] I just thought things would be different. Do you really think that it is true that great parents aren't rewarded? It galls me when I see a few friends of mine who have been lousy parents have their grown kids around them.

T: It doesn't seem fair.

P: You better believe it!

In the next session, Marge was a little more upbeat after having heard from Jessica and Adam.

P: You won't believe it. Jessica actually called me. She didn't actually apologize, but she said that she missed me. Then, a few hours later, Adam called and invited me to lunch. He said he wanted my input about the wedding.

T: How did that make you feel?

P: I'm a bit better. At least I'm out of the funk I've been in. I guess they both care about me in their own ways. You're right that I tend to see things as black or white. If they're not giving me what I want, I think that they don't love me. Still, I don't think it's going to turn out the way I want. I suppose I should get over it already, but I worry about both of them and I can't seem to look forward to anything. This should be a happy time but I keep feeling so sad.

T: It's possible that what's happening now has put you in touch with a lifelong sadness that you have been able to push away a lot of the time.

During the course of Richard's treatment, he became more aware of the constant pressure that he felt to do everything perfectly and showed a greater ability to reflect on the origins of this need. Thus he was able to experience heretofore buried emotions connected with his relationship with his father and his own sexual identity.

P: I realize that I'm anxious all the time. When I'm in a meeting I worry about people's reactions to what I'm saying. I obsess about decisions I have to make. I think about all I have to do and what could go wrong.

T: It's exhausting to have to be perfect all the time.

P: I always feel pressure. I think I've felt it forever. No wonder I have high blood pressure. I don't know how to stop. If I can't do something perfectly, I don't want to do it at all. [Gives examples]

T: How long have you been this way?

P: I can't remember being any other way.

T: It sounds as though someone has been standing over you and evaluating your performance.

P: My mother was a perfectionist. We have talked a lot about my need to please her and my fear that disappointing her would cause me to lose her love. . . .

In another session around the same time, the therapist explored Richard's relationship with his father.

T: We haven't talked much about your father. Your relationship with him seems a little fuzzy.

P: I've told you about his business problems. He was always frustrated in his work life. He couldn't stay in a job and made many lateral moves before he retired early. He held a lot in but then would explode. He could be pretty frightening. [Goes on to describe father's volatility]

T: What's the worst thing he ever did?

P: [Smiling] Once he threw me against the wall. I wasn't really hurt, but I think his loss of control frightened me.

T: You know you are smiling.

P: I guess I am. I don't know why. It was pretty awful.

T: It would be understandable if you tried your best to make him feel better and to keep him from losing his cool.

P: [Voice cracking] I did try to please him and make him happy. He was a sad man. . . . What's this? I'm feeling a lot of emotion. I didn't know I felt this way. [Crying] I wanted to make him proud of me. [Trying to regain control] This is weird. It's so intense. I didn't do a very good job.

T: Why do you say that?

P: I wasn't the kind of son he wanted. He was a Navy man and a hunter. He wanted a son who was a guy's guy. I liked to read and never was very good at sports. I tried to do what I thought would make him happy. I was in the Honor Society; I became a Boy Scout; I even dated girls. I never told him I was gay. I never really accepted it myself, but I knew it deep down and I wonder if he knew too. We never talked about it. He died without knowing who I was.

T: That's sad for you.

In the next several sessions, Richard spoke more of his feelings about not having a close relationship with his father.

P: I've been trying to remember my relationship with him. He wasn't there most of the time, and when he was he was impatient and not very expressive of his feelings. I couldn't reach him.

T: That must have made you feel bad.

P: I thought it was my fault.

T: Did you admire him?

P: Maybe when I was little, but he was into himself and not much of a father. I think I used to try to get his attention. As I got a little older, I remember thinking that he was eccentric. My mother used to argue with him a lot. He would always buy stupid things that we didn't need. He used to buy ten of everything. [Somewhat humorously] We had enough junk in the attic for a sale a week. Mom couldn't stand it, but there was no stopping him when he wanted to buy something. Sometimes it was funny, but mostly it was pathetic.

T: He disappointed you as a father. It was not just that you may have disappointed him.

P: Sometimes I wish he could have been different. I would have liked to have had a real father. I think he loved us but he was selfish and preoccupied with his own anxieties. It's like he didn't care enough to eat properly and take care of himself or see to it that we had enough money. I don't think he did it deliberately.

He couldn't have known he would have a heart attack and die, but you think he would have provided for us. I don't know what all this has to do with what I'm feeling today. That was so long ago.

T: Perhaps you are still trying to make him proud of you.

P: It's strange. Sometimes, lately, I feel his presence in our house.

T: Is it a good presence or a bad one?

P: It's good I think. [Becoming tearful] Maybe I think that he would approve and be happy that I was able to have a grand house once again.

The need to deal with her many losses also was a part of Carol's treatment.

P: I've wasted so much time. I'll never get it back. I'm 45 years old. It's too late to have the career that I wanted, and too late to start my own family. I've missed a lot by being so far away from my parents and siblings. I don't think I could go back home, but, even if I did, I don't think the closeness would be there. Mom and Dad are getting on in years, and my brothers and sister have their own lives that I haven't been a part of. . . . I wish I could have made them proud of me, but I really don't know what would make them happy or change their idea that I've rejected them. . . . I don't have any faith in my ability to find a good relationship. I seem to have radar for men who can't commit, and I'm never happy with the ones who are available and seem to like me. I always find something wrong with them. I don't know if there's anything that I can look forward to except having cats to keep me company in my old age.

T: This is very sad for you. You have a lot of losses to grieve. When a person is doing that grieving, it is hard to see beyond it. That's part of the process. But it does eventually help you move forward.

P: I don't know if that will happen to me.

T: I know you feel that way now but it can happen.

P: I feel very old.

T: Perhaps you feel worn down by all the efforts you have made to so far and don't feel that you have the energy to keep going.

P: I feel so alone.

T: I think you may have felt that for a long time. What do you re-
     member about that from your childhood?

P: It's hard to let myself go back there. There were a lot of people
     around, but I felt so different from them. I loved my parents, but
     I wanted more from life. I think they sensed my not wanting to
     be like them from the time I was a little girl. I never wanted to
     help around the farm or do the things that girls were supposed to
     do. . . . I wish I could have been what they wanted. It would have
     been a lot easier.

T: You often blame yourself. It doesn't occur to you that they let
     you down. You seem to need to protect them from your anger.

P: I don't think they could help who they were, but they did hurt
     me. When I think about how much I've missed by not being
     there all these years, I know deep down that I have a fantasy of
     what it would have been like for me. I don't think I could have
     ever felt like a person in that household. Maybe I've lost the il-
     lusion that I could have had a closer relationship with them.

T: That seems right, but giving up illusions are painful too.

P: I feel bad that I don't have parents who are in my corner and
     who want what's good for me.

T: It makes it hard for you to feel truly entitled to succeed.

Overcoming Feelings of Guilt, Shame, and Fraudulence

Many patients with grandiose self-structures have an exaggerated
sense of responsibility. When they do not live up to their expectations of themselves, they may become guilty and self-punishing in
ways that do not seem to be warranted by the objective situation. For
example, the 39-year-old Italian American woman entered psychotherapy after the death of her younger sister from cancer. Not only
did the loss of her sister deprive her of a close companion who was the
only person who shared her history and "held her memories," but it
led her to berate herself for not preventing her sister's death on the
patient's "watch" (see chapter 3).

Likewise, feelings of shame and humiliation may arise when people feel that they have displayed traits, engaged in activities, or experienced defeats that are not consonant with their idealized or highly valued view of themselves. These reactions may be particularly intense when the outside world becomes aware of a person's seeming shortcomings or when a person's reputation is damaged, rightly or wrongly. For example, it has been suggested that the suicide of Vince Foster, a friend and attorney to Bill and Hillary Clinton and a man who prided himself on his integrity, resulted from his depressive reaction and feelings of humiliation following the appearance of what he felt to be unfounded disparaging and accusatory newspaper stories that he felt were destroying his reputation.

Another common manifestation of underlying narcissistic vulnerability is a feeling of fraudulence. Sometimes this occurs in persons who adopt a certain persona for the outside world that they believe is necessary to gain approval and recognition. They become accustomed to performing in accordance with their own, and what they think are others' expectations of them. Often the feeling of fraudulence is accompanied by a sense of emptiness or inadequacy that reinforces their need to perform. For example, after a year of treatment, the 42-year-old man who was so unable to commit himself to marrying any of the many seemingly "great" women he had dated over the years (see chapter 3) confided that he often felt he had mastered the skill of being the "perfect" boyfriend—but did not know who he really was in a relationship. "I go through the right motions, but I lose myself. Sometimes I don't even know if there is anything in me beyond my routine."

Underlying feelings of fraudulence and inadequacy also may play a role in a person's experience of an unexpectedly negative reaction to a positive event, such as getting an important promotion, earning an advanced educational degree, or purchasing a new house. Instead of producing feelings of pleasure and satisfaction, these achievements precipitate feelings of worthlessness or of not being deserving.

When guilt and a need for self-punishment or feelings of shame and fraudulence are evoked by life events, therapists will need to help patients to recognize what they are experiencing and to explore the origins of their deep-seated attitudes about themselves. Over time, therapists will need to help them to accept their human failings, reshape their views of themselves, make contact with their true selves, and value themselves differently.

In the case of Marge, her feelings of guilt and shame became more evident as the treatment continued.

P: It's quite ironic. I've always prided myself on being a good mother. I was the first to know what my friends were doing wrong with their children. Now they're enjoying their kids and I'm not.

T: It doesn't seem fair.

P: No, it doesn't. But I really have only myself to blame. I was worse with Jessica than with Adam. I wasn't ready to be a mother. I was anxious all the time about everything. I couldn't stand it if she cried or if anything was out of place or if she spilled anything when she was eating. I wanted her to look and act a certain way. I pressured her. I don't think I thought about what she was feeling. It was all about me. I didn't mean to hurt her, but I see that I did. I feel so guilty. What goes around comes around.

T: How do you mean that?

P: Maybe I'm getting what I deserve.

T: You seem to feel that your mistakes mean that you never did anything right and that Jessica is severely damaged rather than just a young woman with certain problems like all of us. If you were not able to be perfect, then you feel that you were a monster, and if she is not perfect, then you feel she's irretrievably deficient.

P: I'm ashamed of myself. I should have known better. I knew what it was like to have a mother like me. I had no excuse.

T: It's hard to totally overcome our upbringing even when we try. You were different from your mother in many ways. You gave a lot to your kids, and it's clear that you are important to both of them.

P: I loved them both. I just wish now that I had more of myself then. Maybe I wouldn't have needed to push Jess so hard.

In another session at about the same time, Marge again spoke about what she felt to be her own lack of success.

P: It's not only that I haven't had the career and success that I wanted. It's that I betrayed myself. I didn't live up to my own abilities. I think it's a sin to not develop yourself. It's different if someone isn't smart or has no talent, but I did have the ability. That's what kills me about Jessica.

T: So you have a sense of guilt toward yourself and it's hard to forgive yourself.

P: How can I forgive myself? I guess that is why I keep trying to fix Jess.

T: That's an important insight. You know you didn't purposely give up your career.

P: I did in a way. I decided to get married, and I never persisted in trying to write. Later I was too insecure to try. I stopped myself.

T: You have this idea that you should have been able to do anything without any help or encouragement. You take all the responsibility and don't acknowledge what you were up against.

P: What's my excuse now? I need to get more of a life. I don't know if there's time or if I can change.

T: It's not too late.

After a year of Richard's treatment, the therapist began to realize that, alongside his perfectionism and need for control, he often had a sense of not being genuine and real.

P: We went to the movies and saw *The Stepford Wives* yesterday. Have you seen it?

T: Yes I have. What did you think about it?

P: It was a little too campy but I enjoyed it. You may think this is strange, but I began thinking about my childhood and adolescence. I think I was a Stepford son. I did everything that I thought I was supposed to do. It didn't matter what I really felt or wanted. How I acted was how I thought I should be, and I did it well.

T: But, like the Stepford wives, you paid a price.

P: They didn't know it. I didn't either. I was brainwashed. I can see that now. But I never felt good about myself. I was performing. It's like I was impersonating someone else. I never felt sure of myself.

T: When do you think that began?

P: As long ago as I can remember, but I don't think I felt I was hiding anything until I got a little older and tried to pass as straight. . . .

T: That must have been a very difficult period in your life.

P: I don't think I let myself feel that, although I do remember go-
     ing to the doctor a lot. I had headaches. They didn't know what
     was wrong with me and couldn't find anything.

Later in the session, the therapist explored the connection between
Richard's past and his current feelings of not being genuine.

T: Are you still a Stepford son?

P: I was thinking about that. Some of my friends over the years
     have told me that they never know what I'm really feeling be-
     cause I don't say much. I have never known what to say. I wasn't
     aware of holding my feelings in. I think I've just been out of
     touch. . . . Sometimes I'm aware of going through the motions of
     having feelings.

T: Give me an example of what you mean.

P: If a friend is really upset. I can be a good listener and give great
     advice and act like I know what he's feeling, but I'm just trying
     to be a good friend. I don't really feel much of anything. . . . The
     mother of one of our friends died recently. I really didn't give
     a shit. I do like him and was aware that he felt bad, but I didn't
     really feel anything. I acted sympathetic and all that. I don't
     think he sensed that I was absent. I feel like I'm a phony. I know
     how to impersonate a person.

T: What's that like for you?

P: I'm not sure. I know I don't like it.

T: What's the downside for you?

P: I was thinking about that, too. I try so hard to be what I'm sup-
     posed to be that sometimes I resent what I take on or what I'm
     doing. It feels like I'm living someone else's life. Don't get me
     wrong. I'm grateful for my life, but in some ways I don't know
     what's really important to me. No one would think that. People
     envy me. They think I have everything. But I'm a constant wor-
     rier. I'm always anxious that I am going to lose everything.

T: Perhaps you don't always feel that you deserve what you have
     achieved or you feel that it's not really yours.

P: It's more the second.

T: We need to work on helping you get more in touch with what you do feel and want.

Months later, Richard began to show greater understanding of the pressures he had experienced as a child and how they were influencing his current behavior.

P: I was watching myself at work. I automatically go into my perfect employee routine, and I'm volunteering for this assignment and taking on more responsibility and doing without more resources because I know that the company is under financial pressure. I'm the good soldier. I'll go anywhere and do anything.

T: It sounds exhausting. You only know how to add to your "to do" list. Do you ever take anything off the list?

P: No, of course not. Not until I can cross something off as completed. . . . I don't even stop to think about what I really want. I'm noticing that more and more. I'm always raising my hand. Then later I bitch and moan.

T: Being the good soldier in your family was the way you learned to be when you were younger, and it may have given you a sense of self-esteem in some ways. You seemed to have quite a sense of responsibility. You had to put your own needs and feelings aside. It is understandable that later you were frightened of disappointing them if they should learn that you are gay, and you tried to put your sexual feelings aside too.

P: Well, I was able to come to terms with that eventually.

T: Yes, and it's good that you did. But your use of words makes me think you may not have accepted being gay as much as you think. You seem to brush your sexual identity aside as if it's not significant.

P: I don't want people to think that being gay is all that I am.

T: Is being gay so bad?

P: [Laughs] You caught me. I guess I am homophobic at heart despite my politically correct beliefs.

T: Maybe there's a part of you that you still are hiding and that contributes to your feeling fraudulent. It's not by any means the whole reason, but it may be playing a role.

P: Well, there are a lot of situations where I think I still have to be
    closeted. That's just reality.

T: It's not just a matter of fearing what others will think or do. It's
    how you feel about yourself that's important as well.

As the therapist worked with Carol, her guilt, shame, and feelings
of fraudulence became evident.

P: My parents are basically good people. It wasn't easy for them to
    raise so many children. They sacrificed a lot for us, and they just
    don't understand that there's a life outside of the town they live
    in or that anyone would want to leave. My brothers and sister
    still live in the area. I was the only one who broke away. They
    think I've rejected them. I've caused them to be unhappy.

T: So your being happy doesn't count.

P: Well, it was important to me. I was selfish. I wanted to get away
    and have a different kind of life.

T: Your calling those wishes selfish suggests that you judge yourself
    harshly for pursuing your dreams.

P: I used to feel guilty all the time when I was in college. I would
    never tell them anything that I was doing. When I went home
    for visits, I tried to fit in. It got more difficult as time went on. I
    couldn't bear feeling that I was making them unhappy and that
    they didn't approve of my life. I thought I had gotten over those
    feelings when I came to New York.

T: It took a lot for you to come here, and maybe you felt less guilty.
    But I wonder if your guilt went underground and found its way
    into your career and relationship pursuits.

P: Are you saying that I messed things up for myself because I felt
    guilty?

T: I think that's a part of it. You were able to get away but not able
    really to fulfill your dreams. Perhaps you also felt that if you
    were a success, you would lose your connection to your family
    completely.

P: I feel so ashamed. I've had such great opportunities, and I haven't
    been able to take advantage of them. Sometimes I think that my
    parents were right after all and I should not have tried to be more
    than I was.

T: How do you mean that?

P: It's one thing to be smart in a small town. Maybe I wasn't cut out to make it somewhere else. Mom and Dad always told me that nothing good could come from trying to be what you're not. I thought that they were just trying to hold on to me. . . . There have been a lot of times in the past few years when I would say to myself, "Who are you kidding? You don't have what it takes."

T: You hear their words.

P: I guess I do. I'm confused. I feel like I can do well and then I feel like I'm a fraud and that deep down I try to act as though I can do it but I really can't.

T: When have you felt that way?

P: When I've had trouble with my writing. I get so depressed. When I was told that I wasn't getting tenure, a part of me was relieved. I thought, "Well, you don't have to keep acting any more and you can go home." But that didn't seem right either. I don't know any more.

T: We have a lot of work to do—to help you feel less guilty about your dreams and less ashamed of yourself for having had problems along the way. There are a lot of reasons that you have had difficulties.

P: How do I do that?

T: I can't answer you exactly. I can, though, point to a direction. We have to examine some of the assumptions about yourself and your family that you have bought in to, think about what your needs were as a child and how they were frustrated, and look at what you need now and how you can get some of those needs met.

P: It may be too late. I'm not getting any younger.

T: It's true that time is moving on and some opportunities have passed by. I can't promise you that you will get everything you ever wanted. You may need to make some compromises, but I do know that you can feel better about yourself and your life.

7

THE FOCUS AND PROCESS OF PSYCHOTHERAPY
Part 2

Chapter 6 began by showing the process of helping midlife patients identify what might be thwarting their self-needs and inflicting blows to their self-concept and self-esteem. Then it illustrated how therapists work with patients to modify the demands of the grandiose self; to mourn their losses; and to overcome feelings of guilt, shame, and fraudulence. Like the treatment of most patients, the successful treatment of those in midlife usually depends on the use of techniques that support and strengthen the self, in addition to those that help them to gain insight into the reasons for their intense reactions and to change their usual patterns of behavior.

Strengthening the Self-Concept and Enhancing Self-Esteem

Helping midlife patients to reshape and strengthen their sense of themselves and enhance their self-esteem are crucial aspects of their treatment. When their bubble bursts, many people become extremely negative about themselves and their past experiences. They do not see themselves as capable, or else they eradicate their own history of achievement and forget previous successes. Often they depend on others' reactions in order to feel good about themselves, or they feel unable to achieve their perfectionist standards of behavior. Consequently, their self-esteem fluctuates dramatically or even plummets.

Providing support and encouragement is certainly a part of most treatment methods. Some self psychologists, however, have emphasized the importance of the therapist's providing a range of selfobject functions to patients, particularly to those who have not experienced sufficient validation of their feelings and experiences or who lack idealizable adults in their lives. Such patients are unable to share a sense of likeness with significant others or have missed other types of crucial selfobject experiences.

It is especially important for therapists to enable patients to retrieve positive memories, connections, and achievements and to regain and retain control of their lives (Butler, 1963; Grunes, 1982; Greenes, 1986). It is advisable for therapists to search for, identify, and affirm their patients' strengths, particularly when their patients have not had any validating experiences earlier in their lives. It may be necessary to help patients to value themselves in new ways when they have held to rigid and unrealistic expectations of themselves or are no longer able to engage in pursuits that have been a mainstay of their self-concept and self-esteem. Even when patients reveal a history of failed opportunities, it may be useful to acknowledge their resiliency in surviving difficult circumstances. Moreover, it can be beneficial for therapists to identify and validate patients' feelings and needs when they are out of touch with their own inner life.

Therapists' genuineness and responsiveness to patients are crucial parts of the treatment. In some instances, therapists may self-disclose, revealing aspects of their own personality, interests, attitudes, background, life experiences, even their thoughts and feelings during the course of treatment. Self-disclosure is by no means always indicated, however, because many patients with narcissistic vulnerability may experience it as intrusive or disruptive. Nevertheless, the use of self-disclosure may help some patients to engage in treatment and develop selfobject transferences. They may reveal and explore traumatic experiences. They may experience validation or acknowledge and take ownership of previously disavowed aspects of their own feelings and behavior. Therapists' self-disclosures also can help patients to feel less alone. They can learn to bear shame and humiliation, and other painful emotions. Patients can thus be helped to discover and strengthen their sense of self and be exposed to alternative ways of thinking and acting. Patients can bridge differences that exist between themselves and their therapists. Self-disclosure can foster experiences of intimacy and sharing (Goldstein, 1994, 1997).

Expanding the Capacity for Empathy

When patients are highly dependent on others to bolster their self-esteem, they tend to be preoccupied with their own reactions and not consider what others are going through. They often misinterpret others' motivations and are not accustomed to experiencing the world through others' eyes. What others say and do is always about them, the patients. Although it is not unusual for the capacity for greater empathy to occur naturally in the course of a successful treatment, sometimes it is useful for therapists to help patients think in new and different ways to expand their empathic understanding of others.

Finding New Selfobjects and Outlets for Self-Expression

Helping patients to identify those in their lives who can support their sense of themselves and guiding patients to restore or develop new outlets for self-expression are important objectives in the psychotherapy of many midlife patients. It is important to offer a vision of what is possible and to actively encourage patients to take actions that are new and frightening if these are consistent with the therapists' assessment of the patients' capacities. It usually is necessary for clinicians to encourage patients to take small steps in giving up what is familiar and safe, in taking risks, and in trying out new behaviors. Selective therapeutic responsiveness to patients' needs shows them that there is a world of potentially more gratifying relationships than the patients may have experienced previously. This helps them to take risks in developing relationships that can reinforce new ways of relating to others and perceiving the self.

Connecting to Positive Aspects of the Self and Others and Moving Forward

As discussed in earlier chapters, when Marge began to relinquish her rigid view of herself as a perfect mother during the course of treatment, she recognized that she had contributed to her daughter, Jessica's, problems and went through a painful period of rumination about what she felt was her destructiveness to Jessica. During this time, Marge also expressed guilt for having felt ashamed of her own mother and the family's poverty when she was a child and adolescent and for not having realized her potential in her work life. She had lost touch with anything good she had done in her life and felt incapable of making desired changes in her life.

In the following excerpts, the therapist attempted to help Marge reconnect with some of the positive aspects of her parenting. The therapist validated some of Marge's childhood needs and helped her to value herself differently. Finally, the therapist encouraged her to move forward in her life.

P: It was so important to me to do it right. I was going to have the brightest and most successful children and the closest family. I really thought I was going to do it even without their father's help. . . . I was so caught up in my own needs, I didn't see who they really were. I know you are going to say that I didn't try to hurt them, but the fact of the matter is that I did hurt them. I don't know if I can forgive myself. I don't know if Jessica will ever forgive me. I want to explain it to her but I don't think she wants to hear it. I don't blame her. I really messed up.

T: It has been very painful to realize that you have made some mistakes. There's been no room for error in your view of yourself, but it seems that this recognition has resulted in your swinging from seeing yourself as all good to seeing yourself as all bad. It's one thing to recognize your human failings, but it's quite another to see yourself as not having done anything right. It's as if you don't remember anything good that you have done.

P: When I think about how hard I pushed Jess and how critical I've been, you're right—I don't see the good. Shouldn't I have known better? So what if I tried to be a good mother? Does it even matter? Jess still has to live with the effects of my mistakes.

T: You measure yourself against an impossible standard, and you measure Jess against an idealized view of who she should be. It's hard for you to accept her limitations and your own. Even the best parents are not always perfect and do not have perfect kids.

P: I was pretty imperfect.

T: I understand that you feel that way. You are feeling really down on yourself. It's hard for you to have any compassion for your own struggles in life. You had to find your way on your own, without a husband or other supports and positive role models.

P: That's true enough. I wished I had a mother or an aunt or a sister who could have guided me. They were wrapped up in themselves.

T: Whatever mistakes you made, it's clear that Jessica cares a lot about you.

P: I do forget that sometimes, particularly when she's mad at me and doesn't want to talk to me. When she calls me and asks me for advice or does something nice, I feel a little better. Then sometimes she makes me feel terrible. I do rise and fall based on how she acts toward me. . . . Our relationship is a little better than it was. Over the weekend, she came over to the house for the afternoon, and I showed her how to make a pie. She's dating a guy, can you believe it? He loves blueberry pie and she wants to make one for him. It was fun and we didn't fight. I almost had a slip when she walked in. She was wearing a torn pair of slacks, but I caught myself and buttoned my lip.

T: Good for you. Was it hard to do that?

P: It's so automatic with me to notice what's wrong with her. She's right about that. I have to make a supreme effort not to say anything, but I see that she's better when I shut up or I try to find something positive to say. That's not easy for me. It's not my nature. I'm just like my mother. I hate it.

T: I can see that you are trying to be different with Jessica, and I'm glad that your efforts are getting some positive results.

Later in the session, with the therapist's prompting, Marge recalled some experiences she had had with Jessica when she was a child.

T: I want to go back to Jessica's asking you to teach her how to bake a pie. That couldn't have come out of the blue. You must have had other kinds of experiences like that with her.

P: Not for a very long time. When she was younger, she used to watch me when I baked. Then, sometimes I would let her lick the frosting from the pan. Those were the days when I made the frosting myself. [Becomes tearful] She used to think I was the greatest.

T: What are you feeling right now?

P: I miss those times.

T: They were important to you. Do you recall other times like that?

P: It's funny that you ask that. When Jessica and I were making the pie, she reminded me of something we used to do together that I had not thought about in years. When I would pick her up from her art class, I would take her out to have an ice cream soda at a really great place for kids. [Still tearful and smiling at the same time] It's so strange.

T: What are you thinking about?

P: My mother used to love ice cream. That's about the only treat she let herself have. She used to send me out to the corner store to get some after dinner on summer nights. I used to like those times. I think it was not only the ice cream that I liked but also that she seemed less unhappy.

T: Those were rare moments when you felt you could do something to please her and make her feel good. You had a positive connection to her at those times.

P: That was unusual. I thought it would be different with my kids.

T: Didn't you once tell me that you had a memory of bread baking when you were a child?

P: Yes. Sometimes, on Fridays, my mother would make her own bread. She didn't do it all the time, but I used to love that smell when I came home from school.

In the following session, Marge brought up her reaction to this discussion.

P: I have to tell you. I was very sad when I left here last time. [Tearful] I started thinking more about my mother and remembered some of her good qualities. I feel bad that I was so ashamed of her. She didn't have much. My father never earned a decent living. They had to struggle. I was the first to be born here, and I was blue-eyed and blonde. She wanted me to be a real American and be a success. I was a selfish brat.

T: What are you referring to?

P: I wanted them to be modern. They both spoke with an accent, and our apartment was so cramped and shabby. She was very clean but she never bought anything for herself or tried to fix things up. We didn't have a television until I was 10 years old. I didn't want to bring anyone home, and I used to get mad at her for not going out. The other kids came from different kinds of homes. No one was rich, but they seemed to have more than we did and their parents were American born and seemed to know how to have a good time. I used to love going to their houses. Ours was so bleak most of the time. I don't know what I was thinking.

T: You are blaming yourself again. Don't you think it's understandable that you wanted to be like your peers, to be accepted by them, to have what they had, especially when your family life was so lonely and difficult?

P: It was hard to be home most of the time.

T: You blame yourself for wanting material possessions and wishing your mother were more modern, but it's possible that these things became associated with the lack of nurturing and the feelings of insecurity that you experienced.

P: It must have hurt my mother that I wanted to spend so much time away from home.

T: From everything you have told me, your parents were very pre-occupied with their own troubles and your mother was very strict, critical, and frightened of the outside world. It must not have felt warm and safe. Your friends' parents responded to you and were nice. They helped you to survive.

P: I depended on the kindness of strangers. I've always liked that line [from the play *A Streetcar Named Desire*].

In the next few sessions, Marge brought up her recent contacts with Jessica.

P: I seem to be taking one step forward and one step back. Jessica and I had a tiff. It was my fault as usual. She started telling me about her new boyfriend, and I thought she was making herself too available to him. I should have kept my big mouth shut, but I gave her a little lecture on how she should play hard to get. I knew I had made a mistake as soon as I said it.

T: Well, that's not so terrible. Parents say stupid things like that. How did Jessica react?

P: Actually, she wasn't too bad. She told me that what was good for my generation was not necessarily good for hers and that she didn't think I was such an expert on relationships with men anyway. I started to defend myself but I heard you telling me to think before I speak or I'd feel worse. I just changed the subject, and everything seemed to be okay.

T: Well, you should be pleased with yourself.

P: I am a little . . . I've been thinking that Jessica seems to be trying with me. I notice that she's has been calling more and is not so testy.

T: She seems to want to have a good connection with you. She appears to see you more positively than you see yourself.

P: I've been thinking about that. I've been trying to remember some of the good things between us. I was pretty awful but not always. . . .

T: That you did care about her must have come through.

P: I have to try to be more there for her now despite myself.

One of the ongoing issues in the treatment was Marge's tendency to become easily depressed and self-disparaging if she felt disappointed or rejected by Jessica or Adam and his fiancée. She would feel better about herself if her interactions with them had gone well. Marge accepted this state of affairs as natural early in the treatment and only later began to acknowledge that she was too dependent for her self-esteem on her children's reactions.

P: I've been realizing lately that it's a little crazy that my moods depend on the kids. I still call them kids. They're far from children anymore even though they act like kids sometimes. Jessica calls, I feel good. She looks depressed, I feel bad. She's testy with me, I get depressed and hate her and myself. Adam invites me to lunch, I'm happy. His fiancée doesn't call me for two weeks, I feel rejected. . . . It happens with my husband too and with friends. If he doesn't pay attention to me at a party or tries to be entertaining without bringing me into a conversation when we're at dinner with friends or his colleagues, I feel like I don't exist. If he surprises me with some flowers, I'm his forever. . . . I don't know if I told you about my friend Amy and her husband. We went to their house for dinner and they served shellfish, which I'm allergic to. Amy knows that. She's been with me enough over the years. When I said something, she said she had a lapse and was apologetic. Don't you know that afterward I felt hurt because she wasn't thinking about me when she planned dinner.

T: It's a hell of a way to live.

P: I hate it but I don't know how to change it. What can I do?

T: I wish I could give you the answer. What strikes me is that you seem to measure who you are on a minute-by-minute or day-by-day basis and according to other people's reactions and behavior. It's hard for you to feel solid within yourself. We all need others, but you do not seem to have any money in the bank emotionally. If someone disappoints you, it wipes out any good feelings you have about yourself.

P: I can't even imagine what it would be like not to be this way.

T: It's not hard to understand how you came to feel this way given how much emphasis your mother placed on your being what she wanted and her tendency to be critical, moody, and depressed. It seems likely that you never knew what to expect and may have equated her anger and withdrawal with your not meeting her expectations. As we've discussed before, this probably had a lot to do with your becoming so perfectionistic. What do you remember about how you felt?

P: I can remember feeling really good sometimes if I seemed to please her, but I don't think that I did too often. I tried, but something always seemed to go wrong. I know I used to feel sick inside when I could see her anger or disappointment. I can't quite explain it. It was an awful feeling, particularly if she didn't talk to me. She could silently punish me for days. I used to try to get her to talk and she wouldn't, even if I cried and got really upset. Eventually she would relent but I never knew when she would. . . . As I got a little older, I didn't care anymore and I wouldn't talk to her and acted like she wasn't getting to me.

T: That sounds pretty grim. Where was your father?

P: Probably working or sleeping. He didn't know how to handle her either. I think he escaped in whatever way he could.

T: I wonder if you were anxious a lot about what would happen when you came home every day.

P: I tried not to come home when I was old enough to stay away. I don't know if I was anxious. I did always have a lot of stomachaches.

In the following sessions, the therapist continued to address Marge's self-esteem fluctuations.

T: Have you ever considered that your mother's reactions were not about whether you were a good child or a bad child but about her unrealistic expectations and her own frustrations? She may not have been able to be there for you but you interpreted this as related to how you performed. Perhaps you also react this way to others now—that their reactions are always about you and how well or poorly you're doing rather than about their own issues.

P: It's hard to make that distinction. I go into an automatic funk if I think someone is not acting right. I feel that it is my fault.

T: Well, we have to help you find a way of interrupting that automatic process and realizing that you are the same person with good qualities. Perhaps it might help to have a red flag or another type of warning signal go up when you begin to feel hurt and angry. It's important to make yourself think of some of the reasons that people might be acting as they do but that don't necessarily have to do with you.

P: [Laughing] Moi? You think I should consider what other people are feeling? That would be a switch.

T: You really have come a long way if you can laugh at yourself that way.

In this same period, the therapist began to explore whether Marge's fluctuations in self-esteem were affected by her relationship with the therapist.

T: We've talked a lot about how your feelings about yourself are influenced by others. I was wondering if you feel that way here.

P: I feel you understand me and aren't trying to judge me. I can really talk to you. I wish I could have had that with my sister. . . . I do worry sometimes about what you really think about me when I leave here. I know that I sound pretty angry and stubborn. But when I come back you seem glad to see me. I think that I've come to count on that. I don't know how I would feel if I saw a different look on your face. I'd probably be upset. I react badly if anyone looks at me sideways.

T: Well, I'll try not to but I'll need you to tell me if I mess up.

P: Don't worry. You'll know.

Soon after this session, Marge brought up an incident that had occurred with Adam's fiancée, Sarah.

P: I had a really hard day on Saturday. I was furious but I was able to get myself out of it. I surprised myself. I think you'd be proud of me.

T: Tell me about it.

P: It started with Sarah calling me to talk about the wedding plans. She told me how many people from our side we could invite. It was such a small number. I was taken aback. It meant we couldn't invite all our friends. I just couldn't believe it. I started to object, and she said that she had discussed it with Adam and he agreed. There was nothing she could do and that she hoped I wouldn't be too unhappy. That shut me up. I started fuming when I got off the phone. I almost called Adam but I knew that wouldn't do any good. So I spent the morning sulking. It was beautiful outside and I had lost interest in going out. Then I remembered what you said about the red flag. I said, "Self, maybe it's not about you." I started thinking that I was feeling insulted and hurt because Sarah didn't consult me. But the fact is that we have a small family and not all our friends will be available and the kids are paying for the wedding themselves because they don't want our help and Sarah's parents don't have much money. Adam says they would rather have a sizable gift. I began to calm down and we went out for a walk and to the movies. I still think she can be a cold bitch, but at least she called me personally rather than let Adam pass the word along.

T: That's a first. I am proud of you. Maybe you could negotiate for a few extra people if it gets too difficult especially if you're not angry when you bring it up.

P: Maybe I could. From our talks about Sarah, I realize that she wants to feel that I respect her autonomy and opinions and, I think, that she's a little afraid of me.

T: It's too bad that she is not a different type of person, but I can see that you are in a better place.

Later in the treatment, Marge frequently brought up her boredom with her job and her frustration with her lack of an interesting career. She recognized that she needed to get more of life and to take more risks, but her lifelong pessimism was evident.

P: I know I need to find something else to do with myself. I can't keep expecting my kids to give me a reason to get up in the morning. My job just doesn't do it for me. My husband can't understand what's wrong with me. His work is his life and he loves it. He's so lucky. He has been more attentive lately and that's nice, but I'm still unhappy. I just keep wishing I had done something more with my life. I still wish I could but I probably won't do anything about it. I'm basically too lazy and a coward.

T: What would you do if you could?

P: I don't know exactly. I would like more friends that I could do things with. They don't have to become bosom buddies, but I would have to reach out more and not be so reclusive. . . . What I really would like to do is something new and different that would be more exciting than spending time in the library. There's probably no point in talking about this if I'm not going to do anything.

T: What would you need to help you take a some small steps to make things better? I don't have a crystal ball, but it's likely that you have a lot of years ahead of you and you have your health and a fair amount of energy and are doing okay financially. You can have more in your life. I don't mean that in a pressuring way.

P: I know that you're not trying to push me. Maybe I could use some pushing, not really pushing but encouragement, like what you are doing. My mother had a way of pressuring me, but I never felt she tried to help me.

Later in the session, the therapist came back to the subject of what Marge might do to move forward.

T: Have you had some ideas, even if you rejected them or they seemed silly, about what you would like to pursue if you could?

P: [Laughs] Aside from becoming a highly acclaimed author, I have thought about doing something with real estate. I love houses, and friends have told me that I have a great sense of color and design. I know I couldn't be an interior decorator because it's too difficult a business. A friend of mine is constantly complaining about how dissatisfied her clients are and how they never want to pay her. But I think I would like to show and sell houses. I know it can be cutthroat, but I'm a good talker and I might enjoy some of wheeling and dealing. Do you think that's stupid?

T: Not at all. It sounds doable. In fact, it sounds as though you have given it some thought.

P: I was going to look into what I would need to do, but I never did. That's me. Great ideas and no follow-through.

T: Perhaps you are in a different place right now and can focus on what you might want to a greater degree.

P: You don't think I'm too old?

T: You know that we are the same age, so I'm not sure I'm the best person to answer that question. It seems to me that there are more opportunities for women our age today than there were for

our mothers. In a way, we're not as old as they were when they
were our age.

P: That's true. I've thought that too.

Over the course of the next several sessions, Marge went back and
forth between her concerns about Adam's approaching wedding and
her wish to make some changes in her life.

P: It's funny, I was reading *The New York Times* on Sunday, and I
      found myself looking at the real estate section of the paper. I
      hadn't done that for a long time. I used to look at it all the time
      just to see what the prices of houses were and where they were.
      It's always interested me. I don't know why I stopped.
T: You've been depressed and have had a lot on your mind. Have you
      thought more about our talk about your interest in selling houses?
P: I put it aside, or so I thought, but then when I was looking at the
      paper I must confess that I felt a little excited.
T: This is the first time that I have sensed you are really enthusias-
      tic about something. What would it take for you to find out
      more about what might be involved?
P: I just have to call an old friend of mine who is in real estate. I'm
      sure she would tell me what she did to get started. She loves to
      talk about herself. I haven't been in touch with her for a while,
      but we've had lapses in our relationship before. I've been think-
      ing about her. I guess I do feel a little awkward about calling her,
      but she's always wanted the friendship. She would probably be
      happy to hear from me. I've been the one who distanced from her.
T: You could kill two birds with one stone, so to speak.
P: You mean I'd be getting the information that I want and reach-
      ing out to a friend in the process. I'm going to do it. My God, it's
      a small thing. I'm not going to wimp out.

In the next session, Marge came in looking pleased with herself.

P: You won't believe it. I actually called my old friend and we ar-
      ranged a lunch date. We met yesterday. It was actually fun to
      talk about old times, and, when we talked about her kids, I got

an earful about her troubles with her daughter and her son-in-law. Life is strange. We both thought that each of us had the perfect family life. . . . Meanwhile she's been able to earn quite a lot of money selling real estate. Her hours are crazy because she is at her clients' beck and call, but she doesn't seem to mind. She gave me a contact for some information on courses that I'd have to take. She said it would take about six months, and then I would need to take a test to get a license. . . . My husband thinks I should do it. I was surprised. He actually said that he knew that I needed a change and that he wanted me to be happy. He used those words. I didn't think he had it in him. The poor guy. I've been really hard to live with for a long time.

Affirming the Self and Developing the Capacity for Empathy

Recall that Richard entered treatment at a time when his self-cohesion was shaky and he was experiencing strong emotions as a result of a series of life events that assaulted his need for control. Whereas in the initial phase of the therapy he looked to the therapist as a strong figure who would help him restore his equilibrium, as he began to feel better he related to her as an expert in human relationships who could coach him on how to improve his work life. It took over a year before Richard began to explore himself in more depth, get in touch with his underlying feelings, and allow himself to depend on the therapist. At this time, Richard spoke of being a robot who knew only how to be what others wanted and who was estranged from his own needs and feelings. He also began to recognize that he still had deep-seated antigay feelings that he had pushed aside. The therapist tried to help Richard connect to his more genuine feelings and needs and to come to a greater acceptance of his sexual identity.

P: I don't want to have to perform all the time and be the most conscientious and hardworking employee, the greatest host, the best son, the most generous friend. You name it. I want to be more genuine and do what I feel like doing, not only what I'm expected to do.

T: Let me give you a multiple-choice question. Do you think that you still think you should be the best and that others expect that of you, or that you are fearful of being yourself? Or don't you know what being yourself means?

P: Can I check all of the above? [Pensive]

T: What are you thinking?

P: I'm ashamed to tell you. There was a long time when I didn't know how to pick out clothes for myself. I know you must think that's strange, but it's true. I wasn't sure what looked good on me or what I liked. In school, we had to wear uniforms, navy blue blazers, white shirts, and khaki pants. At other times, I always wore what my mother picked out for me. It's embarrassing when I think about it now. When I started to shop by myself, I practically had an anxiety attack. I couldn't make up my mind about what to buy, and, when I finally decided, I would bring the purchases home and try everything on a million times. I still wouldn't be sure that I had made the right decision until a friend noticed that I was wearing something new and make a positive comment. I drove Roger crazy when we met, and, with his help, I'm a lot better.

T: You always dress very well.

P: I think I do, but I'm not very adventuresome. I stay pretty conservative. I'd be too self-conscious that I might stand out in some way if I wore something really trendy.

T: It's good that you feel less anxious about your choices. Perhaps you will eventually become confident enough to take more risks. What's the worst thing that can happen?

P: You know me. It's another way I have to be perfect or what will the neighbors think?

After the Thanksgiving holiday, Richard came to a session, flung himself down, and said he was exhausted.

T: What's wrong?

P: I want to tell you about our Thanksgiving dinner. It's a good example of what I go through. You know we were planning this extravaganza. We ended up having 20 people for dinner. We were only counting on 18, but we invited two more people at the last minute. . . . It cost us a fortune. I stopped counting until it was over. Of course, I did everything myself. Roger is hopeless when it comes to entertaining, except that he can serve drinks and help in the cleanup. Everything was perfect from the invitations, table settings, and decorations to the main meal, service, dessert, and afterdinner drinks. I have to admit that it was pretty wonderful, and everyone seemed to have a good time, even my mother. I was exhausted afterward. All that effort and it was over in hours. I thought I wanted to do it, but did I really or did I just think it was expected of me?

T: You seem to be happy about how it turned out.

P: I'm glad it went well, but I know I can entertain. I'm good at it. It's enough already. I don't even like turkey or stuffing that much, and do I need to have all these people for dinner? I can always see my mother and my siblings. I'd rather Roger and I went out to an inn and ordered a nice dinner and be done with it. I would like to skip Thanksgiving next year.

T: What would happen if you did?

P: That's a good question. I don't know the answer. I find myself doing these things when I don't even know if I want to. I don't stop to ask myself if I want to.

T: What do you think drives you? Is it the applause or avoiding disappointing others or not wanting to fall short?

P: I like the applause for a minute, but I think it's more that I'm expected to do these things and would be falling short in some way if I didn't rise to the occasion.

T: Who would think that?

P: I would think it myself, but that's how I was raised. . . .

T: Your whole self-worth seems to rest on your doing what you feel others expect of you even if it's at your own expense.

P: [Looks pensive]

T: What are you thinking?

P: This is the only place where I feel I can be myself, whatever that is. I don't have to put on a performance here. I used to feel that I did, that you wouldn't respect me if I let you see me underneath.

T: You seem sad.

P: Do I? Maybe I am.

T: Try to put your feelings into words.

P: I think I'm seeing that my parents' love was conditional. I don't know how they would have reacted if I didn't do what they wanted. It was never an option. I see how they reacted to Mark [next brother in birth order]. He never fit the bill, and they let him know it. The way they treated him used to upset me a lot. . . . Maybe they would have treated me that way if I had not been the perfect son. It makes me angry to think about that. I never realized how controlled I felt. I just accepted who I was supposed to be. I even sided with my parents sometimes about my brother. I thought that he wasn't trying hard enough. I was hard on him. Their expectations were my expectations. I guess I bought the party line.

T: Did you ever want to rebel?

P: I don't think it ever occurred to me in those days.

Shortly after this session, Richard called for an extra appointment because of another disturbing incident that had just occurred with his landscaper friend, Peter. Richard had found a way to get over his past anger at Peter (described in chapter 6) for not having supervised his shrub planting properly. Now, months later, Peter had made another "horrible" mistake and Richard was beside himself.

P: Thanks for making the time. I just thought it was better that I talk to you because I feel like I'm going to explode and a part of me thinks it's not a good idea.

T: What's going on?

P: Peter volunteered to house-sit so he could be there for a delivery of some furniture for our downstairs sitting room. I arranged for the delivery, which wasn't easy because they're so independent and didn't want to give me a definite day or time, and over the weekend Roger and I moved out the old furniture and cleaned thoroughly. So what happened? Peter got the delivery date and day mixed up! He thought the 10th was a Tuesday, not a Monday. So, of course, the delivery men came and no one was home, and they left. I got a call at the office later that day, after it was too late to do anything about it, and they can't deliver again until next week. We're having company for the weekend, and the place is a mess. I'm furious.

T: It's certainly frustrating, especially after you went to such efforts to prepare.

P: I suppose it's not so terrible if the room is empty, but I just don't know how he could be so dumb and careless. He called me later that evening to apologize again, but I didn't want to talk to him. I told him I would call him in a few days. I didn't trust myself not to yell at him.

T: What did he say when he apologized?

P: He said he had been preoccupied with his daughter's going off to college and his wife's depression. I always have a lot on my mind. It's no excuse.

T: Well, these things happen to everyone. It's difficult for you to cut him some slack and to think that he's not used to coping with a lot of pressure and has his own feelings about his daughter's leaving home. You expect him to be like you, and you certainly never cut yourself any slack.

P: So you think I should accept his apology and let it go.

T: I don't think you should do it because I think you should.

P: I want to know what you think.

T: It's hard for you. You have high expectations of yourself and others, and, when people don't live up to your standards, it frustrates you and you become quite judgmental of them. You don't judge them any more harshly than you judge yourself, but it's not like you to have empathy for what they may be experiencing, just as you lack empathy for yourself if you fall short in some way.

P: It's true that empathy is not my strong suit. Roger has told me that.

T: What brought that about?

P: He thinks I'm too hard on my mother and some of our friends and on myself. He tries to get me to see their side of things or to ease up, but what he says usually rolls off my back.

T: Are you taking what I'm saying with a grain of salt, too?

P: I think there's truth in what both of you are saying. It's just not my nature.

T: We were talking about this last time with respect to your brother, whom you described being hard on you because you bought into the family party line. You were expected not to have feelings or make any mistakes.

P: I can see now that my brother had a totally different temperament from me, and he couldn't do what I did. But, then, I just thought he was overly emotional and lazy.

T: Sometimes it seems that for you to have any feelings at all is overly emotional, until you can't take it any more and even an everyday frustration can make you feel like exploding.

In the following several sessions, Richard talked more about his childhood and adolescence and about being gay.

P: I was thinking about the fact that I never rebelled. Even when I realized deep down that I must be gay, I pushed it away.

T: You must have been very frightened of not living up to your parents' expectations.

P: My father used to make jokes about "fags" all the time, and he would talk about the horrible lives they led. How could I be gay? It would have killed him.

T: You felt that your attraction to other boys was a really bad thing. I wonder if you ever thought that your father died because he somehow suspected you were gay. Kids sometimes do blame themselves when a parent dies at a young age.

P: I don't think I thought that I had caused his death but . . . [Becomes silent]

T: You look sad. What are you thinking?

P: I think that a part of me was relieved when he died, even though it was so hard for us afterward. I think I felt that I could be freer somehow. That's pretty terrible.

T: It's not hard to understand that you would feel that way. You experienced a lot of pressure. You could not be yourself.

P: It's funny. I've always blamed my mother for being critical. The fact is that, when I told her I was gay later on, she was okay about it. I don't know. I tend to think the worst of her. Maybe she was relieved because my being gay meant that she wouldn't have any competition from another woman. . . . She loves Roger. He's actually nicer to her than I am. He has the patience to listen to her.

In subsequent sessions, the therapist continued to explore Richard's self-concept as a gay man and his feelings of low self-esteem.

T: Last time you were talking about how your father used to make a lot of negative comments about gays. How did that make you feel?

P: I guess I believed what he believed. I know it's not politically correct, but I didn't want to be gay in those days. I tried not to be, but it's just who I was. I still don't quite understand it all. What do you think causes boys to be gay?

T: Your words sound as if you're asking how you got such a disease. What if being attracted to other men is natural for you?

P: It feels that way. Does that mean I'm naturally deficient in some way?

T: I don't think so and the scientific community increasingly doesn't think so, but deep down you do. It's hard to overcome the negative messages you got when you were younger.

P: I did always think that something was wrong with me. It's painful to think about it. That's one of the reasons that I've always tried so hard to do everything perfectly. I wanted to show that there was nothing wrong with me, and I wanted to escape being a target of criticism. A lot of gay men are like that. They want to prove to themselves and the world that they're just as good as, if not better than, straight guys. They don't want to be scapegoats.

T: It's quite a burden. Maybe you don't have to keep proving that you are okay to yourself. You seem to have set yourself apart from other gay men.

P: There's a lot to gay life that I don't like. I can't stand the flaunting of queer sex and the bodybuilding craze.

T: That's not all there is. You have a lot of stereotypes of gay life. I guess it's understandable that you bought into your father's views.

P: That's pathetic.

T: It's really hard for a boy to grow up without feeling that his core self is acceptable and prized by his family and the outside world.

P: It still feels hard some times. I want people to know that I'm gay only if I'm really sure that they're okay with it. I stifle a lot of myself at work. I never talk about my life with Roger. I don't think they would insult me or anything like that. I'm sure people suspect that I'm gay, but I think they're more comfortable with my not drawing attention to it, and I don't want to give them a reason to block my career in some way. Roger thinks I'm paranoid. He's more comfortable with letting it all hang out, but he's in a different field where there are more of us. I probably am making too much of it.

P: It's a hard call. It doesn't seem right to have to feel wary of letting people see who you are because of their stereotypes and prejudice. But your concealment also has caused you to pay an emotional price.

P: You say that as if you know what it's like. I didn't initially think you were a lesbian, but lately I've assumed that you are. I never asked you.

T: Why do you think you haven't?

P: I guess I thought you wanted to keep it private, like me. . . . Are you out in your professional life? Has it affected your career?

T: People are aware of it, and I don't think it has hurt me in any major way. Of course, it's possible that some people have reacted negatively, but I don't know for sure. I understand what it's like to feel that people are uncomfortable hearing about one's private life. There are still situations where I don't make a point of being open about my sexual identity, but I inhibit myself less and less these days. I don't want to hide who I am. Of course, I am in a different field from you, and I'm a woman, which may be easier in some ways.

P: Thank you for answering me. It makes me feel that you do accept who you are.

T: What's important is your accepting yourself.

In a session many months later, Richard was reflecting on how he had handled a difficult situation at work.

P: I had a hard week. My boss was in one of his moods. Nothing was right. He wanted everything done over. He was making all of us crazy. He refused to see that there was not enough time before the annual report is supposed to be printed for us to revise the color scheme, replace photographs, and write new copy. Then there's the conference that we've been planning. He's not happy with the guest speakers we've lined up or with the gifts everyone is supposed to get and the 9/11 memorial. You name it. He doesn't like it. But you would be proud of me. I realized that I could do only what I could do, and that was not going to be everything. I'm not going to make myself sick trying to make it all perfect. Whatever I can do will have to be good enough. He won't even remember everything that he said he didn't like. All he will care about is the feedback he will get from others. Last year I knocked myself out and everything was great, but everyone would have been happy if it had been a little less great. What we're doing is so much nicer than what most companies do. I have to confess that I did pop an Ativan to help me calm down. I figured that was better for me than two martinis.

T: I am proud of you. I think that's the first time that you have felt this way.

P: I actually have been practicing in some other ways. I've been trying to catch myself before I commit to taking on a new project or volunteer to take minutes at a meeting or be in charge of an office party or a collection for an employee's aunt's funeral. They're little things, but they add up to more pressure.

T: How does it feel?

P: It feels good. I worry a little about what others are thinking, but that's stupid. Does anyone really care? I was analyzing how much of my time is spent in nonessential activities, and it's a lot. I'd like to be able to breathe again. . . . I also told Roger that I don't want to entertain every weekend and that we have to cut down and be firmer with our families. They can't just show up on our doorstep whenever they feel like it. It's too much.

T: That might reduce some pressure on you. What did Roger say?

P: He's all for it. I think he's been going along with what he thought I wanted.

At around the same time, Richard revealed that he had been a little more open about his personal life with his colleagues.

P: A funny thing happened yesterday at work. Roger and I have worn similar commitment rings for years. They're really wedding bands, and I always have taken mine off when I go to work or am doing something that's job related.

T: I didn't realize that.

P: I guess it never came up but I noticed when I got into the office yesterday morning that I had forgotten to take the ring off. I actually had been thinking lately that it was pretty stupid to keep taking it off.

T: The mind works in mysterious ways.

P: Wait, that's not the whole story. Julie, my assistant, noticed it. I've always assumed that she knows that I'm gay, but we've never talked about it. So she asked me how long I had been with someone. I told her the truth and used Roger's name. I think she was astonished at how many years we'd been together. She was cool and said that she was glad I had someone and that she would like to meet him.

T: What was your reaction?

P: I nodded. I think I felt pleased and a little anxious at the same time. I'm sure she will tell some other people. I think I feel more able to handle it now. It might be a relief not to feel I have to be so guarded and private.

Toward the end of the next session, Richard mentioned that his mother was coming for lunch over the weekend. He recounted that she was feeling depressed and alone because her sister had died recently.

P: It's strange. Usually I get turned off by her when she gets needy, but I actually felt a little sorry for her. I invited her to the house because I wanted to cheer her up, not because I thought she expected me to or that it was my duty. I think it made her feel good.

T: That's a change for you.

P: [Laughs] You mean I'm becoming human?

T: Maybe a little more human.

Validating Healthy Ambitions and Abilities

When Carol entered treatment, she had just had to leave her faculty position at a local university and obtained a job as a word processor to support herself. She knew that, if she wanted to get another academic job, it would be necessary for her to start the application process immediately. She was unable to mobilize herself to take action, however, and in the initial phase of treatment she decided to postpone making a career move for another year. She wanted to use the time to think through what she wanted to do and work on the issues that were troubling her.

Exploring Carol's concerns, the therapist learned of her low self-esteem and pessimism about the future. Carol was doubtful about her ability to succeed in an academic environment or to have a committed relationship with a man who loved her. In the light of her history, it appeared that Carol was quite capable but that her lack of confidence, need for validation and encouragement, unrealistic expectations of herself, and guilt about having left her family to pursue her ambitions were playing a role in her current difficulties. In addition to engaging in the work described in chapter 6, the therapist felt it also was important to validate Carol's healthy ambitions and needs for recognition, help her gain more confidence in her writing, and encourage her job seeking.

Carol began the following session, which occurred after several months of treatment, by bringing up a recent telephone conversation with her mother.

P: I spoke to my mother over the weekend. I hadn't called her for several weeks. Of course, she never picks up the phone to call me. She just waits. Children are supposed to call their parents. It always feels like it's a test of my love and loyalty. It never occurs to her to call and find out how I am.

T: You sound understandably angry.

P: I am angry at her, but I'm more angry at myself. I keep hearing her voice in my head that tells me to call her or I'm not being a good daughter. Sometimes I try to ignore the voice and then I feel guilty. Then, when I do call her, I wind up feeling worse. Our conversations are not natural. I feel that she's punishing me in some way. It's like she's not going to care about me unless I stand on my head to show her that I care about her. In her mind, my being in New York definitely shows that I don't care about her or anyone else but myself.

T: What happened on this call?

P: It was strained as usual. She made some sarcastic comment about my not calling her because of my busy life, but she never asked me about my work or what I was doing. She brought me up to date about what was going on with other family members. I suppose that's a good thing right now. I never told them that I had to leave my faculty position. I can't cope with what she would say.

T: What do you imagine that would be?

P: I don't think she would feel bad for me. She'd probably be happy in some way like I deserved it for trying to get ahead. She would-n't say that exactly, but it would be in her tone of voice. Then she would probably expect me to come home for a while. That would be a disaster.

T: It must be difficult for you to feel that you not only can't turn to her for support but that she would be happy that you ran into difficulty instead of feeling good if you succeeded.

P: I've gotten used to it.

T: Does that mean you don't have feelings about it? You look sad.

P: I try to push the feelings away. What good does it do for me to dwell on them? She's always been like that as far back as I can remember.

T: What was it like for you?

P: I always felt that I was doing something wrong. She would make fun of me for liking school and wanting to read or even doing my homework. No one would help me. They never talked about anything going on in the world. They must have read the news-paper or listened to the news. They weren't stupid people. She would have been happier if I was content to do work on the farm and go to family events and marry someone who lived nearby. That's their life. That's what my siblings have done for the most part. One of my brothers moved away but he's still nearby in the next state and can drive home on a weekend if need be. . . . In truth, their marriages are all pretty awful. I think that my oldest brother is abusive, and he and my sister-in-law both have a drinking problem. Who knows what they are really like? My parents would never talk about the bad stuff.

Later in the session, the therapist returned to a discussion of Carol's desire to make something of herself.

T: It's sad that you not only were never encouraged to develop your abilities but were made to feel bad about your ambitions. It took a lot of strength from you and support from others to help you withstand your family's influence.

P: Do you think it was strength?

T: I guess you don't. It took a lot for you to persevere in the face of their lack of support.

P: They've always told me that I am selfish. Sometimes I think that they are right.

T: A child shouldn't have to feel that pursuing her own abilities and dreams is disloyal and a rejection of her family's values. You've had to pay a high price for being yourself.

P: I owed them something for giving birth to me and taking care of me.

T: It sounds as if your mother is talking.

P: She did used to say that to me but it's true, isn't it?

T: How would you feel about this if it were your child? Would you feel that your child should sacrifice being who she is because of what she owes you?

P: I'd want to give my children every opportunity to develop themselves. That's what I would want for them, and I would love them no matter what. [Starts crying]

T: You should have had that for yourself.

P: They make me choose between them and what I want from life. I am selfish for having chosen what I want.

T: There are certain kinds of selfishness that are healthy.

P: I was different from my siblings. I don't know why. I just never wanted what I was supposed to want. My parents both feel that children are supposed to make their parents' lives easier. I wanted to make them happy, but I didn't fit in with what they wanted. I could never make them understand that. I tried to include them. I didn't want to keep them out of my life until I couldn't take their reaction to me any longer. I didn't want to reject them. It took me a long time before I just compartmentalized my life and never talked about what I was interested in or what I was doing. . . . Thank heavens that there were other people in my life whom I could talk to and who were encouraging of me then. But maybe if they hadn't been there, I would never have had the nerve to leave home and my family would have been happier and more accepting of me.

T: What would that have been like for you?

P: Maybe I would have been happier. I know that's ridiculous. I don't know what would have happened to me if I had stayed there. I'd probably have become an alcoholic, like my sis-ter-in-law. But leaving home has certainly not led to my being happy. I've made a mess of things.

T: You have had a long-standing conflict about pursuing your am-bitions that has had a lot to do with the problems that you have encountered in your work life and personal relationships. It's likely that you haven't ever felt entitled to succeed or to let yourself have a family of your own.

In the sessions that followed, the therapist and the patient revisited this topic repeatedly as well as the issue of Carol's self-esteem fluctu-ations and feelings of fraudulence.

P: How do I know that I'm really cut out to be an academic? Maybe I've been kidding myself all these years.

T: Have you ever considered that this feeling you have of kidding yourself is your parents talking? Others have recognized your abilities and encouraged you. I guess their voices are not as loud as those of your family.

P: I know you think that when I am having trouble writing it's not about a lack of ability but about my letting my parents' voices stop me. I just feel so stupid when I can't write.

T: That's not a good feeling, but at those moments you seem to for-get the times you have been able to write and have felt good about your accomplishments.

P: I do forget. . . . A friend of mine was talking about being proud of herself because she had finished a difficult project she had been working on. I thought to myself that she was so lucky to be able to feel a sense of pride. I wish I could feel that way.

T: Often it's hard to feel pride in ourselves if the people close to us when we're growing up do not show their pride in us. You also expect yourself to be able to do everything yourself immediately and don't have patience with yourself and with the process you have to go through when you write something and it does not flow smoothly.

P: I'm sure it's easy for you.

T: What makes you thinks so?

P: You write a lot. I looked you up on the Internet.

T: How did that make you feel?

P: Good. It made me feel that you could help me.

T: Is it important for you to think it's easy for me?

P: I don't think so. I don't want you to be perfect. I wish you could tell me that it's been hard for you too. I think it would make me feel more hopeful.

T: Well, it has been hard.

P: Really? You are not just saying that?

T: I'm not just saying that. I don't think it has been as difficult for me as it is for you, but writing has never come easily for me. It's not as difficult as it used to be because I know that I can do it. I've had to learn to get past my frustration when I get stuck and to help myself get started if I'm overwhelmed by a difficult or important project.

P: What do you do?

T: Different things. Sometimes I take a rest and try to clear my mind. Listening to music or going out for a walk or for lunch helps. At other times, I just put down any thoughts that I have without trying to make them coherent. After a while, they begin to take on some form that I can use.

P: It feels good to talk about this with you.

In a session during this period, Carol emphasized her own failure when she again talked about her past problems meeting the demands of being a faculty member.

T: It's true that you have had some issues that contributed to your difficulties, but you also seem to underestimate the demands made on you. It used to be a lot easier for faculty to get tenure in many places. Now the pressures on faculty are very great, particularly in the highly rated schools.

P: I always wanted to be at the best. It felt good to have my former position, although there were times when I wondered what I was doing there. I used to feel that way sometimes when I was in college. I would sit in the library, stare at the books, and think that I had fooled the admissions committee. I worried that they would find out that I didn't belong there. I guess I've had to prove to myself that I can do it.

T: It's a burden to have to try to prove yourself. What would it mean if you worked at a school that was good but not necessarily the best? Do you think it would make you feel bad about yourself?

P: Probably. But I feel pretty bad not working in my field. I don't think I would feel worse than I do now working as a word processor. Maybe I've been too black and white in the way I've thought about this. Either I'm a great success or a failure.

T: There are other schools in the world besides the one where you were. There are environments that are a little more humane and that value teaching as well as publishing. They're disappearing but they still exist.

P: I have to think about this more.

After months of agonizing, Carol decided that she did want to pursue an academic career and talked about the type of school that might be good for her and what she could do to strengthen her application.

P: I've been thinking that it's worth a try for me to apply to a school that is not as pressured as those in the top echelon and that values teaching and doesn't expect people to publish quite as much or in the crème de la crème journals. It would be a bit of a comedown, but I realize that the important thing is for me to get another position in which I have a chance to succeed rather than set myself up for failure. I've probably put too much emphasis on being at the best place in order to prove something to myself and my family.

T: That's an important realization. Do you have some ideas about places to which you might want to apply?

P: I took your suggestion and called some faculty members I've met over the years who are at other schools to get their ideas. They were very helpful. One of them said she thought there were some positions coming up at her school, which is in Connecticut. I could commute if I had a car. I do have a license.

In the next session, Carol brought up her plan to work on an article for publication that she had put aside earlier.

P: I thought it would be good if I could submit a few papers for pub-lication by the time I start applying for another a faculty posi-tion. It would give me more confidence, and I think it would show that I am serious and can be productive. I have to be able to explain why I didn't get tenure without selling myself short. I have to convince them that they should hire me.

T: It's good that you are looking forward and trying to help your-self. Do you have some thoughts about what you could write?

P: I have that one paper that was returned to me for revisions that I never made, and I have an idea for a sequel to that paper that I think I could develop if I could get to work. I still am procrasti-nating. I start out with good intentions, and the day goes by without my doing anything.

T: Can I do something to help you get started?

P: [Looks surprised] You can't write the papers for me. It would be nice if you could.

T: You once told me that it helped you to talk over your ideas with your peers.

P: There's isn't anyone with whom I can do that right now.

T: Would it help if we talked about your ideas? I'm not in your field, but I certainly would be interested.

P: [Looks excited] I would really like you to see the paper that I wrote, and the critique and suggested revisions. Would you be willing to take a look at them? I don't know if you have the time. I don't expect you to give me any ideas. I just think it would give me some moral support and help me tackle making the changes.

T: I'd be glad to.

The following session occurred after the therapist had had a chance to read Carol's paper.

P: I'm afraid to ask you what you thought of the paper.

T: Actually, I really enjoyed it. The paper shows a passion for your subject. You have a nice way of making some of your ideas come alive with your examples, and I learned something. I could see the wisdom of your editor's comments, but her suggestions for revisions seem very minor.

P: [Looks pleased] You know, when I reread her critique, I couldn't understand why I got so depressed that I didn't make the changes right away. What she said seemed pretty benign.

T: You must have been feeling so bad about yourself that any criticism at all felt devastating and overwhelming.

P: I must be feeling better. Just looking at the paper again for the first time made me see that I could handle it.

T: You sound motivated.

P: [Explains] I don't think it would take me very long to do the revisions.

T: That seems reasonable, but it's important not to set yourself up to get discouraged if it takes you a little longer than you think it will. Of course, you are not me, but even writing a few pages takes me longer than I think it will.

P: You know me. I'm glad you said that. I do set myself up.

In the next session, Carol recounted her experiences trying to make the necessary revisions on her paper.

P: You'll be surprised when I tell you what happened. I thought I knew exactly what I was going to do with my paper, and I worked for a while and then got stuck. I couldn't get through it, and I began to get discouraged. I remembered what we had talked about and I went out for lunch. When I came back, I sat down at the computer again and bingo! I had an idea and worked the rest of the afternoon. I actually finished it. All I have to do is clean up a few references and write a cover letter.

T: That's great! I am happy for you.

P: It's funny. I actually liked what I wrote. I think it's good.

Later in the session, Carol brought up her next project.

P: I feel motivated to try to start the sequel before I lose my nerve.

T: Do you want to talk about your ideas?

P: [Shares her thinking] I'm not sure how it will all play out, but I think I know the main ideas I want to communicate.

T: That's really important. That's half the job. I can see from how you explained your ideas to me that you are a really good teacher.

With some expectable writing pains, Carol did complete the second paper within a few months. By this time, she was getting ready to submit her applications for three teaching positions that were available in schools that she had researched and thought would work out for her.

P: I don't know if I'm more frightened of being rejected or of being hired. I'm afraid I will have the same problems as before.
T: It's important to remember that you have been able to write to your own satisfaction in the past few months. In fact, you have done a lot.
P: I do feel good about that, but your being there as a sounding board and cheerleader has helped me. I can't always have you at my side to cheer me on.
T: Well, perhaps you can have me inside.
P: How would that happen?
T: That's not an easy question to answer. A part of the answer is believing in your own abilities and being patient with yourself and knowing that I am proud of your achievements. It's important to find others who can appreciate and encourage you.

A few sessions later, after Carol reported that she had sent in her applications for a faculty position, she began talking about reaching out to others.

P: I've really been ignoring my personal life. I had to put it on hold after I broke off with you-know-who. I haven't really missed him, but I do miss having a companion. I've been withdrawn from friends too, but I am going to try to resurrect a few of my relationships. I know that I have to try to meet some new people and put myself back out there as far as meeting men is concerned. It scares me. I don't think that dating has ever been my strong suit.
T: That's something we can talk about more.
P: I'm afraid I don't know the rules anymore.

T: It hasn't been that long since you have dated.

P: It feels like it has.

T: It's difficult to start over.

P: You can say that again. I also don't know what I have the right to expect. I'm not getting any younger, and there are such losers out there.

T: It's good that you are thinking about it. You must be feeling better about yourself.

8
COUNTERTRANSFERENCE, SELF-DISCLOSURE, AND THE REWARDS OF TREATMENT
An Epilogue

Having been a clinician all my adult life, I have traversed midlife with my patients. Trying to convey the struggles of the midlife patients with whom I have worked over the years has been a long journey. The writing process has reminded me of the treatment of particular patients with whom I may have experienced lapses in empathy, painful emotions, and self-doubts. As I found myself sometimes questioning my own solutions to problems, the work also renewed old battles that I had thought I had won and left behind. Some of my reactions undoubtedly were connected to my own degree of self-awareness and mastery of the issues my patients were facing, level of comfort with myself and my life at any given time, and my ability to allow myself to experience, but not become overwhelmed by, my patients' distress.

Notwithstanding the personal discomfort that this work entailed at times, it has been extremely gratifying to be a part of a process in which patients regained their self-esteem, strengthened their self-structures, moved forward in their lives, and discovered new or renewed sources of satisfaction and pleasure. In what follows, I offer some reflections on the challenges and rewards of being a midlife therapist who works with midlife patients.

Countertransference Challenges

Kohut (1984) viewed self-actualization as an important result of self-psychological treatment and held a less prescriptive and normative view of mental health than did more traditional treatment frameworks. He did not see conformity to society's expectations as the sine qua non of healthy functioning, nor did he view difference from the norm as equated with pathology. It is not always easy to be aware of and able to put aside one's own values, attitudes, and biases so as to appreciate the subjectivity of one's patients and help them go their own way.

In the course of my work, I encountered patients whose backgrounds, life situations, and characteristic ways of coping were radically different from mine and who sometimes taxed my empathic capacities. There also were many persons whose life events and experiences paralleled my own, fortunately not always at the same time. Although our similarities may have deepened my ability to grasp the nature of their plight, it also resulted in my having to confront unsettling feelings of various sorts and degrees of intensity about my own recent past, present, and future. It is likely that the sameness that I may have felt with certain patients may have resulted in collusions, blind spots, and outright mistakes. As Stolorow and Atwood (1992, pp. 103–122) remind us, although instances of serious misattunement often occur when the therapist cannot empathize with a patient who is very different from the therapist, a more subtle but often just as problematic countertransference problem arises when the therapist feels too identified with the patient. The seeming similarity between the midlife therapist and the midlife patient may result in the therapist's failure to grasp and appreciate essential features of the patient's life that are different from those of the therapist or may result in an overvaluing of the therapist's solutions.

The following two examples illustrate some of my own struggles with difference and sameness.

A Lapse of Empathy with a Patient's Rage and Confrontational Stance

Bella, a 53-year-old, European-born, married woman, entered treatment after having been deeply insulted and hurt by Ruth, the wife of her husband's business partner, who seemed to be allied with Ruth against Bella. Bella wanted an apology, which was not forthcoming. An extremely tense situation ensued in the family-owned business, and Bella's husband, who was not part of the family, felt concerned that his position was threatened. Additionally, Bella and her husband no longer felt welcome at social events and vacations that the family organized. Marital discord escalated between Bella and her husband, who was furious at her for making problems. He wanted her to "keep quiet" and try to "make peace." In turn, Bella became enraged at her husband for not supporting her and for being "weak" in his customary manner. He prevailed on her not to implement her plan to go to the patriarch of the family, who headed the business, and to tell her side of the story. He felt that Bella would make his situation worse.

"What about me? He doesn't care about me and what I'm feeling. I'm supposed to shut up. . . . Ruth has won. She has succeeded in pushing me out, and I'm afraid she'll find a way of getting rid of my husband too. I'm worried that his days in the business are numbered because the old man can't go on forever. If he dies, Ruth will make sure that my husband goes. Then where will we be? He won't be able to get another position like this one, and he will blame me besides. We're not getting any younger. I'm making myself sick. He wants to put his head in the sand, but I can see the writing on the wall. I can't just pretend this never happened but I'm afraid to go against him. I don't know what to do."

Bella went on to say that she felt that Ruth was making her look bad even though she was right and that she could not stand not speaking out. She felt that she was going against her own values and allowing herself to be victimized. "What also bothers me is that I have been in this place before." She described many incidents in her life when she felt that she had been wronged for trying to do the right thing. The most painful of these seemed to revolve around her relationship with her family of origin and a disastrous set of circumstances that resulted in her becoming estranged from them to protect herself from their wrath. Bella felt that she was doing something wrong. It later became apparent that what Bella meant by "wrong" was that she did not know how to protect herself from untrustworthy and unstable people who took what they could from her and then turned on her.

Prior to seeking individual treatment, Bella had convinced her husband to enter couples therapy with her, but this experience was very difficult for Bella, who became furious at the therapist and stopped after a few sessions. According to Bella, the marital therapist, a well-known professional woman, suggested that Bella's rage at Ruth was out of proportion to the situation. The therapist said that Bella's perpetuation of her problems with Ruth and her wish to confront the head of the business with the "truth" about what had transpired were totally insensitive to her husband and to what was appropriate, given the mores of the family business.

Although she did not agree with the couples therapist's reported intervention, the individual therapist could understand the former's sentiments. Listening to Bella, she, too, found herself feeling more sympathetic to Bella's husband than to Bella and experiencing a strong impulse to try to reinforce Bella's self-restraint. The therapist's initial impression was that Bella was a strong-willed woman who seemed confident in her convictions about right and wrong, was in the midst of a narcissistic rage that had begun with Ruth's failure to appreciate that Bella's efforts to help her came from a good rather than a controlling place, and with Ruth's angry attack on Bella's motivations. It seemed that Ruth probably did feel rivalrous with and envious of Bella, but it was evident also that Bella was unaware of how her attitudes and behavior had provoked Ruth's angry outbursts, Bella's husband's displeasure with her part in the rift, and

his failure to validate and support her position. Although she imagined that he did have a characteristically passive and nonconfrontational stance, she thought that his wish to try to smooth over the
situation, given his tenuous position in the business, was more than
understandable, despite its impact on Bella. What also seemed important was that the current situation seemed to repeat and highlight
a core issue for Bella that involved her own parents and sister and left
her feeling like a bad person, to which she reacted by needing to
prove that she was right.

Although the therapist thought she understood preliminarily that
Bella's self had been assaulted in a profound way, like the couples
therapist, she was concerned that Bella seemed to have little insight
or concern about how her actions might make her husband's situation worse and that she was moving toward being out of control. The
therapist knew that it was important to stay connected to Bella's
rage, her wish to stand up for herself, and her desire to expose her en-
emies and gradually to explore the current situation's link to Bella's
experience in her own family. She suggested that it was important for
Bella to gain some understanding of what the current situation
meant to her, particularly in the light of past experiences with her
family, and to take some time to consider what she wanted to do.

The therapist's initial intervention was not inappropriate, but it
was based on her anxiety. Although she tried in subsequent sessions
to be empathic with Bella, she was aware of feeling judgmental of
Bella's confrontational style, which was significantly different from
the therapist's usual approach to avoiding or diffusing conflict. The
therapist was also irked by Bella's insensitivity to others. These reactions on the therapist's part made it difficult for her to proceed at
Bella's pace and gain a more complete understanding of Bella's subjectivity and selfobject needs. Uncharacteristically, the therapist
prematurely focused on exploring the origins of Bella's extreme
needs for validation and vindication rather than on empathizing
with her sense of injury and learning more about how Bella saw herself and her life. After several weeks, Bella almost ended the treatment because she did not feel that the therapist truly "got her" and
that, like everyone else, the therapist wanted her to keep quiet. "You
think that it's bad that I want to defend myself and expose Ruth?"
The therapist knew she had to take a step back. Later she realized

that her own anxieties and nonconfrontational style were getting in the way of a sound and attuned therapeutic approach. Fortunately, she was able to acknowledge her mistake, and Bella was able to give her another chance.

In the therapist's renewed attempt to relate to Bella's concerns, she began to appreciate that Bella possessed a keen sense of justice and injustice. Bella felt a responsibility to speak out rather than remain silent in the face of what she experienced as unfair. She prided herself on doing this, even if it was at her own expense at times. In some ways she saw self-protection as a "cop-out" and viewed those who took the easy was as being morally challenged. Bella's need to confront a seeming injustice was overdetermined. It seemed to stem not only from her sense of victimization in her own family, but also from her experience of the aftermath of the Holocaust and the effects of the spread of Russia's totalitarian power in Eastern-bloc countries. She identified with those who stood up for what was right and risked their lives. She also suffered some survivor guilt. Bella's fighting for herself had helped her get through life, although it also had negative consequences for her. At a deeper level, which became more apparent only after a considerable period of time, Bella also experienced a profound sense of having done something wrong, which she covered over by a sense of moral superiority and a need to be right.

Perhaps paradoxically but not surprisingly, as the therapist became more able to connect to Bella's subjective experience and to appreciate her lifelong struggle, Bella's acute sense of injury lessened in intensity, and she became less urgent about having to right the wrong that was occurring in her personal life. She continued, though, to feel that she had been "wronged" and would eventually take some action to rectify the situation.

A Blind Spot Related to Overidentification

Jan was an attractive 43-year-old nontenured faculty member at a local private university. She entered treatment because of blocks she was having in writing for publication. She also was in the throes of depression. She worked in a field related to the therapist's, the therapist also being an academic. Coincidentally, they had grown up in the same Midwestern city and attended the same college and university. More important, there were aspects to Jan's upbringing and relationship with her family with which the therapist identified. As a child and adolescent, Jan never had much encouragement and support for her academic interests and abilities from her family. She lacked nurturing and was largely ignored, unlike her brothers, who were the "stars." Fortunately, Jan was well liked by her teachers, whom she eagerly sought out, and their responsiveness to her helped her. These similarities contributed to the therapist's feeling an unusual sense of familiarity with Jan's work issues and background. Therapist and patient quickly formed a positive connection that had elements of a twinship transference and countertransference.

After two years of treatment, Jan had made considerable progress in her writing and was receiving excellent feedback about her work from senior faculty. Students eagerly sought to be in her classes and she had superior teaching evaluations. Although she still felt upset about not having a long-term relationship or more friends, she was less depressed and able to get more satisfaction from her work, cultural interests, and her few close relationships.

At this time, she became embroiled in a work-related intrigue that potentially threatened her position. She became extremely upset about what she described as her coworkers' attempts to sabotage her by spreading false rumors about her relationships with her students—these relationships were being labeled as "inappropriate." She acknowledged to the therapist that she had made a mistake by having an end-of-term party for one of her graduate-level classes at her apartment. Nothing inappropriate had occurred, and all seemed to enjoy themselves. It had never occurred to her that having the party at her apartment could be misconstrued, for this had not been an unusual practice on the part of some of her teachers in graduate school. In retrospect, she realized that having extended herself in this way seemed to arouse the envy of some of her colleagues because of her good relationships with her students, particularly when some of the students who had attended the party spoke about how great it was to have a faculty member who extended herself to them. Jan was mortified and angry about the unfair rumors. She could not believe that her colleagues had stooped so low.

She was terrified that her dean would form an unfavorable impression of her that would go against her and cause her to not have her contract renewed. She knew she had to speak to the dean but felt anxious that, even if she succeeded in getting the dean on her side, the few faculty members that she thought were against her would continue to cause problems for her. For several months prior to this incident, she had been aware that they were giving her a hard time in faculty meetings and committees; she felt uncomfortable but shrugged off their behavior as part of academic "nonsense." When Jan spoke about this in her therapy sessions, the therapist, whose own academic experiences had clearly taught her that faculty members are rivalrous with and envious of one another, particularly of those who are successful, accepted Jan's judgment about the situation. Likewise, the therapist remembered that, when Jan had mentioned the party in passing in one session, the therapist had not thought anything of it other than that it was a nice thing to do.

Listening to her patient's story about what was occurring at school, the therapist felt distressed for Jan but also began to question herself. She did not think that Jan had done anything wrong or inappropriate but wondered if she herself had been remiss in some way in the treatment. This concern continued to bother her after the session, and she gave it considerable thought. She recognized that she identified strongly with Jan's success and felt very warmly toward her. Although the treatment was exploratory and interpretive, the therapist had used herself to mirror selected aspects of Jan's talents and abilities. The therapist recognized that she had imbued Jan with aspects of her own idealized self-concept and with other characteristics that the therapist wished she possessed. This realization prompted the therapist to exercise some denial of the dangers of academic life and to help her patient anticipate and navigate these in a better way. Likewise, the therapist, who had been responsive to Jan's need for validation and encouragement in the treatment, may have missed and failed to explore how Jan's neediness for mirroring from others was having a negative impact on those others.

Jan was able to diffuse the problem by having a talk with the dean, who turned out to be quite supportive but who also advised her to be mindful of respecting the boundaries between faculty and students to a greater degree. She also suggested that Jan not take her colleagues' behavior too seriously but that she might put a little more effort into her relationships with them.

This incident was a turning point in the therapy, as both therapist and patient became more focused on Jan's long-standing problems with peer relationships. Although she had a few close friends, she had difficulty reaching out to others and often felt uninterested in their concerns. From childhood, Jan had felt that she was different from and not accepted by others and spent a lot of time by herself. Although the therapist was aware of this issue, she had not made it a central part of the treatment. Instead, she opted for helping Jan with the more immediate issues related to her writing and depression. The therapist also realized that her minimizing this facet of Jan's life stemmed, in part, from her own way of coping with some of the disappointments she had experienced with peers and colleagues.

Anxiety about Aging and Life's Vicissitudes

In addition to confronting therapists with issues related to difference and sameness, the treatment of midlife patients may force them to face their own anxieties about life. All of us are vulnerable to this period's vicissitudes—career concerns, dissatisfaction with one's life or relationships, loss, illness, aging. Nor are any of us immune from the abundant fears and assaults associated with contemporary life. This was made abundantly clear when therapists and patients met with one another after the terrorist attacks on 9/11, which seemed to bring about a necessary blurring of some of the usual boundaries between them as they both struggled to cope with the meaning and impact of the event and its residue of fear and anxiety. The powerful nature of 9/11 compelled therapists to be more available to and more real with their patients, particularly with respect to disclosing their reactions, fears, symptoms, and coping strategies and in being more there for them in concrete ways. The tragedy seemed to force therapists to reexamine their use of themselves in the therapeutic process. It dramatized and brought to light some of the issues that occur in a less obvious way when therapists and patients share similar life experiences and concerns.

Vulnerability to Anxiety

Eileen was a 56-year-old, recently retired professional in the education field who had been in treatment for five years because of generalized anxiety and depression about getting older and being alone.
Although prone to obsessional thoughts and superstitious rituals
based on her phobic tendencies, Eileen had not been in treatment
previously, except for a six-month stint in a research study involving
the use of a new antidepressant coupled with cognitive therapy. Receiving minimal help from this course of treatment, she decided to
try a more psychodynamic psychotherapy.

Eileen lived alone and had a few close friends with whom she so-
cialized. Her parents were in their early 80s and lived in a condomin-
ium complex in Florida. She spoke to her mother several times a
week and visited them dutifully three times a year. She had one married brother who lived in a nearby state and was fairly close to his wife
and children although she saw them infrequently and described him
as overburdened by troubles in the marriage and his work life. Eileen
identified as a heterosexual woman but had never experienced a
long-term relationship with a man. She had not been eager to marry
when she was younger. When she finally realized she might be alone
all her life, she felt she was too old to do anything about it.

Eileen's main fears were related to her preoccupation with her
health, her aging parents' eventual physical deterioration and death,
and her not having children who would look after her if she became
more dependent as she grew older. She felt that she had never attained work or financial success. She hated her job in the New York
City school system and could not wait to retire. She loved cultural
events and attended plays, concerts, and the ballet frequently. Attendance at these performances was her only self-indulgence, as she
tended to have trouble doing nice things for herself, lest she be punished in some way if she enjoyed herself too much. Not allowing herself to have too much pleasure was the way that she bargained with
God not to make something really bad happen. Consequently she
lived in what she regarded as a "dump," refrained from going on
vacations, and rarely spent money on herself.

The therapist was approximately five years older than the patient.
At the time Eileen entered treatment, the therapist's 81-year-old

mother lived alone in another city. She was still independent, reasonably physically healthy, and mentally intact given her age. The
therapist felt successful professionally and personally and had a good
life, which she enjoyed. But she did not have siblings whom she could
count on or children of her own. Although she was aware of her own
concerns about her mother and her own aging, she was not prone to
worrying and felt she could handle whatever would arise.

For most of the treatment, the therapist did not experience
Eileen's anxieties as contagious and was able to listen to her endless
fears and explore the developmental factors that seemed to be at the
core of how Eileen managed her life. In contrast to the cognitive
therapist's attempts to reason with Eileen about her anxieties and superstitious behavior, the current therapist used her closeness in age
to Eileen; their common life-stage experiences; her recognition of
the arbitrary, uncertain, and tenuous nature of life; and her awareness of some of the sources of her own manageable anxiety to relate to
the patient's concerns. This approach seemed to be reassuring to the
patient, who felt that she was not crazy and the therapist could understand her. She seemed able to use the therapist's empathy, self-
disclosures, and calmness, as well as her new insights into her own
background, gradually to give up some of her need to try to control
life and death and to allow herself some greater pleasure.

In the midst of the treatment, the September 11 terrorist attack on
the World Trade Center took place. In the weeks that followed,
Eileen was terrified, as were almost all the therapist's patients. The
therapist was not immune from this severe anxiety, although she
found herself sufficiently composed to be there for all her patients.
She was able to listen to their fears; deal with their sense of loss, grief,
and rage; share their concerns; and offer some suggestions about how
to deal with their anxieties. Without being flooded with emotion or
having to cut off from her feelings, she and her patients could explore
what the attacks had triggered in terms of their core issues.

In her work with Eileen, however, the therapist was aware of
feeling acutely anxious as Eileen filled the sessions with nightmarish scenarios of how the terrorists could attack in the future. She
verbally drew vivid accounts of the photographs and films of the
event. Not wanting to inhibit Eileen's expression of her fears, the
therapist found it very difficult to listen to her; the therapist's

mind clearly was elsewhere at times in the sessions. Only after quite a few sessions did the therapist realize that Eileen actually wanted to see the therapist's anxiety in a palpable way. Thus she could reassure herself that she was not crazy and that she was trying to regain some control of a world gone out of control by going over the graphic details of the attack and anticipating future ones. When the therapist was able to convey her realization, Eileen slowly began to become calmer herself.

About two years later, the therapist became more concerned about her now 86-year-old mother, who seemed to be more withdrawn socially than was customary and who seemed to be complaining more about her various aches and pains, none of which turned out to be symptomatic of serious health problems. At this time, three of the therapist's close friends, several colleagues at the university, and two of her patients were struggling with the physical and mental deterioration, need for increased caretaking, and deaths of their elderly parents. This problem seemed to be of epidemic proportions. Although the therapist had been able to compartmentalize her concerns about her own mother's health to a significant degree, she found herself having more frequent visions of interrupting her practice and teaching to attend to her mother's needs. And she was more resentful of her brother's ability to ignore and remove himself from the situation.

In the throes of this escalation of the therapist's anxiety, Eileen returned from Florida after having spent several weeks there following the disastrous multihurricane season of 2004. Eileen was agitated and depressed about her Florida experience and filled her sessions with graphic details of her parents' helplessness, physical incapacities, housing problems, and fear during the hurricanes and afterward. She described how they would have died of neglect if she had not been there. She gave horrific accounts of how health professionals and other so-called service people were totally incompetent. Although Eileen had returned home, she felt that her worst nightmare was coming true, and she did not know what she was going to do in the near future to protect her parents. She knew that they were going to die soon, but to her that was secondary to thinking that they would be powerless if they needed help. Finally, Eileen said that she had located a private geriatric care agency that she was going to contact to see what services they could provide. The therapist found herself flooded by Eileen's account of her parents' and her own harrowing experiences. Uncharacteristically, the therapist fidgeted incessantly in the session and wished for it to be over quickly. Although she was able to calm herself and regain her equilibrium later and in subsequent sessions with Eileen, this episode was humbling and confronted the therapist with her own vulnerability.

A Therapist's Selfobject Needs

Countertransference issues also arise when therapists' vulnerability in midlife puts them at risk of looking to patients to meet the therapists' needs or to fulfill selfobject functions. Sometimes therapists participate in, or even recreate, their patients' earlier problematic relationships. Therapists who are themselves experiencing a loss of narcissistic supplies or blows to their sense of self may need their patients' applause, idealization, validation, affirmation, and twinship. Or, as parents may have done earlier in their own lives, therapists may burden their patients with performance expectations to bolster their own professional self-esteem. They may seek intimacy with or power over the patients; they may seduce the patients emotionally only to frustrate and reject them. Or therapists may find themselves violating sexual boundaries. As Maroda (1999) notes, a therapist's own personality and past can get together with the patient's need for pathological forms of enactment, creating a serious therapeutic problem that makes it difficult to know who is doing what to whom.

Sometimes the vulnerability that therapists experience in midlife makes them envious of their patients for being able to enjoy their desired lifestyles and occupational or professional activities. Therapists may envy the new opportunities and relationships their patients enjoy. The patients' health and energy, financial success, and certain attitudes toward life are enviable, too. Then, too, there can be vicarious enjoyment in working with certain patients whose lives seem more interesting or fulfilling than our own. The termination process may be particularly difficult for us when patients either have fulfilled selfobject needs or provide vicarious outlets.

A complicated issue that arises in the treatment of midlife patients is how to help them to make choices or changes in their lives
when these changes create anxiety in us or go against our values.
Such may be the case when we are working with a patient who wants
to divorce because of feeling trapped after many years of marriage or
who is engaged in a extramarital affair. A patient may desire to have a
child as a single parent. He or she may decide to leave a frustrating
job without having obtained a new one. A patient may contemplate
early retirement or want to make a geographic change that necessi-
tates leaving familiar supports behind. It has been suggested that
therapists can help patients go only as far as we have gone ourselves.
Although this idea may not be completely true, it bears careful
consideration.

Therapist Self-Disclosure

When midlife therapists and patients have faced similar life events
and issues, in an effort to be helpful, the therapists may feel the impulse to share what they feel to be their wisdom or experience. This
type of self-disclosure can be beneficial, but not always. I have written elsewhere about the rationale and suggested guidelines for therapist disclosures of this and other kinds (Goldstein, 1994). Despite
increasing attention to this subject in recent years, this is still
unchartered territory, and well-intentioned and sensitive therapists
will make mistakes.

In the following example, the therapist, who had recovered from
having experienced a painful period of grief, disclosed her experience in response to her patient's questioning.

Promoting Hope and the
Courage to Start Over

Angela, a 45-year-old lesbian high school teacher, sought treatment
almost two years after the loss of Emily, her partner of 15 years, who
died of cancer after a long illness. Angela felt depressed and hopeless
about the future. She said that, in some ways, she felt worse than

when Emily first died because she had become more socially isolated and felt angry at anyone whose life was going on. "Even worse, maybe they do know and don't want to be around me," she said. She thought of Emily all the time and that made her feel better temporarily until she remembered that Emily was dead. Angela had not given away Emily's clothes or possessions because they comforted her. "Most of the time I feel dead and that I'm going through the motions of life. I'm really worried about myself. I can't go on like this. I'm not getting any better. I walk around in a fog. I almost got hit by a car last week. I don't know if you can do anything to help me."

The therapist, whose partner had died some years earlier, also had experienced a painful grief process followed by a new and rewarding beginning. She was touched by Angela's plight. She conveyed her empathy and concern for Angela's sense of loss and despair but also held out hope that she would recover: "Sometimes when you lose someone you love, a part of you seems to die." In their second session, Angela said, "I felt better after we spoke. You seemed to understand what it's like for me. You encouraged me to talk about Emily so I felt like she was present, and you didn't seem put off by my pain."

It seemed that Angela was experiencing Emily's death as a loss of part of herself. She had looked to Emily to fulfill her selfobject needs for a sister or twin, and Emily's presence bolstered Angela's fragile sense of self. Significant in Angela's history was that she had grown up in a disconnected and disengaged family and looked to those out-side the family for support and nurturance. She had always longed for a sister, who she thought would be her close companion. Raised in a small town, she had no positive lesbian role models, and she moved to New York after graduation from college. In New York City, she of-ten experienced considerable loneliness but had trouble reaching out to others. After becoming involved with Emily, whom she met through work, Angela felt happy for the first time in her life. Emily was more outgoing and sociable than Angela. They had a close, but by no means trouble-free, relationship. Angela felt that she was too dependent on Emily, who was also fairly controlling and dominating in the relationship.

Once a selfobject transference of a twinship nature was estab-lished between us, Angela began to feel less alone and to be more present. She looked forward to coming to sessions as if they were her lifeline, even though she often used them to share her pain and sense of despair about ever being able to find love again. She seemed to feel reassured by the therapist's empathizing with her feelings and experiences. At one point, the following dialogue occurred.

P: Sometimes I feel you understand me so well that it makes me think you have gone through a similar experience. Have you?

T: I'll answer that if you really want me to, but I'd like to know what it would mean to you if that were true.

P: I'd feel bad that you suffered too, but it would be comforting in a way.

T: How so?

P: Well, it would mean that you survived somehow. You seem so upbeat but not in a fake way. I mean you seem to understand my pain, but it doesn't pull you down.

T: I did experience the loss of my partner.

P: I'm sorry. When?

T: About 10 years ago. It was very hard for several years. I didn't think I would ever recover, but I did.

P: Did you ever find someone else? I hope you did.

T: Yes. We've been together for seven years now.

P: That's wonderful.

T: How does what I've said make you feel?

P: I'm glad you found someone. That gives me hope. Maybe it is possible to start over and have a good life. Did it take a long time?

T: It felt like a long time, but it took about three years.

P: Maybe I don't have so much more time to go. [Laughs]

T: I wonder if you have other feelings about what I told you?

P: I don't think so. I feel good that you trusted me.

Soon after this session, Angela set about sorting out and giving away some of Emily's possessions and reaching out to old friends. She began to explore her tendencies to lose herself, and she started to examine her fear of being "taken over" by others, as well as her guilty attachment to her mother, which heightened when she left home and became more open in her lesbianism. At a later phase of the treatment, the therapist encouraged Angela to pursue interests that she had set aside much earlier in her life. Feeling stronger in herself,

Angela expressed an interest in dating. She and the therapist discussed what it was like to start over, and they talked about the vicissitudes of her dating experiences. Two years after the treatment began, Angela met a woman on a trip to Europe, and they have been together ever since: "It's like a miracle."

In this example, the therapist's hesitant sharing of her own life experience at the patient's request seemed to mark a positive turning point in the treatment that ushered in the patient's beginning to let go of her deceased partner and embracing life.

During the course of treatment, it is likely that midlife therapists will experience some disturbing life events that intrude on the treatment process directly by interfering with session times and necessitating a brief or prolonged hiatus or indirectly because of the therapist's emotional or physical state. Whether or not therapists disclose the nature of these sometimes traumatic events to patients, they almost always are aware of them, at least unconsciously. This state of affairs raises the questions of what therapists should disclose about their lives and whether there are times when patients need to know what is occurring in the therapist's life rather than be left with their fantasies and anxieties, which they cannot name or discuss. The following example (originally described in Goldstein, 1997) is illustrative.

Repairing a Therapeutic Mistake

In the days before therapeutic self-disclosure was popular, the therapist experienced the illness and eventual death of a close companion. As with many therapists who find themselves in similar situations, her work helped her to get through this time. It never occurred to her to disclose her loss to patients because she thought that any self-disclosure of this kind would be intrusive or burdensome. Nevertheless, some patients must have sensed that something was wrong. The truth of this disquieting realization was brought home when Patsy, a 48-year-old patient who had moved to another city upon remarrying, asked for an appointment in order to touch base when she came back to New York City for a visit two years after termination.

In this second treatment, she had a mainly idealizing transference, and, although she might have benefited from more treatment, she made substantial progress even in sessions. During the brief reunion, Patsy asked if the therapist had been going through a difficult time during the end of her previous treatment. Unprepared for her question, the therapist responded that she was not sure what was prompting the question. Patsy said that she had often thought about the last few months of treatment. She felt that the therapist seemed sad at times, and Patsy regretted not having questioned her about this. When the therapist asked what this meant to her, Patsy explained that she first thought that the sadness had to do with her leaving treatment. Later she thought that more was involved but feared upsetting the therapist. Later, she felt bad that she had not summoned the courage to ask.

A self-reflective woman, Patsy spontaneously connected her reaction to an earlier experience with her mother, who was depressed but stoical after the death of the patient's sister when Patsy was a child. She had often mentioned that she could not make contact with her mother, who seemed to prefer Patsy's sister. Patsy had experienced a sense of guilt for not being sensitive to her mother and felt inadequate that she had not been able to make her happy. Although Patsy appeared to have come a long way in dealing with the impact of her childhood experiences, she episodically felt sad about not having had a chance to redo her relationship with her mother, who died some years earlier.

After terminating treatment, when Patsy found herself feeling regretful about not having asked the therapist about her apparent sadness, she decided that she could rectify the situation because, unlike her mother, the therapist was still alive. Patsy then asked if her suspicion was accurate. The therapist responded that she was glad that Patsy could bring this up and that she regretted not having given her an opportunity to do so earlier. With some hesitation, she told Patsy that someone very close to her had been quite ill and had died. She added that she had not shared this with her at the time because she did not want to burden her. The therapist added that she was sorry that she had not realized that she might be burdening Patsy more by suffering silently. She wondered if Patsy's mother, too, had not wanted to burden Patsy and had made a similar mistake.

The therapist went on to say that she had mixed feelings about Patsy's leaving treatment because, although she herself was happy that she had found a loving partner and felt ready to embark on a new phase of her life, she would miss their work together. Patsy became tearful but looked visibly relieved. She asked if the therapist felt better now, and the therapist replied that she certainly did. Although she tried to explore Patsy's reaction to her response, she did not want to continue the discussion nor did she press for any more details.

A month later, Patsy sent a letter in which she thanked the therapist for having shared with her. She wrote that something had lifted for her, and she was feeling much happier and freer than she ever had felt in her life. It seemed ironic that, although the therapist had originally decided not to self-disclose during the actual treatment, she nevertheless had communicated quite a lot anyway. Moreover, she had unwittingly participated in creating a repetition or enactment of the patient's earlier frustrating interaction with her mother and had failed to provide a new kind of experience.

During the treatment, when the therapist sensed Patsy distancing at times, she might have probed for questions or observations about the therapist that Patsy was reluctant to raise. Such probing could have permitted a more open discussion of what she was experiencing. The interaction also suggests that something in this patient moved her to reach for a better solution than the one she had lived out with her mother. Despite the therapist's mistake, Patsy continued to maintain a positive sense of the therapist and was able to differentiate her from her mother. The question of what might have occurred if the therapist had originally self-disclosed to Patsy during treatment remains unanswered. It is not easy to know how and when to be more real and when to keep quiet.

Although some intersubjective and relational writers have suggested that therapists share their thoughts and feelings with patients as an ongoing part of the treatment process (Renik, 1995; Aron, 1996; Maroda, 1999), there are risks in engaging in self-disclosure too freely without considering the nature of patients' selfobject transference needs. Such risks may arise, for example, when vulnerable therapists who work with particularly despairing, withdrawn, self-absorbed, or devaluing patients who show little progress and are filled with negativity have difficulty making connections or who deny the therapist's separate existence. This can lead to a contagion of despair, therapist detachment, unattuned self-disclosures that invade the patient's space, or demands for too much closeness or progress. Aron (1996) acknowledges that the relational emphasis on therapist and patient having an open dialogue about their relationship and the patient's perceptions of the therapist's personality may be experienced by the patient as intrusive and disruptive and constitute an impingement stemming from the therapist's own narcissistic needs.

Rewards and Transformations

Sometimes midlife patients are able to make significant changes in their lives. Their ability to use the therapeutic process to confront and gain acceptance of themselves, to overcome the obstacles in their lives, and to reach for and fulfill their dreams can be gratifying, if not, inspirational. Their progress and growth, sometimes in the face of a long history of dysfunction and distress, have contributed to making me more sharply aware of the positive edge of midlife and has influenced my attitudes and behavior. At a deeper level, there have been times when the rewards of the work have had unanticipated reparative effects. Such was the case as a result of my work with Anthony, a part of which has been described elsewhere (Goldstein, 2001).

Fulfilling a Dream

Anthony, an unemployed 48-year-old gay man of Sicilian background, sought treatment because of his increasing feelings of worthlessness and hopelessness after having been let go from a company he had worked at for many years. He described himself as a failure and had no hope of being able to turn his work life and finances around. He felt that he had betrayed himself by never becoming a writer, which he attributed to his lack of self-confidence and his fear of taking risks. He was "freaked out" to be approaching 50 and having nothing to show for it. Anthony supported himself financially through unemployment insurance and his male partner's help. He worried that he would not find another job and that he would ruin his 12-year relationship. Anthony said that he had been fired because his work was not up to par and that his performance had started to wane when his immediate superior placed increasing pressure on him to produce. He viewed this position as his last chance to better himself and thought of committing suicide when he was let go. He said he did not have the guts to do so, however, and that it would kill his parents and be unfair to his partner.

Sharing his history, Anthony said that from an early age he had always felt he was a disappointment to his parents, particularly his father. Although he looked tough and could handle himself in fights with other boys, Anthony liked to read rather than become involved in sports and was more sensitive than his older brother. He described feeling like an "oddball." He recalled being intense and moody and felt a sense of alienation from his father, who was emotionally removed and whom he regarded as weak. He described his parents as "good people" basically but "old country" and limited in their awareness of the outside world. His mother was more accessible emotionally but was often depressed. Anthony's father worked for the father's older brothers as a mechanic and expected Anthony to work in the garage, which Anthony hated because his peers called him a "grease monkey" and taunted him for being Sicilian. A studious student in a Catholic school, Anthony felt that the priests favored the kids from Irish backgrounds. Anthony described being aware, from an early age, that Sicilians were looked down on by others, including other Italians. He grew up feeling deeply ashamed of his ethnicity and of being poor. He thought it was ironic that he then had to deal with the third stigma of being gay, which he tried to hide from his family and even from himself.

Anthony had had some superficial friendships and dated women occasionally in high school so as to "fit in," but he tended to keep to himself. He graduated from college but did not pursue graduate studies because he did not feel smart enough and had no funds. After graduation, he worked in a series of jobs in journalism but would become discouraged if he received any criticism about his writing. He felt that he could not compete with his coworkers. He also had trouble supporting himself financially. He took a job in the insurance field that paid better, but he hated the work and lacked the confidence and money to go back to school. He worked for different companies and did try to write some articles for publication on the side. He had some small successes over the years, which only made him feel angry at himself for not being able to pursue his writing more seriously. He mismanaged his finances and accumulated considerable debt, requiring him to declare bankruptcy.

Closeted as a gay man until he was in his 20s, Anthony had had several short-lived relationships, often with straight men, until he met his current partner, whom he viewed as the "best thing" in his life. Although Anthony's parents were initially greatly disapproving of his sexual orientation, they became more accepting of Anthony over the years. Because there were few family members still alive and Anthony's brother and his family lived on the West Coast, Anthony did not have to deal with the potentially negative attitudes of a large extended family.

Anthony felt a sense of despair. He was negative about himself, tended to be anxious and fearful, and lacked confidence. He seemed to have lacked mirroring and encouragement from his parents and teachers, idealizable and positive role models, and those with whom he shared a sense of similarity. He had received negative messages about his ethnicity and sexual orientation from his family and the surrounding social environment that he internalized and that contributed to his negative self-concept. He had to suppress his sexuality and protect himself from others' getting to know him. As an adult, Anthony was highly dependent on the approval of others to feel good about himself, but he felt pressured and anxious if anything was expected of him. He was vulnerable to assaults to his self-esteem and suffered bouts of depression when he received minor criticisms or did not get the recognition he wanted. Although Anthony held strong opinions about many subjects, he was unable to sustain a good feeling about his own talents and capacities, pursue his ambitions, or even maintain a job. When depressed, he engaged in self-sabotaging behavior, the results of which reinforced his negative views of himself. A major positive aspect of his life was his relationship with his partner, a caring and supportive man.

Anthony filled his early sessions with his depressive ruminations and spoke of his sense of alienation from others and his feelings of shame. Because of the emphasis that Anthony placed on his ethnicity and sensing his caution in opening up to the therapist, she asked him if he felt that she could understand and appreciate him even if she did not share his Sicilian American background. Anthony replied that the therapist seemed to be accepting of him, and he had always thought that Jews and Italians got along pretty well. Nevertheless, he continued to be guarded in sessions. He acknowledged that he was not used to sharing what he thought and felt with others and waited for others to draw him out.

Because the therapist felt that Anthony needed some concrete evidence of her ability to enter his world, she revealed that like Anthony, she enjoyed his favorite TV program, *The Sopranos*, and that she had visited and loved Sicily. Anthony and the therapist began to discuss various episodes of the program and he began to share more positive parts of himself with her. He began to use Italian phrases and translated them when the therapist showed interest. He commented humorously on his own personality characteristics, such as his sense of doom and gloom and fatalism, which he identified as characteristic of Sicilians. He brought articles about Italian culture to the sessions, and patient and therapist exchanged views on movies and plays. Later, they discussed all the minute details of the patient's employment search.

In addition to trying to connect with Anthony, the therapist initially empathized with his sense of failure and despair. She explored the origins of his negative self-concept in his early life experiences and interpreted the links between Anthony's past and present. A significant part of the treatment was to help Anthony mourn the person that he might have been, to moderate his feelings of self-blame for having ruined his opportunities for success, and to help him accept where he was in life and start over. The therapist also tried to validate and mirror Anthony's talents and capacities and encourage his creativity and literary interests. Although he began to be more positive about himself and his future, he returned to his morose and hopeless stance when he did not feel that the therapist was completely in tune with him or provided him with the validation that he needed. Instead of pointing out his need for perfect attunement and his hypersensitivity, the therapist was nondefensive about her empathic lapses or insufficient mirroring and empathized with Anthony's feelings. She also linked his need for a strong show of support to the lack of responsiveness by others in his life.

During the six years of Anthony's treatment, he made consider-able progress. After a year, Anthony found a position that utilized some of his writing skills, and he was able to overcome his frequent impulses to leave the job when he felt frustrated or criticized. During the next three years, this position enabled Anthony gradually to get his financial situation under better control, which enhanced his hopefulness, lessened his feelings of deprivation, and alleviated some of his concerns about his relationship with his partner. Nevertheless, Anthony continued to feel that he had never fulfilled his ambitions to be a serious writer, and he tended to demean what he considered to be a low-paying and insignificant job, given his age and aspirations.

With the encouragement of the therapist, Anthony began to write some articles for publication in well-known and widely read magazines. The articles were accepted and provided him with posi-tive feedback about his ideas. By the end of the fourth year of treat-ment, with much trepidation, Anthony decided to write a book proposal on a subject that combined his major interests. With the help of a literary agent, and to Anthony's great surprise, he was able to obtain a book contract with a sizable financial advance from a prestigious publisher. The last two years of treatment were fraught with Anthony's fears, feelings of inadequacy, and fears of failure, and transient episodes of procrastination and self-sabotage. He was, nev-ertheless, able to stay focused on his project. Sessions were often filled with his discussing his ideas and his writing blocks, his annoy-ance that his job was interfering with his being a full-time author, and his fear that he would "fall on his face." Because the book dealt substantially with issues of ethnicity, Anthony reflected on his own struggles around his Sicilian American background and his gay sex-ual orientation. Increasingly, Anthony allowed himself to become more fully immersed in his writing and had bursts of creativity that he never had experienced previously. He was excited about his own ideas and showed a new interest and pleasure in living. He was very happy that his editor also was enthusiastic about the work he had done so far. He reported that his relationship with his partner was better than ever, and he drew closer to his parents, who seemed to be pleased with his interest in their lives and his newfound work success. He quickly recovered from disappointments without lapsing into his ususal depressive position.

As Anthony neared the completion of his book and the publisher was already making plans for its release, he could not quite believe what was happening: "It's almost like a dream. I'm afraid I'm going to wake up." In one session at this time, he reported that he had a brainstorm for another book, and he eagerly shared his thoughts about it. The therapist thought it sounded quite promising and feasible. Anthony commented on the changes in himself: "I'm 54 years old, and I've finally found myself. I can't get over it. It's so exciting, and it makes me feel confident and powerful in some way. I can't quite explain what it's like although you seem to understand."

Anthony's progress was very gratifying at many levels. The therapist was pleased that her 54-year-old patient had gone his own way and found himself. He was experiencing increased creativity, freer self-expression, and a capacity for pleasure and joy, goals that Kohut (1984) described as being at the heart of self-psychological treatment. An author herself, the therapist understood and identified with what Anthony was experiencing in the process of his writing and as his project was coming to completion. At another, more personal level, the therapist was aware that, when Anthony had entered treatment, his situation reminded her of that of her older brother, whose work and personal life and self-esteem had deteriorated when he was in his early 50s and who never recovered; he died from cancer during the more recent stages of Anthony's treatment. In contrast to the sadness and helplessness that the therapist experienced with her brother, she felt good and effective in her work with Anthony. These feelings led her to reflect on a core issue in her early life that undoubtedly had been a factor in her choice of career as a therapist: she had not been able to have a positive impact on her own family of origin. Anthony's success was deeply affirming of the therapist's sense of self.

REFERENCES

Adelmann, P. K., Antonucci, T. C., Crohan, S. E. & Coleman, L. M. (1989), Empty nest, cohort, and employment in the well-being of midlife women. *Sex Roles*, 20:173–189.

Aldwin, C. M. & Levenson, M. R. (2001), Stress, coping, and health at midlife: A developmental perspective. In: *Handbook of Midlife Development*, ed. M. E. Lachman. New York: Wiley, pp. 188–214.

American Psychiatric Association. (1994), *Diagnostic and Statistical Manual of Mental Disorders* (4th ed.). Washington, DC: American Psychiatric Association.

Aron, L. (1996), *A Meeting of Minds: Mutuality in Psychoanalysis*. Hillsdale, NJ: The Analytic Press.

Bacal, H. A. (1985), Optimal responsiveness and the therapeutic process. In: *The Evolution of Self Psychology: Progress in Self Psychology, Vol. 7*, ed. A. Goldberg. Hillsdale, NJ: The Analytic Press, pp. 36–44.

Baker, H. S. (1991), Short-term psychotherapy: A self-psychological approach. In: *Handbook of Short-Term Dynamic Psychotherapy*, ed. J. P. Barber & P. Crits-Christoph. New York: Basic Books, pp. 287–318.

Barnett, R. C. (1984), The anxiety of the unknown—Choice, risk, responsibility: Therapeutic issues for today's adult women. In: *Women in Midlife*, ed. G. Baruch & J. Brooks-Gunn. New York: Plenum Press, pp. 341–357.

_____ & Baruch, G. K. (1985), Women's involvement in multiple roles and psychological distress. *J. Pers. Psychother.*, 49:S277–S285.

_____ & Marshall, N. L. (1991), The relationship between women's work and family roles and subjective well-being and psychological distress. In: *Women, Work, and Health*, ed. M. Frankenhausen, U. Lundberg & M. Chesney. New York: Plenum Press, pp. 111–136.

Bart, P. B. (1971), Depression in middle-aged women. In: *Women in Sexist Society*, ed. V. Gornick & B. J. Moran. New York: New American Library, pp. 163–286.

Baruch, G. K. & Barnett, R. C. (1986), Role quality, multiple role involvement and psychological well-being in midlife women. *J. Pers. Soc. Psychol.*, 51:578–585.

_____ & Brooks-Gunn, J., eds. (1984), *Women in Midlife*. New York: Plenum Press.

Benatar, M. (1989), "Marrying off" children as a developmental stage. *Clin. Soc. Work J.*, 17:223–231.

Benedek, T. (1970), Parenthood during the life cycle. In: *Parenthood—Its Psychology and Psychopathology*, ed. J. Anthony & T. Benedek. Boston, MA: Little Brown, pp. 185–208.

Benjamin, J. (1988), *The Bonds of Love: Psychoanalysis, Feminism, and the Problem of Domination*. New York: Pantheon Books.

Brooks-Gunn, J. & Kirsh, B. (1984), Life events and the boundaries of midlife for women. In: *Women in Midlife*, ed. G. Baruch & J. Brooks-Gunn. New York: Plenum Press, pp. 11–30.

Brunell, L. F. (1992), Psychological misweaves of the 80s—Damage control in the 90s: A multi-modal analysis for therapy in the nineties. *Psychother. Priv. Pract.*, 11:123–134.

Butler, J. (1990), *Gender Trouble: Feminism and the Subversion of Identity*. New York: Routledge.

Butler, R. N. (1963), The life review: An interpretation of reminiscence. *Psychiatry*, 26:65–76.

Caplan, G. (1964), *Principles of Preventive Psychiatry*. New York: Basic Books.

Cath, S. H. (1963), Some dynamics of the middle and later years. In: *Crisis Intervention: Selected Readings*, ed. H. J. Parad. New York: Family Service Association of America, 1965, pp. 174–190.

Chodorow, N. (1978), *The Reproduction of Mothering: Psychoanalysis and the Sociology of Gender*. Berkeley: University of California Press.

Coehlo, G. V., Hamburg, D. A. & Adams, J. E. (1974), *Coping and Adaptation*. New York: Basic Books.

Colarusso, C. A. & Nemiroff, R. A. (1981), *Adult Development*. New York: Plenum Press.

Cornett, C. W. & Hudson, R. A. (1987), Middle adulthood and the theories of Erikson, Gould, and Vaillant: Where does the gay man fit in? *J. Gerontol. Soc. Work*, 10:61–73.

Dalton, S. T. (1992), Lived experience of never-married women. *Issues Ment. Health Nurs.*, 13:69–80.

Dan, A. J. & Berhard, L. A. (1989), Menopause and other health issues for midlife women. In: *Midlife Myths: Issues, Findings, and Practice Implications*, ed. S. Hunter & M. Sundel. Newbury Park, CA: Sage, pp. 51–66.

Dautzenberg, M. G. H., Diederiks, J. P. M., Philipsen, H. & Tan, F. E. S. (1999), Multigenerational caregiving and well-being: Distress of middle-aged daughters providing assistance to elderly parents. *Women & Health*, 29:57–74.

Eckenrode, J., ed. (1991), *The Social Context of Coping*. New York: Plenum Press.

———— & Gore, S. (1990), *Stress Between Work and Family*. New York: Plenum Press.

Ellman, J. P. (1992), A treatment approach for patients in midlife. *Can. J. Psychiat.*, 37:564–566.

_____ (1996), Analyst and patient at midlife. *Psychoanal. Quart.*, 65: 353–371.

Elson, M. (1984), Parenthood and the transformation of narcissism. In: *Parenthood: A Psychodynamic Perspective*, ed. R. S. Cohen, B. J. Kohler & S. H. Weissman. New York: Guilford Press.

Erikson, E. (1950), *Childhood and Society*. New York: Norton.

_____ (1959), Identity and the life cycle. *Psycholog. Issues*, 1:50–100.

Fosshage, J. L. (1991), Beyond the basic rule. In: *The Evolution of Self Psychology: Progress in Self Psychology, Vol. 7*, ed. A. Goldberg. Hillsdale, NJ: The Analytic Press, pp. 64–74.

Freud, S. (1905), On psychotherapy. *Standard Edition*, 7:257–268. London: Hogarth Press, 1953.

_____ (1914), On narcissism: An introduction. *Standard Edition*, 14:67–102. London: Hogarth Press, 1957.

Galatzer-Levy, R. M. & Cohler, B. J. (1990), The selfobjects of the second half of life: An introduction. In: *The Realities of Transference: Progress in Self Psychology, Vol. 6*, ed. A. Goldberg. New York: The Analytic Press, pp. 93–112.

Gibson, R. C. (1989), Black adults in aging society. In: *Black Adult Development*, ed. R. L. Jones. Berkeley, CA: Cobb & Henry, pp. 389–406.

Gilligan, C. (1982), *In a Different Voice: Psychological Theory and Women's Development*. Cambridge, MA: Harvard University Press.

Goldstein, E. G. (1990), *Borderline Disorders: Clinical Models and Techniques*. New York: Guilford Press.

_____ (1992), Borderline personality disorder. In: *Mental Health and the Elderly: A Social Work Practice Perspective*, ed. F. J. Turner. New York: Free Press, pp. 220–248.

_____ (1994), Self-disclosure in treatment: What therapists do and don't talk about. *Clin. Soc. Work J.*, 22:417–433.

_____ (1995a), *Ego Psychology and Social Work Practice*, 2nd ed. New York: Free Press.

_____ (1995b), When the bubble bursts: Narcissistic vulnerability in the middle years. *Clin. Soc. Work J.*, 23:401–416.

_____ (1997), To tell or not to tell: Self-disclosure of events in the therapist's life to the patient. *Clin. Soc. Work J.*, 25:41–58.

_____ (2001), *Object Relations Theory and Self Psychology in Social Work Practice*. New York: Free Press.

_____ & Horowitz, L. C. (2002), *Lesbian Identity and Contemporary Psychotherapy: A Framework for Clinical Practice*. Hillsdale, NJ: The Analytic Press.

Goode, W. J. (1960), A theory of role strain. *Amer. Sociol. Rev.*, 25:483–496.

Gottschalk, L. A. (1990), Origins and evolution of narcissism through the life cycle. In: *New Dimensions in Adult Development*, ed. R. A. Nemiroff & C. A. Colarusso. New York: Basic Books, pp. 73–91.

Gould, R. L. (1978), *Transformations: Growth and Change in Adult Life*. New York: Simon & Schuster.

Greenes, J. M. (1987), The aged in psychotherapy: Psychodynamic contributions to the treatment process. In: *Treating the Elderly with Psychotherapy*, ed. J. Sadovy & M. Leszcz. Madison, CT: International Universities Press, pp. 64–75.

Greenglass, E. R. (1985), Psychological implications of sex bias in the workplace. *Acad. Psychol. Bull.*, 7:227–240.

Greer, G. (1992), *The Change: Women, Aging, and the Menopause*. New York: Knopf.

Grinker, R. R. & Spiegel, J. D. (1945), *Men Under Stress*. Philadelphia, PA: Blakiston.

Grunes, J. M. (1982), Reminiscence, regression and empathy—A psychotherapeutic approach to the impaired elderly. In: *The Course of Life, Vol. 3*, ed. S. I. Greenspan & G. H. Pollock. Washington, DC: National Institute of Mental Health, pp. 545–560.

Guttman, D. (1975), Individual adaptation in the middle years: Developmental issues in the masculine midlife crisis. *J. Geriatr. Psychiat.*, 9:41–59.

Hartmann, H. (1950), Comments on the psychoanalytic theory of the ego. *The Psychoanalytic Study of the Child*, 5:74–96. New York: International Universities Press.

Havighurst, R. J. (1968), A social-psychological perspective on aging. *Gerontology*, 8:67–71.

Hayes, L. S. (1986), The superwoman myth. *Soc. Casework*, 67:436–441.

Heckhausen, J. (2001), Adaptation and resilience in midlife. In: *Handbook of Midlife Development*, ed. M. E. Lachman. New York: Wiley, pp. 345–394.

Helson, R. (1997), The self in middle age. In: *Multiple Paths of Midlife Development*, ed. M. E. Lachman & J. B. James. Chicago, IL: University of Chicago Press, pp. 21–44.

Hill, R. (1958), Generic features of families under stress. In: *Crisis Intervention: Selected Readings*, ed. H. J. Parad. New York: Family Service Association of America, 1965, pp. 32–52.

Hunter, S. & Sundel, M., eds. (1989), *Midlife Myths: Issues, Findings, and Practice Implications*. Newbury Park, CA: Sage.

———— Sundel, S. S. & Sundel, M. (2002), *Women at Midlife*. Washington, DC: National Association of Social Workers Press.

Jacobowitz, J. & Newton, N. A, (1999), Dynamics and treatment of narcissism in later life. In: *Handbook of Counseling and Psychotherapy with Older Adults*, ed. M. Duffy. New York: Wiley, pp. 453–469.

Jacobson, E. (1964), *The Self and the Object World*. New York: International Universities Press.

Jacobson, G. E., Strickler, M. & Morley, W. F. (1968), Generic and individual approaches to crisis intervention. *Amer. J. Public Health*, 58:338–343.

Janis, I. (1958), *Psychological Stress*. New York: Wiley.

Jordan, J. (1990), Relational development through empathy: Therapeutic applications. In: *Works in Progress, Vol. 40*. Wellesley, MA: Stone Center for Developmental Services and Studies, pp. 11–40.

Jung, C. (1933), *Modern Man in Search of a Soul*. New York: Harcourt Brace.

———— (1971), The stages of life. In: *The Portable Jung*, ed. J. Campbell. New York: Penguin, pp. 3–22.

Kaplan, A. & Surrey, J. L. (1984), The relational self in women: Developmental theory and public policy. In: *Women and Mental Health Policy*, ed. L. Walker. Beverly Hills, CA: Sage, pp. 79–94.

Kaplan, D. (1962), A concept of acute situational disorders. *Soc. Work*, 7:15–23.

Kernberg, O. (1970), Factors in the psychoanaltyic treatment of narcissistic personalities. *J. Amer. Psychoanal. Assn.*, 18:51–85

———— (1974), Further contributions to the treatment of narcissistic personalities. *Internat. J. Psycho-Anal.*, 55:215–240.

———— (1977), Normal psychology of the aging process revisited, II. *J. Geriatr. Psychiat.*, 10:27–45.

———— (1980), Pathological narcissism in middle age. In: *Internal World and External Reality*. Northvale, NJ: Aronson, pp. 135–153.

———— (1984), *Severe Personality Disorders*. New Haven, CT: Yale University Press.

Kertzner, R. & Sved, M. (1996), Midlife gay men and lesbians: Adult development and mental health. In: *Textbook of Homosexuality and Mental Health*, ed. R. P. Cabaj & T. S. Stein. Washington, DC: American Psychiatric Press, pp. 289–303.

Kim, J. E. & Moen, P. (2001), Moving into retirement: Preparation and transitions in late midlife. In: *Handbook of Midlife Development*, ed. M. E. Lachman. New York: Wiley, pp. 487–527.

Kimmel, D. C. & Sang, B. E. (1995), Lesbians and gay men in midlife. In: *Lesbian, Gay and Bisexual Identities over the Lifespan*, ed. R. D'Augeui & C. Patterson. New York: Oxford University Press, pp. 191–213.

Kohut, H. (1966), Forms and transformations of narcissism. *J. Amer. Psychol. Assn.*, 14:243–278.

_____ (1971), *The Analysis of the Self*. New York: International Universities Press.

_____ (1977), *The Restoration of the Self*. New York: International Universities Press.

_____ (1984), *How Does Analysis Cure?* ed. A. Goldberg & P. Stepansky. Chicago, IL: University of Chicago Press.

_____ & Wolf, E. (1978), The disorders of the self and their treatment: An outline. In: *Essential Papers on Narcissism*, ed. A. Morrison. New York: New York University Press, pp. 175–196.

Krause, N. & Geyer-Pestello, H. F. (1985), Depressive symptoms among women employees outside the home. *Amer. J. Community. Psychol.*, 13: 49–67.

Krystal, S. & Chiriboga, D. A. (1979), The empty nest process in midlife men and women. *Maturitas*, 1:215–222.

Lachman, M. E., ed. (2001), *Handbook of Midlife Development*. New York: Wiley.

_____ & James, J. B., eds. (1997), *Multiple Paths of Midlife Development*. Chicago, IL: University of Chicago Press.

_____ Lewkowicz, C., Marcus, A. & Peng, Y. (1994), Images of midlife development among young, middle-aged, and older adults. *J. Adult Dev.*, 1:201–211.

Langsley, D. & Kaplan, D. (1968), *Treatment of Families in Crisis*. New York: Grune & Stratton.

Lazarus, L. W. (1991), Elderly. In: *Using Self Psychology in Psychotherapy*, ed. H. Jackson. Northvale, NJ: Aronson.

Lazarus, R. S. (1966), *Psychological Stress and the Coping Process*. New York: McGraw-Hill.

Levinson, D. J. (1996), *The Seasons of a Woman's Life*. New York: Knopf.

_____ Darrow, C., Klein, E., Levinson, M. & McKee, B. (1978), *The Seasons of a Man's Life*. New York: Knopf.

Lifton, R. F. (1979), *The Broken Connection*. New York: Simon & Schuster.

Lindemann, E. (1944), Symptomatology and management of acute grief. In: *Crisis Intervention: Selected Readings*, ed. H. J. Parad. New York: Family Service Association of America, 1965, pp. 7–21.

Long, J. & Porter, K. (1984), Multiple roles of midlife women: A case for new direction in theory, research, and policy. In: *Women in Midlife*, ed. G. Baruch & J. Brooks-Gunn. New York: Plenum Press, pp. 109–160.

Marks, S. (1977), Multiple roles and role strain: Some notes on human energy, time and commitment. *Amer. Sociol. Rev.*, 42:921–936.

Maroda, K. (1999), *Seduction, Surrender, and Transformation*. Hillsdale, NJ: The Analytic Press.

McGrath, E. (1992), New treatment strategies for women in the middle. In: *Gender Issues Across the Life Cycle*, ed. B. R. Wainrib. New York: Springer, pp. 124–136.

McQuaide, S. (1998a), Opening space for alternative images and narratives of midlife women. *Clin. Soc. Work J.*, 26:39–53.

——— (1998b), Women at midlife. *Soc. Work*, 43:21–31.

Miller, J. B. (1977), *Toward a New Psychology of Women*. Boston, MA: Beacon Paperback.

Miller, J. P. (1991), Can psychotherapy substitute for psychoanalysis? In: *The Evolution of Self Psychology: Progress in Self Psychology, Vol. 7*, ed. A. Goldberg. Hillsdale, NJ: The Analytic Press, pp. 45–58.

Mitchell, V. & Helson, R. (1990), Women's prime of life: Is it the 50s? *Psychol. Womens Quart.*, 14:451–470.

Modell, A. H. (1975), A narcissistic defense against affects and the illusion of self-sufficiency. *Internat. J. Psycho-Anal.*, 56:275–282.

Neugarten, B. L. (1968), Adult personality: Toward a psychology of the life cycle. In: *Readings in General Psychology*, ed. W. E. Vinacke. New York: American Books, pp. 332–343.

——— & Associates, eds. (1964), *Personality in Middle and Late Life*. New York: Atherton Press.

Nolen-Hoeksema, S. & Larson, S. (1999), *Coping with Loss*. Mahwah, NJ: Lawrence Erlbaum Associates.

Olfson, M., Marcus, S. C., Druss, B. & Pincus, H. A. (2002), National trends in the use of outpatient psychotherapy. *Amer. J. Psychiat.*, 159:1914–1920.

O'Neil, J. M. & Egan, J. (1992), Men and women's gender role journeys: A metaphor for healing, transition, and transformation. In: *Gender Issues Across the Life Cycle*, ed. B. R. Wainrib. New York: Springer, pp. 107–123.

Palombo, J. (1985), Depletion states and selfobject disorders. *Clin. Soc. Work J.*, 14:32–49.

Parad, H. J., ed. (1965), *Crisis Intervention: Selected Readings*. New York: Family Service Association of America.

——— & Caplan, G. (1960), A framework for studying families in crisis. In: *Crisis Intervention: Selected Readings*, ed. H. J. Parad. New York: Family Service Association of America, 1965.

——— & Parad, L. G., eds. (1990), *Crisis Intervention, Book 2*. Milwaukee, WI: Family Service Association of America.

Parks, S. H. & Pilisuk, M. (1990), Caregiver burden: Gender and the psychological costs of caregiving. *Amer. J. Orthopsychiat.*, 61:501–509.

Pearlin, L. I. (1985), Life strains and psychological distress among adults. In: *Stress and Coping: An Anthology*, 2nd ed., ed. A. Monat & R. S. Lazarus. New York: Columbia University Press.

Pearlman, S. F. (1993), Late mid-life astonishment: Disruptions to identity and self-esteem. *Women in Ther.*, 14:1–12.

Person, E. (1982), Women working: Fear of failure, deviance, and success. *J. Amer. Acad. Psychoanal.*, 10:67–84.

Polasky, L. J. & Holahan, C. K. (1998), Maternal self-discrepancies, interrole conflict, and negative affect among married professional women and children. *J. Fam. Psychol.*, 12:388–401.

Pollock, G. H. (1987), The mourning–liberation process: Issues in the inner life of the older adult. In: *Treating the Elderly with Psychotherapy*, ed. J. Sadovy & M. Leszcz. Madison, CT: International Universities Press, pp. 3–30.

Pulver, S. E. (1970), Narcissism: The term and the concept. *J. Amer. Psychoanal. Assn.*, 18:319–341.

Rapoport, R. (1963), Normal crises, family structure, and mental health. In: *Crisis Intervention: Selected Readings*, ed. H. J. Parad. New York: Family Service Association of America, 1965, pp. 75–87.

Reich, A. (1960), Pathologic forms of self-esteem regulation. *The Psychoanalytic Study of the Child*, 15:215–232. New York: International Universities Press.

Renik, O. (1995), The ideal of the anonymous analyst and the problem of self-disclosure. *Psychoanal. Quart.*, 26:303–357.

Riegel, K. F. (1975), Adult life crises: A dialectical interpretation of development. In: *Life-Span Developmental Psychology*, ed. N. Data & L. H. Ginsberg. New York: Academic Press, pp. 99–128.

Rodin, J. & Ickovics, J. R. (1990), Women's health: Review and research agenda as we approach the 21st century. *Amer. Psychol.*, 45:1018–1034.

Rosenfeld, H. (1964), On the psychopathology of narcissism: A clinical approach, *Internat. J. Psycho-Anal.*, 45:332–337.

———— (1971), A clinical approach to the psychoanalytic theory of the life and death instincts: An investigation into the aggressive aspects of narcissism. *Internat. J. Psycho-Anal.*, 52:169–178.

Rossi, A. (1980), Life-span theories and women's lives. *Signs*, 6:4–32.

Ruderman, E. B. (2003), Plus ça change, plus c'est la même chose: Women's "masochism" and ambivalence about ambition and success. In: *Therapies with Women in Transition*, ed. J. B. Sanville & W. B. Ruderman. Madison, CT: International Universities Press, pp. 1–26.

Ruth, J. & Coleman, P. (1996), Personality and aging: Coping and management of the self in later life. In: *Handbook of the Psychology of Aging*, 4th ed. New York: Van Nostrand-Reinhold, pp. 308–322.

Sang, B. (1993), Existential issues of midlife lesbians. In: *Psychological Perspectives on Lesbian and Gay Male Experiences*, ed. L. D. Garnets & D. C. Kimmel. New York: Columbia University Press, pp. 500–516.

Schwaber, E. (1983), Psychoanalytic listening and psychic reality. *Internat. J. Psycho-Anal.*, 10:379–392.

Selye, H. (1956), *The Stress of Life*. New York: McGraw-Hill.

Sheehy, G. (1974), *Passages*. New York: Dutton.

Sieber, S. D. (1974), Toward a theory of role accumulation. *Amer. Sociol. Rev.*, 39:567–578.

Spira, L. & Richards, A. K. (2003), On being lonely, socially isolated, and single: Multiple perspectives. *Psychoanal. Psychother.*, 20:3–21.

Spurlock, J. (1984), Black women in the middle years. In: *Women in Midlife*, ed. G. Baruch & J. Brooks-Gunn. New York: Plenum Press, pp. 245–260.

Staudinger, U. M. & Bluck, S. (2001), A view on midlife development from life-span theory. In: *Handbook of Midlife Development*, ed. M. E. Lachman. New York: Wiley, pp. 3–39.

Sterns, H. L. & Huyck, M. H. (2001), The role of work in midlife. In: *Handbook of Midlife Development*, ed. M. E. Lachman. New York: Wiley, pp. 447–486.

Stewart, A. J. & Ostrove, J. M. (1998), Women's personality in midlife: Gender, history, and midlife corrections. *Amer. Psychol.*, 53:1185–1194.

Stiver, I. P. (1991), Beyond the Oedipus complex: Mothers and daughters. In: *Women's Growth in Connection: Writings from the Stone Center*, ed. J. Jordan, A. Kaplan, J. B. Miller, I. P. Stiver & J. Surrey. New York: Guilford Press, pp. 97–121.

Stolorow, R. D. & Atwood, G. E. (1992), *Contexts of Being: The Intersubjective Foundations of Psychological Life*. Hillsdale, NJ: The Analytic Press.

Strickler, M. (1965), Applying crisis theory in a community clinic. *Soc. Casework*, 46:150–154.

Sze, W. C. & Ivker, B. (1987), Adulthood. In: *Encyclopedia of Social Work*, 18th ed. Silver Spring, MD: National Association of Social Workers, pp. 75–89.

Tiedje, L. B., Wortman, C. B., Downey, G., Emmons, C., Biernat, M. & Lang, E. (1990), Women with multiple roles: Role compatibility, perceptions, satisfaction, and mental health. *J. Marriage Fam.*, 52:63–72.

Tyhurst, J. (1958), The role of transition states—Including disasters in mental illness. In: *Symposium on Preventive and Social Psychiatry*. Washington, DC: Walter Reed Army Institute of Research, pp. 149–167.

Vaillant, G. E. (1977), *Adaptation to Life*. Boston, MA: Little Brown.

Wainrib, B. R. (1992), *Gender Issues Across the Life Cycle*. New York: Springer.

Wallerstein, R. (1986), *Forty-Two Lives in Treatment*. New York: Guilford Press.

White, R. F. (1966), *Lives in Progress*. New York: Holt, Rinehart & Winston.

Williams, J. H. (1977), *Psychology of Women*. New York: Norton.

Wolf, E. (1988), *Treating the Self*. New York: Guilford Press.

INDEX